www.wadsworth.com

www.wadsworth.com is the World Wide Web site for Wadsworth and is your direct source to dozens of online resources.

At *www.wadsworth.com* you can find out about supplements, demonstration software, and student resources. You can also send email to many of our authors and preview new publications and exciting new technologies.

www.wadsworth.com
Changing the way the world learns®

From the Wadsworth Series in Theatre

ACTING
Is Believing

Eighth Edition

CHARLES MCGAW

Late of the Goodman School of Drama
A School of the Art Institute of Chicago

LARRY D. CLARK

Dean Emeritus, College of Arts & Science
University of Missouri – Columbia

KENNETH L. STILSON

Chair, Department of Theatre & Dance
Southeast Missouri State University

THOMSON

WADSWORTH

Australia • Canada • Mexico • Singapore •
Spain • United Kingdom • United States

THOMSON

WADSWORTH ™

Publisher: Holly J. Allen
Assistant Editor: Shona Burke
Editorial Assistant: Laryssa Polika
Technology Project Manager: Jeanette Wiseman
Media Assistant: Bryan Davis
Marketing Manager: Kimberly Russell
Marketing Assistant: Neena Chandra
Advertising Project Manager: Shemika Britt
Project Manager, Editorial Production: Mary Noel

Print/Media Buyer: Kris Waller
Permissions Editor: Sarah Harkrader
Production Service: Hockett Editorial Service
Text Designer: Andrew Ogus
Photo Researcher: Linda Sykes
Copy Editor: Bradford Cox
Cover Designer: Sandy Drooker
Cover Photo: Andrée Lanthier
Compositor: G&S Typesetters, Inc.
Text and Cover Printer: Phoenix Color Corp

Printed in the United States of America
1 2 3 4 5 6 7 07 06 05 04 03

For more information about our products, contact us at:
Thomson Learning Academic Resource Center
1-800-423-0563
For permission to use material from this text, contact us by:
Phone: 1-800-730-2214
Fax: 1-800-730-2215
Web: http://www.thomsonrights.com

Library of Congress Control Number: 2002117117
ISBN 0-15-505982-3

Cover: Titus Andronicus (William Langan) rages at the treatment of his daughter Lavinia (Julie Oda) in the Oregon Shakespeare Festival's 2002 Elizabethan Stage production of William Shakespeare's *Titus Andronicus*. Directed by James Edmondson; scenic design by William Bloodgood; costume design by Susan Tsu; lighting design by Robert Peterson.

Wadsworth/Thomson Learning
10 Davis Drive
Belmont, CA 94002-3098
USA

Asia
Thomson Learning
5 Shenton Way #01-01
UIC Building
Singapore 068808

Australia/New Zealand
Thomson Learning
102 Dodds Street
Southbank, Victoria 3006
Australia

Canada
Nelson
1120 Birchmount Road
Toronto, Ontario M1K 5G4
Canada

Europe/Middle East/Africa
Thomson Learning
High Holborn House
50/51 Bedford Row
London WC1R 4LR
United Kingdom

For Jack Dempsey Cook, my dad
KLS

THIS BOOK PRINTED ON ACID-FREE RECYCLED PAPER

Contents

Preface

"I don't believe you." These simple words, spoken by a "very fine and sensitive theatre director," made a deep impression on the legendary Margo Jones, who recalled the event in her foreword to Charles McGaw's *Acting Is Believing,* a groundbreaking text that has helped train many generations of actors. "An actor must believe to make his audience believe." This phrase served as a guidepost for the original book. McGaw's ideas, based to a considerable extent on the teachings of Constantin Stanislavski, are as vibrant and relevant today as they were in the mid-1950s. The materials were originally organized in such a way as to make them practical for classroom use, although they were intended for any reader seriously interested in the art and discipline of acting. McGaw, like Stanislavski, believed that to find true emotion on stage, to uncover the "mystery of inspiration," talent must be nurtured. Acting can and must be taught.

Today, with hundreds of acting programs across the country graduating a multitude of talented young professionals each year, technique training is more important than ever. In the twenty-first century, acting continues to be one of the world's most glamorous, yet elusive, professions. Thousands of actors vie for a limited number of jobs on stage and in film, television, and other forms of media. Competition is fierce. Without training, connections, and an unstoppable will to succeed, actors cannot hope to survive in this profession—no matter how great their talent.

Between 1955 and 1986, Charles McGaw's brilliant interpretation of Stanislavski's theory inspired thousands of young actors across the country. It endured through four editions until the torch was passed to Larry D. Clark, who expanded the next three editions to meet the demands of actors in the late twentieth century. From 1985 to 1991, I studied under the direct tutelage of Dr. Clark, and studied and implemented the theories and exercises in various editions of this book. And now, as this same torch has been passed to me, I am humbled by the achievements of my predecessors and honored to be associated with their work.

New to This Edition

For the Eighth Edition, I have followed Clark's approach and, whenever possible, have integrated new methodology to teaching and acting that are compatible with McGaw's original blueprint. The teachings of Stanislavski speak as loudly as ever, so in this edition McGaw's and Clark's basic organization remains unchanged. The text begins by focusing on the actor alone, moves to the actor and the play, and concludes with the actor and production. However, the world has changed— it is faster, tougher, wiser, and infinitely more competitive. Thus, this new edition has been revised to better meet the needs of today's acting students:

+ Important Stanislavski theory has been expanded in each chapter, and some of the terminology in the book has been changed to reflect more closely the Russian master's own teachings.

+ A new chapter, "Approaching the Creative State," replaces "Taking It Easy." The new chapter, filled with exercises designed to promote creativity, moves logically through eight basic phases: focusing, meditating, tensing and releasing, centering, shaking, stretching, moving, and vocalizing.

+ The previous chapters "Getting into the Part" and "Getting into Character" have been streamlined and merged into a new chapter, "Creating the Character."

+ The chapter "Getting the Job" has been completely revised and updated to feature auditioning and marketing tips for actors in the twenty-first century.

+ A new Appendix A, "Suggested Plays for the Undergraduate Scene Study," features contemporary trio and duet scenes that encourage a great diversity of casting. In addition, a new Appendix B, "Theatre Resources"—which includes an expanded list of theatres and organizations, plus a comprehensive list of audition sites, publications, professional and student conferences, and acting web sites—replaces "Theatres and Groups."

+ The text's play selections, examples, exercises, and photographs have been expanded and updated to better reflect today's undergraduate students.

✦ A detailed new glossary greatly expands the terminology found in the former chapter, "Learning the Lingo."

Even with these numerous revisions, the Eighth Edition of *Acting Is Believing* maintains the same uncomplicated formula for learning how to act that has served students well for generations.

Acknowledgments

Over the past eighteen months, many people have graciously donated their time, energy, and resources to the completion of this project. I particularly wish to thank Dr. Larry D. Clark, who has given me many opportunities over the years and who has taught me many lessons on life and the profession. He guided me through graduate school and my dissertation, as well as my first published book. He remains my mentor to this day.

I greatly appreciate the help of my publisher, Holly Allen, and former editorial assistant, Mele Alusa, at Wadsworth/Thomson Learning, and my project editor, Rachel Youngman, director of Hockett Editorial Service.

I want to thank Dr. Robert W. Dillon, Jr., for our daily "chats" about acting and his comments regarding this revision. I also want to thank Dr. Martin M. Jones, Paul Zmolek, Megwyn Sanders, Meagan Edmonds, Daniel Graul, and my other colleagues and students at Southeast Missouri State University.

I appreciate the comments of the reviewers of this edition—Eddie Bradley, Jr., Spelman College; Stephanie Campbell, Montana State University; and Susan Shaughnessy, University of Oklahoma.

For their contributions to the appendixes, I wish to acknowledge Jonathan Cantor, University of Miami; Sydell Weiner, California State University; Dominguez Hills; and Professor Matthew T. Gitkin, Department of Theatre, University of Miami.

For their assistance with the new photographs and permissions, I want to thank Cathy Taylor and Steppenwolf Theatre; Ann B. Goddard, Office Manager, Steve Yates, and the Utah Shakespearean Festival; Amy Richard and the Oregon Shakespeare Festival; Jennifer Manzo and Long Wharf Theatre; Kathleen Chalfant; Suzi McLaughlin, Jenae Yerger, Buddy Myers, and the Allied Theatre Group (Stage West & Ft. Worth Shakespeare Festival); Jeff Glover, Public Relation Manager, and Casa Maña Theatre; Amy Lacy, Creative Associate/Graphic Designer, and the Dallas Theater Center; Linda Blaser; Shakespeare Festival of Dallas; Jac Alder, Executive Producer, Christine Lee, Pat Harrison, and Theatre Three; J. Brent Alford; Pat Atkinson and the University of Missouri-Columbia Department of Theatre; Dr. Mary Lou Hoyle and Texas Woman's University Department of Performing Arts; Karla R. Goldstein, Director of Public Relations, and St. Louis

Black Repertory Company; Dr. Steve Simons and Texas Wesleyan University; Dr. James C. Wright and Stetson University; Katalin Mitchell, Director of Press & Public Relations, Richard Feldman, and American Repertory Theatre; Michele Baylin, Marketing Manager, and Center Stage; Brooke Hildebrand; Maia Rosenfeld; David Tucker and Seattle Repertory Theatre; Sara Gruber, PR Associate and Web Editor, Barry M. Colfert, Director of PR and Marketing, and The Shakespeare Theatre; Benita Edwards-Brown, Senior Communication Manager, and the Alabama Shakespeare Festival; and Jessica S. Elliott, Marketing Associate and the Philadelphia Theatre Company.

Finally, I wish to thank my beloved wife, best friend, toughest critic, and colleague, Rhonda Weller-Stilson. Without her insight and patience, this project could not have been completed.

Kenneth L. Stilson
Cape Girardeau, Missouri
February 2003

PART I

The Actor

Al Pacino in Long Wharf Theatre's
production of Eugene O'Neill's *Hughie*.
Directed by Al Pacino.

CHAPTER 1

Training Your Talent

"Acting is believing": what a simple definition, yet how complex the concept. Nevertheless, there it is—a challenge, a goal for your study and practice. To train as an actor is to train your ability to believe, to become able to exist in your believed but imaginary circumstances as if they were real, to command the technique to commune with other actors as if they were who they pretend to be, and to possess the tools to transmit clearly and artfully your beliefs to an audience.

As an actor, you are searching for truthful behavior within the given circumstances of the play. Each production, however, has different parameters with regards to truth. It is your responsibility to understand this new reality and then believe your actions while behaving truthfully within the world of the production. **Constantin Stanislavski,** whose pioneering work for the Moscow Art Theatre at the turn of the twentieth century laid the foundation for much of our current acting technique, wrote:

> Truth cannot be separated from belief, or belief from truth. They cannot exist without each other and without both of them it is impossible to live your part, or to create anything. Everything that happens on the stage must be convincing to the actor, to their associates and to the spectators. It must inspire belief in the possibility, in real life, of emotions

analogous to those being experienced on the stage by the actor. Each
and every moment must be saturated with a belief in the truthfulness of
the emotion felt, and in the action carried out by the actor.[1]

Of significance to an actor is what Stanislavski called the "reality of the inner
life of a human spirit." You will be searching for the soul of an imaginary person,
the inner spiritual world, with your own resources. As an actor you will face the
daunting task of building a new, three-dimensional human being with history, desires, fears, biases, emotions, and images. You and your character may be polar
opposites with regard to a variety of social and moral issues, but you must never
judge your character. Otherwise, you will never be able to sustain belief in your
actions. You must justify every verbal and physical action. You must wear your
character's shoes and clothing. You must look at the world of the production
through your character's eyes.

Although this imagined character, this new human being, will have a completely different inner and outer world from your own, you must find your work
of art by stirring your own inner life, for each character you create must spring
from your own being. Each character is a unique creation derived from three
sources: the given circumstances, the actor's imagination, and the actor's personal
history. For each character, you must touch a different wellspring from within
your lifetime of emotions and experiences. You are your own instrument. Pianists
have their pianos, painters have their canvases, but actors have only their own
bodies and spirits. Unlike artists in other fields, they are their own creator and the
material and the instrument, all in one.

According to Stanislavski, "There are two kinds of truth and sense of belief in
what you are doing. First, there is the one that is created automatically and on the
plane of actual fact, and second, there is the scenic type, which is equally truthful
but which originates on the plane of imaginative and artistic fiction."[2] Over the
years, many acting theorists have attempted to define this type of acting. The fact
is, however, that no single, appropriately comprehensive definition of Stanislavski's scenic acting exists. Throughout this book we will attempt to define this type
of acting while discovering the mystery of inspiration and the conscious control
of the subconscious.

At a more basic level, we can say that acting is behaving as if things that are
not real *are* real, a broad definition that covers even the make-believe games of
childhood. A little later in life, everyone gathers experience in acting in another
context and for another purpose. These performances, which we may suitably
term *social acting,* will vary, depending on the circumstances and the intention of
the "actor." Described at times as good manners, at times as "little white lies," and
at other times as downright deceptions, these performances can vary from cor-
dially receiving guests whom one has no desire to see to feigning ignorance at a
surprise party in your honor. We all tell stories of people and events with the in-

tent of sharing the original experiences with our listeners. And most of us attempt on occasion to mimic the speech and behavior patterns of others. This natural human capacity to perform, listen, react, and affect the performance of others is at the heart of the actor's art; however, these rudimentary experiences are no substitute for formal acting technique training.

Nevertheless, skills developed through social acting — alongside personal observations and self-taught stage experiences — are frequently all an actor brings to school, college, or community theatre productions. These skills, when intermingled with general intelligence and an imaginative director, provide the basis for a certain level of success. Indeed, repeated experiences under such conditions can occasionally produce actors of modest overall ability. But the person who aims to perform consistently at a level of professional competence needs more thorough and demanding technique training. Like musicians and dancers, actors must learn their art step by step. Stanislavski said that the most dangerous dilettante is the one who denies the need for technique and insists that it interferes with inspiration. Performing a major role requires both talent and technical skills fully as great as those necessary for a professional pianist to perform a major concerto, and this talent can be developed and these skills acquired only through proper training. In today's world, such training plays a vital role in an actor's success. In *Acting Professionally: Raw Facts About Careers in Acting,* Robert Cohen writes:

> In the old days, actors without formal training were the rule. . . . Now,
> this sort of attitude has become very definitely the exception. Training
> in the art and craft of acting is a virtual necessity for a successful career,
> and if you are hired at first without training, as child actors or retired
> athletes often are in TV, you will need it before going much further.[3]

During those "old days," fledgling actors received their training by working as walk-ons and bit players in stock companies or by touring road shows, learning their skills in schools of very hard knocks. At a time somewhat later, stories abound of actors discovered in drug stores and young aspirants who descended on Broadway or Hollywood and found fame and fortune merely on the basis of their charm, physical attractiveness, or unique personality.

Those days are over. Stock companies have practically disappeared. The number of touring shows has been reduced greatly, and employment with those that remain is certainly not available to untrained actors. Today, stage, film, television, and even CDs afford the aspiring actor an extremely competitive market, in which thorough training is necessary for even moderate success. For the first time in history, most of our professional actors at least began their training in a college, university, or conservatory.

Furthermore, the best opportunities for stage actors today are often in small professional or regional theatres, which usually offer a mixed repertory of classics, modern plays, and musicals that require actors with range and versatility. In

Carol Pratt

Figure 1.1 Helen Carey as Lady Macbeth and Stacy Keach as Macbeth in The Shakespeare Theatre's 1995 production of *Macbeth,* by William Shakespeare. Directed by Joe Dowling. Many established actors maintain a close working relationship with professional regional theatres across the country.

the past several decades, the growth of these theatres, alternative theatres, children's theatres, theatres associated with colleges and universities, conservatories, and community theatres has given both actors and playwrights many opportunities to practice their profession away from the boom-or-bust syndrome of Broadway and from the major production centers for TV and film.

Even so, it is still commonplace for acting teachers to announce to their students that "there are no jobs" in acting. It is true that professional union actors earn, on average, less than $12,000 a year (and included within that average are several actors who make several million dollars annually!). Out of more than 100,000 professional actors in the United States, less than 50 percent earn an income higher than the national poverty level in any given year, and less than 10 percent of those actors consistently earn a middle-class income.[4] Acting is one of the most deceivingly difficult art forms and arguably the most difficult art with which to make a living. Nevertheless, the best acting students are those who are so irrepressibly committed to this ephemeral and often heartbreaking career that they persist in trying it against all odds. Furthermore, all who study acting know that the skills a student acquires in an acting class have many applications beyond the perimeters of professional theatre. First, studying acting and drama gives a better understanding of oneself and others. Second, creative dramatics, theatre for the aged, and the application of acting skills to the "human potential" movement in psychology provide new opportunities for actors to put their training to work. Moreover, increased leisure time and the recent emphasis on fitness, healthy diet, and meditation open interesting employment opportunities to trained actors willing to put their skills to other than a theatrical use. People trained in theatre successfully populate all sorts of jobs, but especially those requiring effective communicators with the ability to listen carefully and understand or evaluate a role other people are attempting to perform.

Acting with Professional Competence

Although everyone acts and in a simple way achieves some measure of success, the talent and skill involved in game playing and social acting fall far short of that necessary for professional accomplishment in the theatre. The successful stage performance is a carefully planned feat of artistry that communicates with the greatest possible effectiveness a viable interpretation of the meaning of a particular play to an audience. Rather than a casual world in which actors behave impulsively in chance events, the stage is a world of controlled design in which all parts of the pattern serve to illuminate a purpose, usually that of a playwright as interpreted by a director. Of course, inspiration and improvisation can be an exciting part of the art of the theatre, and we will talk about that later. But, from the beginning, students must realize that acting is not doing what "feels natural" and that spontaneous responses are most valid (and most likely to appear) only after careful preparation. Legendary acting theorists have for years attempted to harness the **mystery of inspiration.** There are endless examples of actors who are brilliant on opening night and then fail to achieve any semblance of this initial inspiration in subsequent performances. True inspiration must not be an opening-night discovery. Professional actors search for moments of inspiration at every rehearsal and call upon it at every performance. Inspiration comes as a result of technique training and hard work! Tyrone Guthrie, one of the most eminent twentieth-century directors, wrote:

> Drama is absolutely and elaborately prescribed, and the greatest acting contains a minimum of spontaneous invention and a maximum of carefully calculated effect repeated with only minute variations at every

performance of the same part. Dramatic performance, therefore, is concerned with repeating a series of intelligibly prescribed actions in order to form an intelligibly prescribed design.[5]

As an audience member, we all recognize when we have experienced an inspired performance in which we completely **"suspended our disbelief."** Perhaps it evoked strong feelings of anger, joy, pity, or fear. We identified with the characters, and their journeys may have served as an emotional catharsis for our own lives. However, describing the actor's inspired work of art is extraordinarily difficult. Perhaps we may say that great actors have the uncanny ability to:

✦ **Analyze** and appreciate the playwright's text, the given circumstances, and the character's role within the world of the play. (We attempt to underscore this important aspect of acting throughout *Acting Is Believing* but take it up in particular in Part Two, "The Actor and the Play.")

✦ **Interpret** the character's actions by way of the actor's personal experiences and imagination. (Part One of *Acting Is Believing,* "The Actor Alone," is designed to provide the actor with the capability to unleash these valuable tools.)

✦ **Externalize,** both physically and orally, the character's inner thoughts, desires, and fears, creating a form that will make the meaning comprehensible to others and will have intrinsic artistic value. (The last three chapters of Part Two focus on creating a basis for and communicating an effective interpretation of a play.)

✦ **Project** the character with an appropriate dimension, energy, and clarity that can communicate the meaning to an audience of a certain size occupying a certain space. (The last three chapters of Part Two—especially those labeled "Interpreting the Lines" and "Communicating the Lines"—also deal with this aspect of acting.)

✦ **Repeat** an inspired performance as if the character were living the events on stage for the first time. Part Three, "The Actor and the Production," delineates tools for coping with this portion of the actor's work.)

All we have said thus far makes acting seem to be incredibly complex and demanding, and indeed it is. Nevertheless, in addition to the proper motivation to succeed, we can state the remaining essential qualities of a successful actor quite simply. Remember them as the **three *t*'s:** talent, training, and tenacity.

Talking about talent is easy, but defining it precisely is extremely difficult. Talent is relevant to the observer. Certainly, a "stagemother" and a casting director have two different opinions with regard to talent. But even to a trained professional, it frequently seems to be unrecognizable in its undeveloped state, because biographies of many actors of great prominence tell how they were advised early in their careers that they had no potential for success. Certainly, talent must not be confused with being stagestruck or "screenstruck." Many such people lack the requisite talent and are attracted to the profession only by the most superficial elements of "show business."

Perhaps the best way to define **talent** is to delineate the qualities of successful actors. Successful actors have:

✦ an indescribable aura—also referred to as personal magnetism, stage presence, star quality, and the unspoken television rating system known as TVQ—that makes people want to watch and listen to their every action and thought.

✦ confidence and control over their own personality.

✦ a full understanding and acceptance of their own inner and outer self—both strengths and weaknesses.

✦ a body and voice capable of unending expression.

✦ an insatiable desire and need to share experiences with others.

✦ an increased sensitivity to the world at large.

✦ an unflagging curiosity and understanding about diverse people's modes of behavior and the human condition.

✦ courage and self-confidence and are unafraid to reveal their inmost feelings on a public stage.

✦ a keen sense of histrionics.

People with these attributes will probably be considered "talented." They will probably be cast in major roles that test their abilities on a regular basis at their university or community theatre. Although they may lack technique and experience, their talent will probably be recognized at an early age. Without it, the actor will face an uphill and perhaps insurmountable battle.

Some people claim that a talented actor does not need **training,** the second "*t.*" They shout, "Great actors are born!" However, painters, musicians, and dancers must also be born with talent, and yet do any of these other visual or performing artists achieve greatness through talent alone? Stanislavski said, "The bigger the talent, the more development and technique it needs." **Sonia Moore,** perhaps the most celebrated contemporary teacher of the Stanislavski System, writes,

> To talent, technique must be applied. By the same token, not everyone who studies music for many years will become a great musician; not everyone who studies dance technique for many years will become a great dancer; and not everyone who studies acting technique for many years will become a great actor.[6]

Stanislavski himself said that he had never spoken to any actor, no matter how immense the person's talent, who declared that "technique is unnecessary and talent necessary or that technique is first and talent secondary. Just the opposite— the greater the actor, the more he is interested in the technique of his art."[7] In book after book, biography after biography, this simple fact becomes abundantly clear: Good actors work hard, train hard, and take their work seriously. They know that great achievement can come only after practicing their technique so frequently and so thoroughly that it becomes a natural part of everything they do.

Training requires time, patience, hard work, and self-discipline. Enthusiasm, a striving for perfection (although it can never be achieved), and a willingness to work cooperatively with others all are important. In fact, as necessary as abundant talent is to an actor's chance for success, it can be a trap in the early stages of development if it tempts them to get along with a minimum of effort. Before they know it, persons of lesser talent but with uncompromising discipline and a better attitude will be accomplishing more. You must take complete control of your art, your discipline. Otherwise, you will become no more than a talented proletarian actor, what the legendary actress and teacher, **Uta Hagen,** refers to as a "hack." You will soon be disappointed and discouraged. Talent in itself is a waste, but a talented actor with a strong work ethic has the potential to become an extraordinary artist.

To arrive at an understanding of what an **actor's training** involves, we can divide the process into six parts.

1. **Cultural development:** an important and inadequately emphasized aspect of the training process. Actors—as well as other artists—must be students of life. Hagen says, "To be more than an adequate or serviceable actor, it takes a BROAD EDUCATION in the liberal arts."[8] The material from which the actor draws is the entire realm of human knowledge and experience. They cannot afford to be ignorant of historical or contemporary events, linguistics, literature, music, visual arts, design, psychology, sociology, religion, politics, sports, economics, travel, business, circus arts, eroticism, etc. The list is endless. "An artist who has not mastered his profession is a dilettante," wrote Goethe, "and an artist who has limited himself to his profession is a corpse."

2. **Internal techniques:** a keen understanding of human psychology, historical imagination, and learning how to control and to make effective use on stage of sensory and emotional responses.

3. **External techniques:** the development of the body and voice as responsive and expressive instruments. Vocal dexterity, speech, movement, and gestures are the actor's principal tools, as well as a highly developed awareness of the connection between the mind and body—what Stanislavski refers to as the psychophysical union.

4. **Interpretative skills:** the ability to read a script, examine the plot, explore the characters and their relationships, break the dialogue into small structural units, determine the simple objectives (by way of action verbs) and obstacles (both physical and psychological), unearth the subtext of the verbal

and physical actions, and determine the through line of action, all of which lead to the discovery of the play's super-objective.

5. **Rehearsal techniques:** learning how actors prepare for rehearsals at home; how they experiment, make discoveries, and learn from failure; how they explore various tempo-rhythms; how they commune with themselves, the environment, the images, the text, and with other actors; how they relate to the director, the stage manager, the production staff; and how they observe the principles of rehearsal ethics and discipline.

6. **Performance skills:** the capacity to prepare before a performance; how to relate to, and to share the play with, the audience (without pandering or **indicating**); how to maintain and control impulses, energy, and various tempo-rhythms; and how to keep a performance fresh — "the illusion of the first time" — each time you put on your character's clothing.

With the exception of cultural development, which must come as a lifelong commitment to expanding your knowledge of and sensitivity to the world around you, these processes roughly comprise the information presented in this book. You must be cautious, though, about thinking of acting as a step-by-step, logical process. Good actors never stop honing their abilities in all these areas. Students should always be careful not only to bring the skills and understandings of previous lessons to bear on their current exercise but also to continue a regimen of practice and exploration that expands their abilities to perform the skills they are accumulating. Good actors never cease to study and practice their basic skills, just as accomplished musicians devote a tremendous portion of every day to practicing the foundations of their technique.

The third "*t*," **tenacity,** is perhaps the most difficult of all. Whatever else acting might be, it is a business, and a very cold and heartless business at that. Although you may — and perhaps should — be getting cast on a regular basis at your university or local community theatre, the world of professional acting is extraordinarily competitive. Whereas you may be one of two or three leading ladies at your university, in the professional world it may seem that there is always someone else who is taller, shorter, blonder, more ethnic, less ethnic. The person in line next to you will be able to sing a higher note, handle more complex dance choreography, or manage Shakespearean verse better than you. Beautiful and distinctive people, who are equally talented and equally well trained, will surround you. You may feel they have better connections into the business and that they receive more financial and emotional support from their families. Professional acting is a business of rejection. The odds are always against you. For every fifty auditions you attend, you may receive one offer. Even established professionals — unless you are Brad Pitt or Julia Roberts — must frequently face rejection by producers and casting directors. And once you have secured a job, unless the production has an unlimited run, you must start the process all over again — even before your current job has ended.

A hunger to succeed isn't enough. Ambition alone will not land you a callback. Being discovered is a myth. You must have talent. You must have proper training. But perhaps equally important, you must have the tenacity and confidence to handle rejection on a daily basis. You must learn how to present yourself in a professional manner and sell your talent in an extremely tight job market. Thus, the following set of skills should be added to the above list of an actor's training:

7. **Auditioning and business skills:** the ability to prepare marketable headshots, résumés, business cards, postcards, thank-you notes, and various audition materials; the communication skills to handle yourself in a callback or interview situation; the knowledge to explore the Internet and trade journals and magazines for pending auditions; the capacity to negotiate with agents and managers; the savvy to understand the unions, contracts, health insurance, and pensions and basically serve as the CEO of your own company in which you are the only employee. (Chapter 13 deals specifically with auditioning, headshots, and résumés, but we suggest you read Robert Cohen's and the multitude of related books for more information regarding the "business" of theatre.)

However talented or tenacious their desire to succeed, students must realize that technique training cannot be accomplished simply from studying this or any other book, that it requires the guidance of able teachers, coaches, and directors. Because theatre is a highly cooperative endeavor, working with others in exercises and in scene study is essential. After acquiring the basic skills, the student should be given an opportunity to work before an audience, preferably first in a laboratory situation and later under conditions that approximate those in the professional theatre.

Good acting, then, does not result entirely from some God-given talent that enables special people to perform instinctively. Rather, it ensues from the practice of certain skills that can be learned if one has the aptitude and the determination to do so. Much of this book is based on a twenty-first century interpretation of Stanislavski's System. "As a seeker for gold," he said, "I can transmit to future generations not my searching and my privations, my joys and disappointments, but the precious 'mine' that I found." He went on to say:

> This "mine" in my artistic field is the result of my whole life's work. It is my so-called "System" the technique that permits the actor to create a character, to reveal the life of a human spirit and to incarnate it naturally on stage in an artistic form. This method is based on laws of the organic nature of an actor, which studied in practice. Its strength is in the fact that there is nothing in it, which I "invented," and nothing that I did not verify by applying it to my students and myself. It developed naturally out of my long experience.[9]

Once mastered, technique training provides the actor with an external and an internal means for performing a role as if the events were happening for the first time at each rehearsal and subsequent performance by executing a sequence of specific actions. With proper technique a role cannot grow stale, no matter how long the run. When these actions are harmoniously and artfully integrated, they help reveal the purpose of the play as interpreted for a particular production. Only then can acting be said to be "good," no matter how "beautiful" it may have looked or sounded nor how "exciting" the event itself may have been to an audience. Only then will "acting" and "believing" become synonymous.

The final goal of the great actor is to have the audience believe completely in the reality of the performance.

What part should a textbook play in the complex task of training an actor? It should organize your study in a logical progression; it should create an awareness of recurring problems and suggest solutions, thus guiding you toward technical proficiency; and it should provide you with useful practice exercises. No text can be comprehensive, and this one, although not ignoring any aspect of the acting process, focuses on the development of internal and interpretative skills—including the audition process—through both theory and exercises.

Exploring Your Resources

This book proceeds from the fundamental belief that student actors begin their training with self-exploration. The tools you will use as an actor, although they may be sharpened by practice and stretched by learning and exercise, are present within you even as you read these words.

The need for the actor to develop a well-trained body and voice—which we will refer to as the actor's **external resources**—should be obvious. A musician forced to perform on an inferior instrument is at a disadvantage. And actors are at a similar disadvantage if their muscular and vocal controls are not all that they could be. In fact, the training of the actor's voice and body as an instrument occupied almost the exclusive attention of acting teachers well into the twentieth century.

Today's theatre practice demands that this training—as essential as it is—be accomplished in conjunction with other studies and exercises fundamental to the actor's development. A fine speaking voice and a well-coordinated body in themselves do not make an actor, any more than possessing a Stradivarius makes a violinist. Along with the instrument, the *how* by which artists reach their audience, must come the *what*. The primary task of the actor is to create a character who "behaves logically in imaginary circumstances" provided by the playwright and interpreted by the director, and the raw material for accomplishing this task we shall call your **inner resources.** They will join with your external

Figure 1.2 Keith Hamilton Cobb as Tullus Aufidius in The Shakespeare Theatre's 2000 production of *Coriolanus*, by William Shakespeare. Directed by Michael Kahn. All actors must strive to maintain their external resources.

resources through the psychophysical process as the fundamental basis for the study of acting.

The need for inner resources surfaces the moment you start to think seriously about performing a role in a play. Suppose you have been cast in a part that requires you to enact the funeral rites for a native of Bandjarmasin. If you are like most untrained actors, you will go to your first rehearsal without a clue about what to do when you get there, perhaps already visualizing a storm of applause on opening night, after which hundreds of spectators murmur that you "have it in you" to be a great actor.

In fact, arriving at such a moment will come only after an arduous journey in which you systematically discover what you "have in you" that might help you bring to life on the stage a native of Bandjarmasin engaged in the solemn ritual of disposing of the dead. The chances are ten to one against your ever having heard of the place, to say nothing of your having a familiarity with its customs. Once you realize you must create an unambiguous character in these unfamiliar circumstances, despite your overwhelming lack of knowledge about either of them, you will probably experience a sense of defeat. How could you possibly perform, or indeed even imagine, an action that you could be certain would be truthful to this character?

You have now encountered the world of the actor at rehearsal. All actors face the same dilemma when they prepare to perform a role in any play, no matter how common or how exotic the situation and the setting. Your goal as a student of acting is to be able to bring to the rehearsal a method of studying the role together with the tools that will enable you to access the necessary raw materials for creating and performing it. These raw materials, simply put, constitute the accumulation of your own experience.

Your inner resources, then, are composed of everything you have done, seen, thought, or imagined in your lifetime. Your actions on stage are limited to these resources. For the role in question, you will need to find elements in your inner resources that will allow you to create and believe in the circumstances of the unfamiliar character from Bandjarmasin. Just as you are dependent on your voice and body to carry out your actions, you are also dependent on your inner resources to tell you what actions to carry out.

Fortunately, your resources are not confined to what you have personally experienced; they also come from reading, listening, and observing countless sources. Research and the expansion of your **historical imagination** are important parts of your quest for unearthing the truth in the world of the play. And a part of talent is the ability to deepen and extend experiences in the imagination.

The need for inner resources is not confined to exotic and unlikely dramatic circumstances. For instance, let us suppose you have been cast as Shakespeare's Romeo or Juliet, and that the scene for rehearsal is Act III, Scene 5, sometimes called the second balcony scene. To illustrate the current point, we need only recall the chief facts of the situation. Romeo and Juliet are the son and daughter of two powerful and wealthy families who have long been bitter enemies. Having met by chance, they have fallen deeply in love and have married secretly. Within an hour after their marriage, Romeo, involved in an outbreak of the ancient hostility, has killed Juliet's cousin and has been banished from his native city of Verona. There seems to be no hope of happiness together as the young couple say farewell in the dawning light.

What an exciting prospect to play one of these famous lovers! You have now learned that you must be prepared to explore your own inner resources before you can possibly create a character in whose behavior you, the other actors, and the audience can believe. But how do you know what inner resources to explore? How can you begin to match your own experience with that of the character? You begin with the script, first discovering the physical actions the character must perform. The process of defining and using these actions is the first topic we shall explore.

Notes

1. Constantin Stanislavski, Elizabeth Reynolds Hapgood, trans., *An Actor Prepares* (New York: Theatre Arts Books, 1973), p. 122.

2. Ibid., p. 121.

3. Robert Cohen, *Acting Professionally: Raw Facts About Careers in Acting* (Mountain View, CA: Mayfield Publishing Company, 1998), p. 27.

4. Ibid., p. 3.

5. Tyrone Guthrie, *New York Times,* August 28, 1966.

6. Sonia Moore, *Stanislavski Revealed* (New York City: Applause Theatre Books, 1991), pp. 9–10.

7. Constantin Stanislavski, J. J. Robbins, trans., *My Life in Art* (New York: Theatre Arts Books, 1948), p. 568.

8. Uta Hagen, *A Challenge for the Actor* (New York: Macmillan Publishing Company, 1991), p. 36.

9. Sonia Moore, *Training an Actor: The Stanislavski System in Class* (New York: Penguin Books, 1979), pp. 26–27.

CHAPTER 2

Discovering the Physical Actions

*"An actor becomes an actor when he
masters the choice of actions."*

Stanislavski

We have already stated that a part of the definition of acting is "behaving truthfully in imaginary circumstances." Your first step toward achieving this goal is to discover the physical life of the character you are playing.

Think again about that exciting moment when you arrive at the first rehearsal of *Romeo and Juliet.* You are about to enter the personal world of these characters at a special dimension, and your first task as an actor will be to find out what they do. You will read the play more carefully than you have ever read anything before to discover what specific actions these characters carry out, and what logical sequences these actions follow from the beginning to the end of each scene and from the beginning to the end of the play.

You will discover these actions, the basic raw material for performing your role, by studying carefully the play's **given circumstances,** the unchangeable facts of the play. In some cases your discovery of these facts found in the script will provide enough material for a fully developed character, but more often the answers are only suggested or inferred in the text. Such is the case with *Romeo and Juliet.* As you study the play, however, remember that not all characters speak the truth, for like real human beings they look at their world subjectively. They have a unique point of view about every issue and every other person in the play. Like us, they bring with them certain beliefs, values, and prejudices. Characters sometimes exaggerate. Sometimes they lie. It is your responsibility to discover the truth as perceived by your character. Once you have firmly established your character's point of view regarding "the facts" and understood their implications, you will be ready to augment the circumstances with material drawn from your own imagination. The latter aspect is significant, for it is the technique from which actors place their distinctive interpretation on the role.

Creating a unique point of view is one of the most exhilarating facets of acting. Unfortunately, this excitement can seduce actors into rushing into that phase of their work before they have sufficiently completed their study of the script. The behavior of the character must always be firmly grounded in the character's perceived circumstances. Stanislavski said:

> Let each actor give an honest reply to the question of what physical action he would undertake, how he would act (not feel, there should for heaven's sake be no question of feelings at this point) in the given circumstances created by the playwright. . . . When these physical actions have been clearly defined, all that remains for the actor to do is to execute them.[1]

Please take special notice of two important phrases in Stanislavski's lesson. He admonishes the actor to "act in the given circumstances created by the playwright" and declares that "there should be no question of feelings at this point." Recalling these two pieces of advice will serve the actor well during the entire creative process.

The search for the given circumstances begins in the script, with a study of the dramatic elements of character, plot, dialogue, and locale. In most instances, the playwright uses these facts to tell the actor about the character. Actors must carefully study their characters' words, their every action. Where and when do these physical actions occur? At a later point in the rehearsal process, the given circumstances will also include directorial choices, stage business, costumes, and scenic environment; but mastering these elements is an aspect of acting that will be discussed in a subsequent chapter. For now, let us focus on answering four questions:

✦ Who?

✦ What?

✦ Where?

✦ When?

Each of these four "W's" (we will add an essential fifth in the next chapter) asks questions to which you must find unambiguous answers either in the text or in your imagination. Until these answers are clear, your acting, from simple exercises to complex characterizations, will be at best confusing and at worst meaningless. The answers to the "W" questions generate physical actions, and these actions, when clearly performed, communicate the circumstances of the play to the audience. *Never embark on an acting assignment until you have specific answers to these questions.*

Your acceptance of the role of either Romeo or Juliet has committed you to act in the given circumstances of the play. Both of these roles are specific characters created by a master dramatist. You will be expected to play the character to the fullest extent that your experience and imagination enable you to understand the playwright's prescription. You have no choice, of course, but to play the role with your own body, your own voice. You must use your own past experiences and imagination to deliver appropriate live responses. It follows, then, that in seeking to discover the physical life of the character, you must always find a logical sequence of actions you can understand, that you can *believe* are *necessary*. The vital question is, "What would I *do if I were this character* in these circumstances?" To ask only "What would I do in these circumstances?" inevitably means that you play only yourself rather than the character the playwright has drawn.

You must use the four "W's" to trigger your imagination, whether you are beginning to prepare a role or just about to step on stage. Each must be answered precisely and fully. It is not sufficient, for example, for an actor in *When You Comin Back, Red Ryder?* to answer the "Where?" question with "in a restaurant." A more satisfactory response would be, "In a small, grimy, dusty diner in the New Mexican desert." The actors playing Jerry and Peter in *The Zoo Story* cannot sufficiently stimulate their imaginations by thinking of themselves "in a park." They must concentrate on being "in Central Park, near 75th Street and Fifth Avenue in New York, about nine blocks north of the Central Park Zoo." As a young actor, however, you may never have experienced a dusty New Mexican diner or visited Central Park. Nevertheless, it is still your responsibility to make the "Where?" as truthful and specific as possible. You have your whole life from which to draw, and you have no doubt experienced restaurants that were filthy and yet overflowing with ambiance. You have enjoyed many excursions to a local park. You probably have vivid memories of playing with your dog or throwing a Frisbee®. You know the trees, the landscape, and the specific details of your favorite outdoor hideaway. You certainly have at least some understanding of life in a large city. By transferring these life experiences—added to proper analysis and research—you will have the ability to create a stage environment that is equally specific and detailed.

The questions "What?" and "When?" demand the same specificity. What has happened previously? What has occurred the precise moment before? What is happening in the play right now? What are your character's expectations? What is the year? The season? The day? The weather? At what time does "your" selected life begin? How do the conditions discovered in the "When?" and "Where?" affect the "What?"

The "Who?" question must not merely trigger the preconceived — and usually stereotypical — notions of a lawyer, a cheerleader, or a prince because these terms stand for an infinite variety of people. All lawyers are not the same any more than individual members of a cheerleading squad are the same. Prince Hamlet is vastly different from Prince Harry. "Who am I?" demands thorough investigation using all your resources. In creating a **character autobiography,** you certainly must record your character's laundry list of experiences, relationships, and achievements. More important, though, you must explore your character's dreams, fears, values, and spirituality. What is your character's present state of being? What are "you" wearing, and how does it affect "your" actions?

Perhaps the most important question you must ask yourself about "Who?" is "How do 'I' perceive myself?" Actors cannot judge their characters if they are to wear their clothing and behave truthfully in the given circumstances. Prostitutes do not necessarily consider themselves amoral. They may regard themselves as extraordinarily decent and honest people — although industrious and streetwise. Mass murderers can justify their every action. Although we may consider Adolph Hitler to be one of the most evil men in history, Hitler professed himself to be the spiritual savior, the purifier of his race. He may have perceived himself as a charismatic leader, who had the vision and means to accomplish his political and honorable goals. Judging characters — no matter how different they are from you — will only stifle the creative process. Actors who cannot or refuse to drop their own point of view and moral sensitivities regarding the character's actions and beliefs will create nothing more than a hollow stereotype. Actors who will only look at their characters from the outside will never have the ability to fully invest in their actions.

Without specific and detailed responses to all four "W's" leading to plausible, consistent behavior, you — as well as the audience — will never *believe* in your character's reality.

Each of the four "W's" is not always equally important in every scene. Sometimes, for instance, logical actions growing out of "Who?" dominate the moment. At the beginning of *A Streetcar Named Desire,* when Blanche sneaks a drink before Stella comes home, she needs to dispose of the glass. An appropriate physical action selected by the actor will speak volumes about Blanche's character. In the original Broadway production, Jessica Tandy, standing in front of the kitchen sink, ignored the seemingly logical choice of rinsing out the glass. Rather, she shook it vigorously and replaced it in the cabinet. In this way, the preliminary picture the audience had probably formed of a delicate but fading southern belle was cracked, if not shattered.

As you perform the exercises at the end of this chapter, try altering the dominant "W" in the scene. Notice how each selection will offer a different range of choices of physical actions.

"Making physical actions your own" and "building on your own live responses" are important problems to be considered in later chapters. We are also postponing for the moment a thorough discussion of the actor's use of emotion, complying with Stanislavski's warning that "there should be no question of feelings at this point."

Emotions, of course, play a critical role in acting, but they are unpredictable. You cannot act an emotion, nor can you call forth an emotional response at will. You must learn to begin with tangible and controllable physical actions. You cannot play happiness any more than you can play anger; however, you can at every performance carry out a series of actions whenever you *will* to do so. What is more, because physical actions and internal emotion are inextricably linked, performing the needed actions in the given circumstances may bring forth the desired feeling. We will speak of this in greater detail at the beginning of Chapter 3. But whether the physical actions generate an emotional response, the careful playing of them will realize the intention of the scene and accomplish the actor's primary responsibility. Success is not to be judged by whether emotion is aroused in the actor.

Committing Yourself to Action

The above reference to the actor's *will* introduces you to one of your most valuable inner resources. So important is your *will,* or full commitment to your actions on stage, that it became the cornerstone of one of the greatest twentieth-century American acting teachers, **Sanford Meisner.** He believed that the foundation of acting is the "reality of doing." Meisner's "reality of doing" is our *will,* our commitment to actions. In life, we don't pretend to get dressed in the morning. We actually put on our shirts, our pants, and our socks. We really tie our shoelaces. The stage is a secondary reality, a mirror to nature. However, you must invest as fully in your stage actions as you do in life. At the beginning of his acting classes, Meisner invariably asked his students to solve in their head a multiplication problem. "What is nine hundred thirty-one times eighteen?" His students sat in silence. Some of them pretended to concentrate while others attempted to answer the question. No one solved the problem. The correct answer is 16,758. The answer, however, is not important. What is important is your *will* to work out the problem.[2] In attempting to solve your simple and complex problems on stage, you must search always for solutions that are subject to your *will.* You must find appropriate actions to which you can fully commit and that can be repeated and kept under control at every rehearsal and performance.

The will to action is one of your most powerful inner motive forces, both on the stage and off. Creativity is directly related to your complete investment in the physical life of your character. The strength of your desire to "do fully" determines how interesting your performance will be to yourself and, to a large extent,

Figure 2.1 Terry Seago, Jim Ponds, and Grover Coulson in August Wilson's *Joe Turner's Come and Gone* at Stage West Theatre in Ft. Worth, TX. Directed by Jerry Russell. Note the focus and commitment to verbal and physical action by all three actors in this shot.

how remarkable it will be to your audience. Your commitment to your actions is effective only as long as those actions are directed toward logical activity, supported by the given circumstances, and meaningful to the character. Your activity must also be capable of motivating strong desire. There is no place either on the stage or in the rehearsal room for half-heartedness or indifference. Actors who pretend to drink, pretend to read a letter, pretend to smoke, pretend to kiss will never arrive at "true emotions" on stage. Their actions will simply be false indications of the truth. You must learn to commit yourself without reservation to the purposeful acts of your character. Doing so, you will find that this personal commitment is one of the principal generators of feeling.

Unfortunately, a dedication to strong will does not in itself sufficiently guarantee believability. You must also recognize that, through lack of knowledge or experience or imagination, you can fully commit to doing the inappropriate or illogical thing—a thing totally unsupported by the given circumstances. The result will be a performance that is at odds with the play.

Strong commitment to proper action must not be confined to performance. You must practice this wholeheartedly in every classroom exercise. You must give your total being to your actions during every moment of every rehearsal. Such commitment is an important part of all creative talent.

EXERCISE   To illustrate what is meant by "exploring your inner resources" and "discovering physical actions," we talked about playing a native of Bandjarmasin or Romeo or Juliet. But these problems, involving knowledge of exotic customs or an understanding of what you would do in a scene of emotional crisis, are too complex for beginning practice, so we shall start with a simpler exercise.

In Act I, Scene 2, of *The Miss Firecracker Contest,* by Beth Henley, Delmount is listening to the nervous and eccentric Popeye prattle on about one thing and another, including a recitation of common terms for groups of farm animals, such as "a gaggle of geese." As he listens, he eats a dish of vanilla ice cream, finally interrupting her with, "Oooh! Now the ice cream has given me a headache. Lord Jesus! A gaggle of geese! Oh, my head! My head!" He exits.

Here is an acting problem providing an opportunity to explore your inner resources for the purpose of finding the logical sequence of actions demanded by the given circumstances. If you had never suffered an ice cream headache or if you had never observed the behavior of anyone who had one, it would be impossible for you to solve this problem until you had enlarged your experience. You would have to investigate the nature of this occurrence to find out what actions would be truthful. Fortunately, an ice cream headache is not an uncommon occurrence, so it is relatively easy for you to find in your own experience what you would do if you were Delmount in this situation. You perhaps would take a bite of ice cream, start to swallow it, feel the sharp pain in your forehead, and try to stretch the muscles of the face and head to alleviate the sensation.

This is a simple but very real acting problem. Ignore the sex of the character and the context of the scene for the moment, and work on it until you can *believe your actions.* Here, as in all succeeding exercises, choose your actions so they constitute a definite dramatic structure. This means they should have a *beginning* (acquainting the audience with the problem), a *middle* (developing the problem), and an *end* (resolving the problem). Each of these three structural elements should be played clearly and precisely. In the early exercises the structure will be simple. In this exercise the beginning is Delmount's discovery that his head aches. The middle is stretching the muscles to restore a normal feeling. The end is his exit after his recovery, after he has solved his problem.

Plays are filled with situations like this one that require you to perform in such a way that you convince the audience you believe the actions you must undertake.

Other examples are: Your foot goes to sleep; you try to keep from sneezing; you have a toothache; or, you try to keep from scratching an itch. Perform each of these actions as you exit the stage, drawing on your own experience until you can believe what you do, thus making your work as believable as possible to your audience.

Believing Your Actions on Stage

Several times already, beginning with the title of this book, we have referred to "believing your actions" or to "creating a character in whom you can believe." You must believe what you are doing. Your fundamental responsibility to the audience is to induce their belief in your actions. So the objective of the exercise is not to pretend you have an ice cream headache but is to make yourself *believe* you do *through the actions you take* to ease the sharp, throbbing sensation. Acting is literally a matter of make-believe, fueled by an attitude almost identical to that which comes naturally to children.

Children with their mud pies, their kings and queens, and their cowboy-and-Indian games provide for themselves a set of circumstances very similar to those given to the actor by the dramatist. They instinctively behave in whatever fashion their experience or imagination leads them to think is true to the imposed conditions. The pleasure they receive from the game is in direct proportion to their ability to give themselves over to what they are doing—in other words, to the extent they are able to believe their actions. As the game wears thin and their belief decreases, they invent new circumstances to stimulate further action. One child may propose: "Let's make believe the king wasn't really hurt when he fell off his horse but was only pretending. He did it so the prince would feel sorry for him and help him fight the Black Knight." A whole new sequence of actions is justified, allowing the child and his playmates to continue the game with renewed belief.

Of course, the throne is actually their parents' dining chair. The king's crown is from a fast-food restaurant. The swords are plastic. When the game is over, the precious crown that has been guarded so carefully is kicked to one side of the living room floor. The children never think these things are real, yet while the game is on they treat these "**props**" as if they were true.

It is the same for the actor. During the day King Lear's robes hang limply on a hook in the dressing room, and the imperial crown lies unguarded on the prop table. But when the performance begins, if the actor playing Lear is to convince the audience he is every inch a king, he must believe in the circumstances given him by Shakespeare, by the director, by the designers as thoroughly as he believes in the actual world around him. "No half-belief," as Michael Redgrave said. "Belief . . . does not begin and end by an intellectual process, but . . . is so deep-rooted that it fires each movement, echoes in each silence, and penetrates beyond 'the threshold of the subconscious,' where it becomes creative. . . ."[3]

None of this is to suggest that actors are subject to a kind of hallucination that blurs their view of the surrounding reality and induces them to accept the pieces of glass in the crown as diamonds. The actor playing Lear knows that the life of the character he is playing lives only in the imagination, and, like the children, he knows that the crown and the robes he will wear are not real. He knows, in short, that he is not actually King Lear. He is an actor, so toward all of these things he says: "I will act as *if* they were real." And this conviction in the truth of his actions enables him to believe also in the *truth* (not the *reality*) of the cardboard crown. *If* is a word that can transform our thoughts. *If* allows us to transport ourselves into any situation. "If I were in love . . ." "If I won the lottery . . ." "If I were on death row . . ." "If I were a tenth-century prince and my mother married my uncle not two months after the death of 'my' father." The word *if* is incredibly powerful. *If* gives us a sense of certainty about our new world. If the actor playing Lear loses his sense of truth, it will not be because the crown is not real but because he cannot believe his own actions in relation to it.

Learn this first axiom well: The best way actors can evoke a feeling of belief in what they are doing is to concentrate on simple physical actions. Stanislavski frequently emphasized that "small physical actions, small physical truths and the moments of belief in them . . . acquire a great significance on the stage. . . ."[4]

Sustaining Belief

Once actors learn to believe in the truth of their actions, sustaining that belief is a difficult and ever-present problem. They must work in front of an audience and in the midst of all the inevitable distractions of a theatrical production. They must be able to summon their belief on cue whenever the moment to enter the stage arises. The slightest doubt as to the rightness or truth of what they or the other actors are doing is likely to upset them immediately. An actor playing Lear who treats his crown like the cardboard that it really is can destroy the belief of everyone on stage, just as a cynical child can destroy the magic of the game by protesting they can't fight with "plastic." The actor may renew a wavering belief, just as the child does, by discovering new circumstances that will excite new actions.

EXERCISE   When, for instance, you need further stimulation in the exercise from *The Miss Firecracker Contest,* try introducing circumstances such as these:

✦ Delmount is deeply in love with Popeye. He does not want his actions to make him seem foolish.

+ Delmount's speech and actions are a ruse to allow him to call for somebody to save him from Popeye's boring conversation.

+ Delmount wants Popeye to know that her tiresome conversation has somehow caused his headache.

+ Study the play to find suggestions for other circumstances that might alter the way Delmount performs these actions.

Discovering additional circumstances helps to renew the actor's belief. Asking the fundamental question, "*What* would I *do if* I were this character in these given circumstances?" helps uncover the true answer. Thus, the actor is provided with fresh reasons for action.

At this point you will find it useful to review what you have learned thus far about the way an actor works. Here is a summary:

1. Actors simultaneously develop their inner and outer techniques. Their outer technique depends on a trained voice and body to provide an effective instrument for communicating the meaning of a play to an audience. Their inner technique allows them to use their own life experience and historical imagination as a means of finding and understanding the subtext of their character's behavior.

2. The first step actors must take is to discover a logical sequence of physical actions the character they are playing would carry out in the given circumstances. They begin with physical actions because they are tangible and subject to their will.

3. To make these actions personal and, at the same time, to satisfy the intention of the dramatist, actors ask: "What would I do if I were this character in these given circumstances?"

4. Finding the answer to this question induces actors to believe the truth of their actions, even though nothing in the imaginary world of the character is real.

5. Actors must find strong reasons for these actions and commit wholeheartedly to carrying them out.

6. The actors' belief can be sustained and renewed by finding additional circumstances, true to the script, that stimulate fresh action.

7. Carefully chosen and clearly performed physical actions are one of the surest ways of communicating the play to the audience, which is the actors' primary function.

Solo Improvisation

To accomplish the exercises in this chapter and most of those in the remainder of the book, you will need to gain some skill in the actor training technique called **improvisation,** the spontaneous invention of lines and business without a fixed text. Improvisation as a method of learning, rehearsing, and performing has dominated actor training during the past several decades. Much of the theory underpinning this approach grows out of the research on games and play conducted by psychologists, anthropologists, and sociologists. The charm and indeed the value of the method lie in its ability to tap into your natural propensity to pretend, to make believe, to create, and to perform in a game of the imagination.

One reason improvisation has become such an important technique in actor training is that it places an emphasis on intuition and spontaneity. Viola Spolin, one of America's greatest proponents of improvisational acting, brought this aspect of the improvisational method to light when she wrote: "Spontaneity is the moment of personal freedom when we are faced with a reality and see it, explore it and act accordingly."[5] What better objective for a student who would learn the art of the actor?

Improvisations retain the quality of a game because their performance situation is not controlled by a playwright's words or a director's movement scheme. Actors are given the bare parameters of a situation and are left to perform the actions suggested by their physical involvement in the moment. Do not be fooled, however, for improvisation requires you to develop the given circumstances prior to and as the scene unfolds. Like everything related to acting, an improvisation must provide actors with specific objectives that they must decide to accomplish in a specific way.

It is important for you to develop a sense of personal freedom and self-expression during improvisational exercises. There is no right or wrong way to perform your actions. However, before you begin the improvisation, try to bring yourself into the psychophysical state in the circumstances you have built. Do not attempt to be anyone but yourself in these improvisations, although you will be yourself in different circumstances: a parent, a child, an athlete, a politician. Each improvisation must have a beginning, middle, and end, and it is sometimes easier if you begin the scene with an entrance and end with an exit. Some improvisations—particularly those executed by the solo performer—should be performed without the need to speak. Do not attempt to explain your actions to your audience through indicated or false dialogue, and do not pretend to talk to a nonexistent person at this early stage in your training. But keep in mind that people do sometimes sing to themselves or speak aloud in fragmented ways when the situation necessitates them to do so. In explaining her famous solo exercises, Uta Hagen wrote, "If in action you discover that you sigh, grunt, or groan, use expletives or otherwise verbalize your wishes, don't hesitate to include such responses in your score."[6] Finally, do not choose any actions that cannot be played fully in your acting classroom, such as opening or closing doors or windows that do not exist. In fact, avoid pantomimed actions altogether. Use only real objects and bestow upon them the physical and psychological properties that will help you to believe in their reality.[7] Your instructor will serve as the master of the game, because he or she will possess a mature mastery of both the artistic and technical aspects of the theatre. You will bring your own insight, imagination, and experience to performing the actions; because they are your own, they cannot be known until you discover them and create them for your audience.

EXERCISE   As an introduction to improvisation, perform an imaginary scene using one of the words from the list below as the basis of your actions. Remember, the scene must adhere to the instructions explained in the above paragraph. Play yourself and perform alone, but ask yourself the four "W" questions, just as you would if you were preparing a role from a play. Your instructor will provide the given circumstances of the scene.

1. Dressing (e.g., for bed, for a special occasion, for work)
2. Waiting (e.g., at a dangerous subway stop, at home, at the airport)
3. Searching (e.g., for a lost object, a telephone number, a word in the dictionary)
4. Sitting outdoors (e.g., at the beach, in the woods, in the park)
5. Reading (e.g., a textbook, a "Dear John" letter, a romance novel)
6. Stealing (e.g., in a department store, in a friend's home)
7. Hiding (e.g., from a stranger, from a friend)
8. Packing (e.g., to go on vacation, to move to a new home, to run away)
9. Digging (e.g., to plant a tree, to bury a pet, to look for treasure)
10. Any other simple task

Making a Score of Physical Actions

Early in their training, actors need to master a dependable method of working that will not only guide their study but yield practical results. Some would-be actors have a notion that practical effort, especially if it involves the use of pencil and paper, will dampen spontaneity and hamper creativity. This notion is ill founded. Inspiration comes from conscious technical effort, and a talent that cannot be nourished by hard, practical work is not very robust to begin with. Writing down thoughts stimulates further thinking, and practice carried on in the imagination can provide a solid theoretical foundation for a method of working that will sustain you throughout your career.

You now know how to discover the physical actions for your character in a given scene. Once you have done so (and this does require pencil and paper), you should list them. Your list of actions (and don't be afraid to number them) should form a sequence that is logical and appropriate for the character in the situation, and each action should be such that you are psychologically and physically capable of carrying it out. Your list for the following exercises should be short and not excessively detailed, as it will not be practical unless you can keep it easily in mind. It should, on the other hand, be complete — no gaps that make it difficult for you to go from one action to the next. Your imagination, stimulated by the given circumstances, will provide the necessary strong desire to accomplish the sequence.

Making this list is the first step of a practical technique that Stanislavski called "making a **score of the role.**"[8] It is just a beginning, because much of the remainder of this book is devoted to finding ways of expanding and deepening the score. When completed, the score becomes a comprehensive working design of your role and will include your physical and psychological actions, your major and minor objectives, images, subtext, and line readings. Scoring a role provides three advantages:

1. The preparation of it forces you to dig deeply into the play and into yourself.

2. Augmenting it during rehearsal keeps you alert to the stimulation of the director and the other actors.

3. The existence of the score makes it possible for you to review your creative effort whenever the need arises.

The score begins with a simple list of actions, and you should practice by deriving such a list for the exercise at the end of the chapter. The following is an example:

In *Of Mice and Men* by John Steinbeck, Lennie, a giant, childlike farmhand, sneaks a week-old puppy away from its mother and plays with it, even though he has been warned that it is too young to be handled. He kills the puppy and tries to conceal his mistake by hiding it in a pile of straw. (*Note:* This scene actually occurs before the curtain rises for Act III. As we shall see, some of the most profitable improvisation work an actor can do involves scenes that are important to the development of the play but that take place offstage.)

The Beginning: "Temptation and Anticipation"

1. Sneak into barn concealing a puppy.

2. Kneel on pile of straw.

3. Get comfortable on heels.

4. Place puppy on straw.

5. Poke puppy with finger.

6. Check to see if anyone has followed.

7. Pick puppy up.

8. Hold puppy gently to chest.

The Middle: "Ecstasy and Agony"

1. Laugh (speech and sounds are actions).

2. Hold puppy at arm's length in front.

3. Toss puppy in the air and catch it.

4. Feel puppy bite finger.

5. Drop puppy.

6. Slap puppy with the back of hand.

7. Hear puppy cry in pain.

The End: "Remorse and Cover-up"

1. Pick up lifeless puppy.

2. Try to shake puppy back to life.

3. Hear somebody approaching.

4. Hide puppy in straw.

Just as you did with the above improvisation exercise, note that this score has been divided into structural units—a beginning, a middle, and an end—that will give the exercise form, clarity, and dramatic interest. Also, each of the units has been given a name suggestive of the essential quality and the basic reason for the series of actions. Choosing a right name for each part of the structure is an extremely helpful technique, as it unifies the actions and helps the actors understand the appropriate attitude. It also helps establish proper relationships with the objects they are handling and with other characters in the exercise or scene.

Although the parts of the score should be closely related, progressing logically and inevitably from one to the other, the actor must clearly make a *transition* from one part to the next. Clear transitions bring each unit of the score to a definite terminal point and start the new unit with a firmly positive attack, a new impulse manifesting itself in movement, gesture, or speech. Terminal points and new attacks make the structure evident and give both actor and audience a sense that the play is moving forward.

The beginning, middle, and end of a score of physical actions are not arbitrary but represent distinct components of the overall action. For example, the routine of the beginning must come to a complete end (terminal point) before the action of the middle can commence. The conclusion of an action like "getting comfortable on your heels" results in an instant of stasis, a momentary vacuum, a transition from which comes a strong impulse for new action—preparing to play with the puppy. Recognizing the terminal point of an action is essential to building a score of actions, and pushing off or attacking a new task gives actors an opportunity to reinforce their belief in the human actions they are reproducing.

A sequence of individual actions can be distinguished further because each action will be influenced by the speed or pace of its environment (*tempo*) and by the internal performance pattern of the character (*rhythm*). Environmental influences are almost limitless, but some predominant sources of tempo are the prevailing mood, the weather, and other external circumstances, and even (or often especially) such artistic considerations as the placement of the action within a scene. The major sources of rhythm are within the character, and deciding on their rhythmic range is a consequential choice for the actor.

Life rhythms are extraordinarily important. The widely popular stage production *Stomp* is based primarily on our daily routines and rhythms. As in life, you must have a clear understanding of and feeling for your character's internal rhythms. In a workbook for actors based on Stanislavski's techniques, Mel Gordon suggested:

> All human activity follows some rhythmic pattern, which can be felt by
> the actor and expressed physically. Every stage movement should be con-
> ceived in Rhythm. Also, each character has a private Rhythm. Finding
> the character's Rhythm is an essential key to discovering his personality.[9]

Once a character's rhythm is discovered, combining it with the proper tempo is a subtle process, yet one at which experienced actors often seem to be intuitively right. When they correctly sense what their characters are saying and doing on stage, correct tempo-rhythms are likely to come without conscious effort. In learning a technique, however, it is usually necessary to make a *conscious* effort before mastery of the technique produces *unconscious* results.

Because the two are so closely related, Stanislavski used the term **tempo-rhythm** to designate the combined rhythmic flow and the speed of execution of the physical action (including speech) in a given scene. Tempo-rhythms have a natural appeal to both actor and audience—an almost magic power to affect one's inner mood. This power is, of course, most evident in music. Recall the different moods created by your responses to swing music, rap, ragtime, R & B, and country music. Indeed, the popularity of rock is primarily a result of the effect of its pervasive tempo-rhythm.

In the exercise from *Of Mice and Men,* make clear transitions between the units by using the technique of terminal points and new attacks. Then, experiment until you find an effective and distinct tempo-rhythm for the actions of each part. Be conscious of how it changes as you move from the actions of one part to those of the next. The tempo-rhythm may even change within a single passage. For example, in the sequence from *Of Mice and Men,* Lennie's tempo-rhythm will be dominated by a combination of the rhythm the actor chooses for Lennie's character as it is affected by the tempo of the circumstances of the scene—he fears he may be followed. Should Lennie hear a noise, the tempo-rhythm would change even if the activity he was performing had not been completed. A major change in the external circumstance will produce a major change in the tempo-rhythm.

Tempo-rhythm is applied ordinarily to the basic flow and speed of execution in each individual unit rather than to whole scenes of a play. In a sense, a scene's various tempo-rhythms add up to its overall pace. Scenes tend to have a pace that remains constant. The term *pace* refers to the speed at which the actors speak their lines, pick up their cues, and perform their actions.

To **pick up cues** does not imply that actors should race through a passage or scene. Usually, a director asks actors to pick up their cues to avoid the constant "line-pause-line" syndrome so common among new actors. In real life our communication with each other has a flow, and our silences have a significance that a dramatist can only hint at in transferring the spoken word to the written page. Actors then translate the playwright's words back into the sounds and silences of real "speech."

Next is a second score of actions taken from Brian Friel's *Dancing at Lughnasa.* Rose, a simple-minded young woman, left the house several hours ago with her older sister to pick berries. Feigning illness, she informed her sister that she wished to return home to rest. However, she slipped away to secretly rendezvous with a young man. In this scene, Rose returns home from her encounter carrying a red poppy. She is wearing her good shoes and skirt, but they have been soiled and wrinkled. Lethargically crossing through the family's garden, she sees her sister's cans of fruit. After a moment, she decides to sample the contents before entering the house to confront her worried family. Study both this example and the one from *Of Mice and Men* until you can understand and apply the technique of scoring to your own work.

The Beginning: "Dreams"

1. Slowly, lethargically enter into yard.
2. Stop.
3. Turn back to look at trail leading to house.
4. Smile in quiet reflection.
5. Upon hearing a bird, look into a tree.
6. Smell the red poppy.
7. Gently place flower in front pocket of dress.

The Middle: "Defiance"

1. Resume march toward the house.
2. See cans of fruit.
3. Stop beside them.
4. Check to see if anyone is watching.
5. Place hand in jar and thrust handful of berries into mouth.
6. Wipe mouth with dress sleeve and back of hand.

The End: "Womanhood"

1. Look once again at trail.
2. Notice stained fingers.
3. Hear noise inside house.
4. Turn and notice movement through window.
5. Wipe hands on dress.
6. Calmly move toward front door in quiet determination.

EXERCISE

Make and perform scores for several of the problems suggested below. Use pencil and paper; *write them out.* Remember that a score is a sequence of physical actions constituting logical and appropriate behavior in particular circumstances. Make the circumstances specific; find definite answers to the questions of *who, what, where,* and *when.* Choose actions that will communicate your meaning to an audience; that is, do not develop a habit of acting only for your own benefit. Your score should designate the beginning, the middle, and the end, and each of these units should have a suitable name.

After you have made the score, plan a simple arrangement of exits, windows, furniture, and whatever you need for the action, but let your imagination create as much detail in the environment as possible. Note that this detail provides a rich source for discovering physical actions. Give yourself actual or substitute objects (magazines, coffee cups, and so forth); do not try to pantomime nonexistent props. As you are working by yourself in this exercise, do not invent unnecessary dialogue. Use speech or sound only as necessary to call out or to release inner responses. Do not try to feel emotion. Do not try to be dramatic: simplicity is one of the first (and one of the hardest) things to learn. All of these "do nots" should make you aware that actors always work within a set of prescribed limitations. Only after boundaries have been established can freedom be achieved.

Note the difference between this carefully planned improvisation and the spontaneous exercise suggested before. Perform each score many times. Technique is developed through repetition, and each repetition should stimulate your imagination to greater belief. It is not necessary in these exercises to realize all the circumstances of the play; rather, the situations described should stimulate you to provide circumstances from your imagination.

1. In *Barefoot in the Park,* by Neil Simon, Corie, an energetic young newlywed, enters an unfurnished apartment holding a bouquet of flowers. She looks around the room and sighs. After examining the room, she fills a paint can with water for the flowers, throwing the wrapping on the floor. She searches for an appropriate place to put the arrangement.

2. In Harold Pinter's *The Caretaker,* Mick, a young man, sits alone on a bed. He looks at each object in the sparsely decorated room before he stares at the ceiling and at a hanging bucket collecting rainwater from a crack in the ceiling. He sits still for a long moment before hearing a bang at the door and muffled voices. Mick turns to look at the door and quietly moves toward it.

3. On a sultry summer evening, Maggie, in *Cat on a Hot Tin Roof,* by Tennessee Williams, charges into her bedroom from the supper table to assess the damage one of her nephews has done with a hot buttered biscuit to her pretty dress. She opens the curtains to allow more light in the room and decides to change her dress.

4. In *Coastal Disturbances,* by Tina Howe, it is August, and Leo, a lifeguard, gets ready for a day's work by doing his stretching exercises standing in the sand by his lifeguard's chair. Holly Dancer, a pretty young woman, enters. The pace of Leo's exercises varies as he tries to attract her attention.

5. In David Henry Hwang's *The Dance and the Railroad,* Lone, a twenty-year-old Chinese railroad worker sits alone on a rock on top of a mountain. He rotates his head so that it twirls his ponytail like a fan. He then jumps to the ground and practices opera steps.

6. In *Desdemona: A Play About a Handkerchief,* by Paula Vogel, Emilia, an attendant to Desdemona and scullery maid, having been ordered to peel potatoes. As she pares the potatoes, she vents her resentment by gouging out eyes, and stripping the skin from a potato as if flaying a certain mistress (Desdemona) alive. She then stops to contemplate a proposition offered to her by her mistress that would allow her to escape her husband and live a life of luxury. She begins to energetically, resolutely, and obediently slice the potatoes.

7. In August Wilson's *Fences,* Corey, a young Marine corporal, enters his recently deceased father's yard carrying a duffel bag. He studies his surroundings before seeing Raynell, his father's illegitimate daughter. Keeping the posture of a military man, he slowly crosses to the sister he has never known.

8. In *Losing Time,* by John Hopkins, a young single woman living alone returns home after just having been mugged and raped while outside.

9. In *Lu Ann Hampton Laverty Oberlander,* by Preston Jones, the teenaged Lu Ann is left alone in the living room of their modest, small-town Texas home

after her mother leaves for work. She turns on the radio, dances to the country-and-western tunes it plays, sneaks a smoke from a cigarette her mother has discarded, and then has to greet her brother and a stranger who arrive unexpectedly.

10. In *Purlie Victorious,* by Ossie Davis, Purlie has involved Lutiebelle, a backwoods serving girl, in a scheme in which she will try to pass herself off as Purlie's educated and sophisticated Cousin Bee. After Lutiebelle has examined the beautiful clothes Purlie has bought for her to wear—slips, hats, shoes, nylon stockings—she picks up her own humble belongings and tries to escape.

11. In *Request Concert,* by Franz Zavier Kroetz, a woman comes home from work and goes about the specific and mundane details of her household chores. She seems to be "putting her house in order." At the end, she commits suicide. (This scene could be played by a male.)

12. In *Summer and Smoke,* by Tennessee Williams, Alma is an intelligent, tensely sensitive girl who has developed an abnormally reserved attitude toward young men. On an autumn evening she walks in the park, realizing that her prudishness has been responsible for her losing a brilliant young doctor with whom she has been deeply in love for a long time. She drinks from the fountain and quiets her nerves by taking a relaxation pill. When an unknown young man appears, she decides to make up for her past mistakes by attempting to attract his attention.

13. In *When You Comin Back, Red Ryder?,* by Mark Medoff, nineteen-year-old Red is alone finishing his night shift at a truck-stop restaurant in an out-of-the-way New Mexico town. He plays the jukebox, smokes, and reads a newspaper but prepares to make Angel feel bad for being late when she comes to relieve him.

Notes

1. Constantin Stanislavski, *Creating a Role* (New York: Theatre Arts Books, 1961), p. 201.

2. Sanford Meisner and Dennis Longwell, "Acting Class, Day One, With a Master Teacher," *The New York Times,* 31 May 1987, H, 5 & 30.

3. Michael Redgrave, "The Stanislavski Myth," *New Theatre 3* (June 1946): 16–18. "Copyright, 1946," quoted in Toby Cole and Helen Krich Chinoy, eds., *Actors on Acting,* new rev. ed. (New York: Crown Publishers, 1970), p. 405.

4. David Magarshack, "Introduction," *Stanislavsky on the Art of the Stage* (New York: Hill and Wang, 1961), p. 49.

5. Viola Spolin, *Improvisation for the Theater: A Handbook of Teaching and Directing Techniques* (Evanston, IL: Northwestern University Press), 1963, p. 4.

6. Uta Hagen, *A Challenge for the Actor* (New York: Macmillan Publishing Company, 1991), p. 140.

7. Ibid.

8. See Stanislavski, *Creating a Role,* pp. 56–62.

9. Mel Gordon, *The Stanislavsky Technique: Russia; a Workbook for Actors* (New York: Applause Theatre Book Publishers, 1987), p. 71.

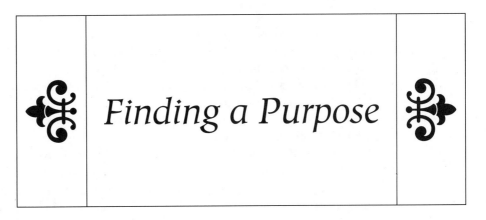

CHAPTER 3

Finding a Purpose

Throughout his career, Stanislavski sought a deeper understanding of the mystery of inspiration on stage. Great actors, he observed, had the uncanny ability to present an inspired performance each and every night. But he did not understand the source of their inspiration. How do great actors reach into the depths of their souls to play a role that demands extreme anguish, hate, or joy when they know that everything around them is a lie? Actors cannot "play" emotions, for they are ambiguous and uncontrollable. Yet inspired performers seem to have the ability to conjure them at will. Stanislavski made it his mission to pursue and analyze inspiration and true emotion on stage and create a system that would allow any proficient actor to exert conscious control over them.

Although it is unclear as to whether Stanislavski had any direct contact with the famous Russian scientist Ivan Pavlov, their experiments investigating the connection between internal experience and its external expression (conditioned response) coincided with one another. Both Stanislavski and Pavlov came to the conclusion that the body and soul are so closely attached that they stimulate and influence each other. Before that point in time, many scientists believed that the body and soul were separate entities with minimal effect on one another. These two men, however, proved through scientific means that every feeling, every thought, every decision, every mental process is transmitted through the body and manifests itself through external expression. Human behavior, in this new light, becomes a continuous, uninterrupted psychophysical process—what Stanislavski referred to as the **psychophysical union.**

The discovery of a character's appropriate physical actions is a key component to uncovering a conscious means (actions) to the subconscious (thoughts and emotions). Stanislavski referred to this as the **Method of Physical Actions**—a breakthrough in acting training and his gift to all future actors. We must, however, define the difference between **physical action** and **physical movement.** Physical action—which may also be verbal—has purpose. It exists within the play's given circumstances and has a point. According to Sonia Moore, "If you fulfill only the physical side of an action, it will be dead, and if you are interested only in the inner side, it will be equally dead. You are learning to involve your psychophysical process."[1] Through Stanislavski's Method of Physical Actions, we learn that the process of life itself may be reversed on stage. In life, external stimulus triggers an appropriate internal feeling that manifests itself in external expression. On stage, the actor responds to stimulus through external expression (action) that triggers truthful internal feeling.

Life

Stimulus → Internal Feeling → External Expression (Action)

Stage

Stimulus → External Expression (Action) → Internal Feeling

Therefore, the Method of Physical Actions is the sum total of the relationship between your psychological and physical being—the psychophysical *union.* The stage is not a place of reality; otherwise, the actors playing Romeo and Juliet would actually have to kill themselves at the end of the play. The tragedy does not really occur. However, playing the appropriate physical actions through the eyes of the character within the world of the play allows an actor to experience true emotion on stage without artificial means. Therefore, as a result of the psychophysical union, emotion is approached indirectly through the discovery of physical actions.

In Chapter 2, we learned that you begin your task of believing by making a score of appropriate physical actions and learning to perform them honestly. We also know that it is counterproductive at this time for you to be concerned about how either you or the character "feels." Even in scenes of tragedy, you must concern yourself with *actions* rather than *feelings*. The question never is, "How would I feel if I were this character in these circumstances?" but rather, "What would I do?"

You should now know how to make a score of actions as the very first interpretative step in performing a role. You know each action must follow another in a logical sequence. You know your actions must be truthful, and you must believe

Mark Garvin

Figure 3.1 John Pankow and Julie White in the 2002 world premiere of *Barbra's Wedding,* by Daniel Stern, produced by the Philadelphia Theatre Company. Each actor must have a clear, simple objective that motivates a sequence of simple actions.

each action is what you would do if you were the character in the given situation. Now we will learn how to make actions purposeful.

Whatever happens on stage must have a purpose, must serve some end beyond the accomplishment of the action itself. Moment by moment, the intent or meaning or significance of the performance, both for the actor and the audience, rarely lies in the action itself but in the purpose for which it is done. Even melodramatic actions such as loading a gun or mixing poison are not in themselves dramatic. We must know why, toward whom the lethal effort is directed. Clearly played for the right reasons, any number of simple, everyday actions—packing a suitcase, moving the furniture, lying down on the floor—may be dramatic.

So, to the four "W's" discussed in Chapter 2, we now add a fifth: *Why?* Answering this question gives the actor a reason to carry out the physical action. The young actor can learn no lesson of more significance. *Actions performed without a reason that is compelling to the actor and clear to the audience have no dramatic interest for either.*

Again, to discover "Why?" you look first in the dramatist's text, the place where all analysis begins. A careful reading should provide explicit reasons for most of the actions you have scored. If not, or if these reasons are unclear, you should follow the same procedure you followed with the other "W's." You turn next to what is *implied* by the text. (During this step the director usually becomes the chief interpreter for a particular production.) Finally, you seal the decision and make it personal by drawing on your own insight and imagination.

Knowing how to make action purposeful is among the most valuable of all acting techniques. It allows you to believe more strongly in what you are doing as the character. It gives you a reason for being on the stage and thus relieves your tension. And it provides a principal means of conveying the import of the play to the audience.

In this edition of *Acting Is Believing* we are going to call the purpose for which you carry out your physical actions your **simple objective,** or *objective* for short. Others call it different names. Earlier editions of this same book refer to it as *intention.* Stanislavski himself called it *zadacha,* which translates as *problem.* You may also hear it referred to as goal, motivation, desire, impulse, or intended victory. Uta Hagen states it as a question—"What are you fighting for?" Robert Lewis had an interesting slant on this problem in terminology. He wrote:

> It has been called many things in many books and some people don't
> call it anything; but it is a process that is going on, if they are really act-
> ing. I myself don't care if you call it spinach, if you know what it is, and
> do it, because it is one of the most important elements in acting.[2]

"Spinach" might prove confusing, but *objective* is a term commonly used by actors and directors. By definition, an objective is "a determination to act in a certain way or to do a certain thing." So let's agree that *action* will mean the sequence of physical actions, the *what,* and that *objective* will mean the reason for doing them, the *why.* Put simply, objective is what you want, what you need to accomplish with your action.

Stating the Objective

Return to the exercises in Chapter 2, and extend them by carrying out your actions to satisfy a clearly stated, simple objective. This important step forces you to dig again into the circumstances. Once you have found the objective by examining both what the playwright gives you and your own experience, it is important for you to state it in a form that compels you to execute a sequence of simple but psychologically motivated actions.

Here is the way it might work in the problem from *Of Mice and Men.* We have already made a score of physical actions and separated them into structural units, so we will add this circumstance, discovered by studying the script: Lennie is apprehensive and secretive about the puppy because his friend and protector, George, has repeatedly scolded him for being addicted to soft, furry objects and for being too rough with them — literally loving them to death. In addition to the physical action of playing with the puppy, we now have a psychologically motivated objective. Lennie is frightened that George will find him and scold him again, and so he must hide. We state the objective as "I must prove I can handle the puppy to keep George off my back."

Stating and playing simple objectives in the problems from this exercise will be relatively easy. Mastering this early work will pave the way later for understanding the complex problem of *units of action* and *super-objectives*.

EXERCISE   **1.** Improvise the score of actions from *Of Mice and Men* with the objective "I must prove I can handle the puppy." Keep the objective closely in mind throughout the presentation, and let your imagination work!

            2. Carry out the same actions, but change your simple objective to "I want to punish George for scolding me." Hold firmly to this objective, even during the action of burying the dead puppy. Use your imagination to justify this objective.

Let's look at two more examples of determining actions and objectives from a script. In *When You Comin Back, Red Ryder?* by Mark Medoff, the scene is a diner in the desert of New Mexico in the late sixties or early seventies. Stephen/Red is a nineteen-year-old who wishes to escape the mundane world and become as famous as his movie hero. Angel, the waitress, is a few years older and accepts her life. She has a "crush" on Stephen and wants him to stay. In the opening scene, the conversation is about coffee, their names, and coupons, but Stephen/Red's objective is "I want to steer Angel's attention away from me," and Angel's is "I must force Stephen to pay some attention to me." This scene has many actions to be played, including reading a newspaper, drinking coffee, and eating a donut.

The Crucible, by Arthur Miller, deals with the famous witchcraft trials in Salem, Massachusetts, in 1692. The theme is the frightening effects of injustice and the misapplication of authority. John Proctor, about thirty years of age, is a hard-working farmer of independent spirit. His wife Elizabeth, also about thirty, has discovered that John had an adulterous affair with Abigail, a girl who worked for them and has since been dismissed. Abigail is one of the children bringing charges of witchcraft against innocent people, including Elizabeth. Earlier, she admitted to John that their allegations were not true. Elizabeth's Puritan ethic has magnified her husband's single infidelity into a situation of major proportions. At the opening of Act II, her objective is "I must compel John to go to Salem to expose and denounce Abigail." John's is "To restore normality to my house, I must satisfy my wife's wishes."

Doing, Not Being

To make your character's need to execute the sequence of physical actions personal and compelling, note carefully the way a simple objective is stated: "I wish . . . ," "I want to . . . ," or "I must . . . ," followed by an **action verb.** Common verbs such as running, leaving, reading, fighting, or kissing may all be classified as action verbs in the literal sense; however, these verbs are *static,* an end in themselves. To an actor, action verbs must motivate a sequence of smaller actions. "To provoke," "to seduce," "to belittle," "to protect" are examples of action verbs that stir the actor's imagination and germinate subsequent simple actions. You must even avoid the use of more complex *static verbs.* Take, for example, the word "power." To say "I wish power" is too general. If you phrase it as a question, "What must I do to obtain power?" it will move you more toward purposeful activity; however, the word "power" still remains too large and relatively static. It cannot be executed at once. Try playing a scene in which you wish for power in general. Stanislavski wrote, "You must have something more concrete, real, nearer, more possible to do. As you see, not any verb will do, not any word can give an impetus to full action."[3] This discussion may sound trivial to the beginning actor, but learning to identify the proper action verb is a necessary and learned skill.

Once an actor articulates a good action verb, he or she instinctively surges forward with an appropriate sequence of physical actions. Think always in terms of what you must *do* by way of action verbs, not in terms of what you want to *be.*

✦ Poorly phrased: "I am jealous of my colleague's recent accomplishments."

✦ Well phrased: "I must belittle my colleague's accomplishments to make myself look better."

✦ Poorly phrased: "I am frustrated by my friend's dispute."

✦ Well phrased: "I wish to negotiate a truce between my friends."

Jealousy and frustration are states of being and cannot drive action, whereas "to belittle" and "to negotiate" stimulate specific activity.

One of the most common mistakes made by young actors is to attempt to act by *being* rather than *doing.* The actor who concentrates upon *being* drunk, *being* angry, *being* happy, *being* sad, or *being* afraid is thus certain to fail. Concern yourself, just as you do in actual life, with what you would do in each situation, not with what you would be or how you would feel. Remember, through the method of physical actions and as a result of the psychophysical union, the emotion will be there if the actions are carried out to the fullest extent of the actor's will.

When you are angry, your mind does not focus on being angry. Rather, you are concerned with the cause—the person or thing that has made you angry—and you may deal with the cause in any number of ways. You may overlook it. You may seek release from your anger in some act of physical violence. You may forgive. You may plan some dreadful revenge. But certainly you are not saying to yourself,

"I must be angry." You *do* something about the intentional scratch on your new car or about the person who has placed you in an embarrassing situation.

When you are frightened, you do not *want* to be afraid. Instead, you want to dispel your fear in some way. You may want to escape or to seek comfort from someone. You may want to calm your fears by turning your attention to something else. You may want to investigate the source of peril. As an actor, you must always place an emphasis on concrete details. Never try to act in general and never attempt to convey a feeling such as love or hate in some vague, nebulous manner. In life, we express emotions in terms of specifics: a nervous man smokes a cigarette while fidgeting with his lighter; an angry woman slams the door on her fiancé and pulls a handkerchief from her purse to wipe her eyes; an anxious teenage girl quickly closes the window blinds and sits on the sofa clutching a pillow. Actors must find equally specific activities; otherwise they will simply be feigning a generalized emotion.

You cannot act a state of being, an emotion, or a condition. If an unknowing director tells an actor "In this scene, you are really angry. I want you to play the anger." The actor will undoubtedly respond with, "Okay, but how do I do that? What do you want me to do?" This type of vague direction will simply leave the actor stuck scratching his or her head. What is anger, anyway? For that matter, what is happiness? What is depression? People have their own interpretation of these states of being, and we are never simply one particular emotion. At any given moment, we may be happy with our lives but anxious about a forthcoming presentation. At the same time, we are frustrated with our family and yet concerned about our child's health. We are a bit intoxicated from the wine we had at dinner, angry with the driver who cut in front of us on the freeway, and overjoyed about our recent promotion. States of being are subjective and inconsistent, and they vary greatly depending upon the circumstances. Trying to play a state of being will only lead you into stereotyped movements and gestures (e.g., clenching your fists to show your anger, putting your hand to your forehead to show you are being thoughtful, or contorting the muscles of your face to show your pain).

Burning your hand may *be* painful. But you *want* to alleviate the pain by applying salve, butter, cold water, or some other remedy. When an actor such as Al Pacino is pointed out in a crowd, you may *be* curious. But you *want* to secure a position where you can see and perhaps get his autograph. To be in pain or to be curious is not actable. But to relieve pain or to satisfy curiosity is. You can easily carry out the actions of applying a remedy to your burned hand or of working your way into a favorable position.

EXERCISE   To realize more fully the importance of *doing* rather than *being* and of stating your simple objective with an active verb, work carefully on the following problems:

1. Choose a word from the list below, and make it the basis for a series of actions. Do not let this instruction lead you into a trap. As you study the list, you should now realize that you cannot act any of these words. They are an end result, an effect. You must imagine a circumstance providing a reason for the *action that will produce the effect.* Then forget the effect, and concentrate on carrying out the actions. For example, the following circumstance would provide an action for the word *cautious: You have just escaped from a war prison. In darkness, starved and exhausted, you are making your way across an area filled with booby traps. You find a knapsack that might contain rations.* State your objective as "I must work my way through the area without exploding a trap."

   The following circumstance would provide an action for the word *spiteful: You have not been getting along with your roommate. You resent your roommate constantly asking to borrow money to satisfy an extravagant taste for clothes. You return home to find that your roommate has "borrowed" money that you were saving to buy a present for your fiancé. You take several articles of your roommate's new clothing, cut off all the buttons, and put them in the box where your roommate keeps coins.* State your objective as "I must teach my roommate a lesson for being so selfish."

   Now, look over the list and select a word. Devise appropriate circumstances. Make a score of your actions. State your simple objective. Structure your score, and name each of the three units. Carry it out in an imaginative improvisation. Observe the instructions given for the exercises in the preceding chapter.

embarrassed	breathless	genteel
distracted	detached	maudlin
bashful	ruthless	cautious
excited	tantalizing	violent
frantic	spiteful	jealous
exhausted	lethargic	dazed
nervous	awkward	jovial
infuriated	bewildered	sickly
terrified	coarse	grouchy
condescending	drunken	panicky

The above list is taken from playwrights' directions to actors in a single volume of modern American plays. They illustrate how dramatists (and often directors) ask for effects. Actors must be able to think of effects in terms of actions and objectives. A frequent comment to actors from directors is

"Don't play the effect (even though he may have just asked for it), play the action!"

2. Choose one of the following "everyday" actions. Create circumstances, and provide an objective you can attack with unfeigned interest and excitement. Take, for example, polishing silver: You are in an antique shop in a foreign country. You discover among many dusty articles a blackened silver bowl that you think is the work of Benvenuto Cellini. Beneath the tarnish may be revealing marks. If you are right, the proprietor obviously does not suspect its origin. State your simple objective as "I must remove the tarnish from this bowl without attracting the proprietor's attention."

    Take, for another example, "walking five steps": You are in the hospital with a serious illness. You are very weak and short of breath. You are under strict doctor's orders to stay in bed. You decide to test your strength by walking a short distance to a chair. You reach the chair exhausted but convinced you are beginning to recover. State your intention as "I must regain the strength in my legs if I am ever to return to full health."

    Now it is your turn. To solve the problem suggested by one of these "everyday actions," you need specific circumstances, a properly stated objective, a score of physical actions, and imagination. Execute all physical actions precisely, clearly, and with complete commitment. Avoid any activity that requires pantomime. Take your time. Give your actions form.

    - ✦ reading a newspaper
    - ✦ looking through a window
    - ✦ opening a door
    - ✦ hunting for a lost object
    - ✦ writing a letter
    - ✦ lying down on the floor
    - ✦ applying or removing makeup
    - ✦ arranging furniture
    - ✦ getting dressed or undressed
    - ✦ drinking alcohol or a soft drink
    - ✦ examining a photograph
    - ✦ wrapping or unwrapping a package
    - ✦ crawling on your hands and knees
    - ✦ packing a suitcase
    - ✦ walking five steps
    - ✦ examining a bundle of clothes

- ✦ waiting for someone
- ✦ stretching

Plays are filled with simple actions for which actors must find objectives that stimulate their imagination and make the actions communicate the playwright's meaning.

Working against an Obstacle

By now you probably realize that within each *objective,* an **obstacle**—whether stated or implied—stands in your path. Obstacles are the foundation on which great dramas and comedies are built. Land mines present a formidable obstacle in the way of successfully escaping from a prison camp. A shrewd antique dealer looking for profit is an obstacle to picking up a Cellini masterpiece for a few *lire.* The interest in a play or scene (or in an acting exercise) lies in the possibilities it offers the actor to gain an objective against odds—odds sometimes so great that the struggle ends in defeat, either glorious or ignoble. The greater the obstacle, the more engaging the action will be to the audience. On the other hand, plays without conflict have little interest for either actor or audience.

As you formulate each simple objective, ask "What is the *obstacle?*" or "What stands in my way of accomplishing my goal?" With no obstacle, there is no problem—no scene—no play! The obstacle, like the objective, may be physical or psychological, internal or external. Internal obstacles always grow from the character's own personality and experience; external obstacles come from all other sources, such as family, societal expectations, religion, politics, nature, laws—even such natural phenomena as the weather and the time of day.

Frequently the physical and psychological are so closely related that it is not possible, or desirable, to separate them. The problem from *Of Mice and Men* is an example of this interrelation. The physical obstacle to Lennie's accomplishing his objective is that the puppy is not old enough to play with him. No matter how gently he treats it, the puppy cannot return the affection. He is not yet trainable. The psychological obstacle is more complex. On a simple level, it is that neither Lennie's emotional nor his intellectual development is mature enough to comprehend the potential outcome of his action. He is a child in a very strong man's body; in fact, his great physical strength is one of the obstacles to his attaining the returned affection of the animals he needs so desperately. As he gratifies his longing to pet them, an ever-increasing desire for this gratification spurs him to handle them more and more roughly. Once he realizes it has sustained injury, Lennie tries to revive the puppy, protect it from pain. He hides the puppy only after he realizes it has died. Note that his objective does not change through this sequence. At first, he wants to get George off his back by proving he can handle the puppy. When he is forced to abandon this strategy, he hides the dead puppy for the same reason. The psychological complexities of the objective and the character's strength of commitment to its completion give it varied textures at different moments during its performance, but the objective itself does not change.

Every actor could select any number of objectives for the character. This selection process constitutes a large part of *interpreting* a role.

On the stage, as in life, psychological objectives and obstacles stimulate us to accomplish what we set out to achieve. In sports, a winner's motivation is nearly always psychological. The runner does not want simply to cover the distance faster than anyone else. Rather, runners are motivated by desire to bring honor and prestige to themselves and to the team and to win admiration and fame. Perhaps they are motivated by a determination to set someone right who said they could not do it. People do not build homes just to complete the physical structure; they also want to provide protection, security, and beauty for themselves and their family. A proud collector may have a special desire to obtain a Cellini bowl. These illustrations from life suggest three important points for the actor:

1. Psychological objectives and obstacles can stimulate actors' imaginations more strongly than can physical objectives and obstacles.

2. Actors must make a personal commitment to overcome the obstacle and accomplish their objective. As we have seen with the Method of Physical Actions, this commitment generates true emotion.

3. Actors must feel the challenge physically as well as intellectually. A runner does not win a race by *wishing* to, *thinking* about strategy, or *feeling* victorious. Goals are achieved through purposeful *action*.

Beginning actors must pay particular attention to the importance of the obstacle. Their psychophysical actions, if they are to have any dramatic interest, must be performed to overcome a counteraction that exerts a strong force against the accomplishment of their objective. They must not be indifferent to this opposition. Dispassion toward the challenge of overcoming the obstacle, too common among student actors, will inevitably render a performance ineffective. An even more basic error occurs when actors fail to understand clearly what the obstacle is. Until they define the obstacle, actors cannot discover what means the dramatist has provided, either directly or by implication, for overcoming it. Actors will then be deprived of the only true and defensible stimulus for drawing additional strategies from their imagination.

Strategy is another term that turns up often in our discussion. The military definition of strategy is "the art and science of employing armed strength to meet the enemy in combat." Although conflict between the character and the obstacle is not always open warfare, actors would do well to conceive their whole performance as a strategic plan to overcome the forces working against them. Far too often in answer to the question, "What are you doing in this scene?" the young actor says casually "Oh, I'm just talking to this banker about loaning me some money." Or "I'm just asking my husband what he did while I was away this afternoon."

"Just" marks a telltale flaw in these answers. Actors must have discovered, either from the script or in their own imagination, an urgent need to get the money or to find out what was happening during the afternoon, and a hardheaded banker or a secretive husband provides a genuine obstacle that must be overcome. Even when the circumstances demand subtle tactics of which the opponent will be unaware (actors often have secrets about their character that should not be shared with their fellow actors), the inner urgency must be undiminished and may be all the greater.

Attempt always to simplify the conflict by finding the character's elemental need; do not try to complicate it. Satisfactory answers in these instances might be "I must secure some money to pay the debts I have incurred before my father finds out about them" and "I must discover whether the gossip about my husband and the girl next door is true." If these answers sound melodramatic, remember that such material is the stuff of which drama is made. The content of Shakespeare's plays in the hands of a hack writer produces soap operas, and the Greek tragedies become horror stories. British critic Kenneth Tynan wrote:

> Good drama, of whatever kind, has but one mainspring—the human being reduced by ineluctable process to a state of desperation. Desperate are the cornered giants of Sophocles; desperate, too, as they huddle in their summerhouses, the becalmed gentry of Chekhov; and the husband of French farce, with a wife in one bedroom and a mistress in another, is he not, though we smile at his agony, definably desperate?. . . . How, in this extremity, will they comport themselves? It is to find out that we go to theatres. . . .[4]

Actors must conceive the carrying out of their objective as a "desperate quest" to overcome an obstacle.

EXERCISE   You were asked to use the problems at the end of Chapter 2 as exercises in making and carrying out a score of physical actions. Without being aware of it as a technique, chances are you performed the actions for some purpose, because it would be unnatural to do otherwise. Now that you have been introduced to the technique, choose again a problem from Chapter 2, and extend it consciously to include finding the objective—both physical and psychological—and playing the action to accomplish your objective. To make the procedure most helpful, be sure to:

1. Find the objective in the given circumstances. It must allow you to satisfy the needs of your character and the demands of the play.

2. Make it attractive to *you*. You personally must feel compelled to carry it out.

3. Make it truthful. You must without reservation believe it is what you would do if you were the character in the circumstances.

4. Provide an obstacle—either physical or psychological—derived from the circumstances or appropriate to them.

5. Be sure your objective suggests a range of physical actions.

6. Start the statement with "I must . . . ," "I wish . . . ," or "I want to . . . ," followed by an action verb that motivates a sequence of simple actions.

Expectation and Adaptation

While on stage, actors must constantly remain in the state of "I am." They must play each moment as if it were occurring for the first time—what the nineteenth-century actor William Gillette referred to as "the illusion of the first time." As in life, your characters cannot be clairvoyant. They cannot *know* the future. Someone once asked the legendary twentieth-century actor Sir Laurence Olivier how he remembered all his lines in *Hamlet*. He responded with "I don't. I simply remember the next one." According to report, great actors such as Gillette and Olivier seemed always surprised by the events of the play. They lived in the present. Some actors may "think" they know the future while on stage. They "know" the next line and have rehearsed or performed the actions countless times, but no one, including actors, can truly know what will happen next. Attempting to anticipate another person's actions will only result in your delivering indicated actions with artificial effects. Therefore, you must play each scene moment-by-moment, remaining in the present. This, however, does not mean that your character does not think ahead or speculate about the future. In fact, everything you do in the present is conditioned by your **expectations** about the future, and what actually happens is never fully what you expected to occur. Uta Hagen wrote:

> When the actor anticipates what he will see, hear, and feel and what the others will be doing (because he has seen, heard, and felt them doing the same thing since the early days of rehearsal), it is because he has failed to include the logical expectations that condition his actions, or merely paid them lip service.[5]

Adaptation, on the other hand, is synonymous with perhaps the most vital question actors must ask themselves. Along with the five "W's," adaptation obligates actors to answer the essential sixth question, "How?" Of this question, Stanislavski once said, "*Adaptations* are our 'paints.'" and "Your first duty is to adapt yourself to your partner." As an actor, you must understand that an action is incomplete unless you fully incorporate answers to the three questions:

+ What?
+ Why?
+ How?

What you are doing. Why you are doing it. How you plan to accomplish your goal.

Adaptations depend on the given circumstances, and that is why you must have specific information and images before you attack the question, "How?" There are dozens of ways to break up with your fiancée, burn a letter, fire an employee, or seduce a person with whom you are attracted. Exploration of "How?" is one of most important and satisfying parts of rehearsal technique. The richer your imagination, the more choices you allow yourself in rehearsal. The more choices you explore in rehearsal, the more interesting your final product.

As you are exploring the various means with which to achieve your objective, your partner must have counteractions to create unforeseen obstacles. There must be dramatic conflicts on stage; otherwise theatre would be amazingly dull. Stanislavski wrote:

> Every feeling you express, as you express it, requires an intangible form
> of adjustment all its own. All types of communication—for example,
> communication in a group or with an imaginary, present, or absent ob-
> ject—require adjustments peculiar to each. We use all of our five senses
> and all the elements of our inner and outer makeup to communicate.
> We send out rays and receive them, we use our eyes, facial expression,
> voice and intonation, our hands, fingers, our whole bodies, and in every
> case we make whatever corresponding adjustments are necessary.[6]

Richard Schechner once proposed the maxim that "the theatrical event is a set of related **transactions**."[7] Certainly one of the essential transactions is among performers. Your performance must always be conceived in relation to other characters who either help or hinder you in accomplishing your objectives, and you must consider these other characters in planning your actions. You have the ability to adapt and sometimes to abandon your plans as you are confronted with the unexpected. You watch and listen and remain ready to adjust what you do and say to the needs of the moment. Thus, your adaptation to the actions of other characters turns your actions into transactions.

In life everybody must be able to adapt to changing circumstances. Those who cannot adapt will never get across the street alive, much less manage the more subtle interpersonal challenges they face. We deal with people both logically and psychologically, and the kind of adaptation we make—whether it is bold, delicate, daring, cautious—is important to our success. Each day brings an infinite number of situations requiring a wide range of adjustments.

In contrast, stage action often seems dull because a lifelike sense of adjustment has disappeared in the actor's struggle to remember and repeat lines and movement. A technique that allows for adaptation to the needs of the moment is a necessity in the actor's training, and learning to think of acting as a transaction is the first step in mastering this important lesson. When performing a transaction, actors concentrate on how they can affect the behavior of the other performers, as well as on what they are doing to cause them to adjust their strategy. The focus, then, is on what happens among the performers, not on the individual or on the mechanics of acting.

EXERCISE

1. For work in the technique of adaptation, try this "coach and actor" exercise. Work in pairs. One actor serves as "coach," telling his or her partner firmly and quietly (the class should be able to hear, too) what actions to perform. The instructions should constitute a logical sequence of physical actions having a beginning, a middle, and an end. The coaches should prepare carefully in advance. They should be certain the sequence can be psychologically motivated, but they should *not* share their objective with their partners. As they proceed, actors must discover an objective and adapt accordingly. The coaches should vary the tempo-rhythm of their instruction as the actions develop toward a climax and as they sense their partners' responses. Later discussions should compare the objective the coaches had in mind with what the actors discovered. The actors' job is to find an objective, not to guess what the coaches intended. There is no absolute right and wrong. Although some objectives might be illogical under the circumstances, two quite different motivations could be well justified.

2. In the following problem, the "coach" becomes an actor within the imaginary circumstances. The two characters are a window dresser and an assistant. The window dresser is on the sidewalk directing the assistant where and how to place the objects for display. A plate-glass window separates them, so all communication must be visual rather than oral. The physical objective clearly is to get the window dressed, and the physical separation provides a definite obstacle. From your imagination supply additional specific circumstances. Know exactly what objects are being arranged for display. Some other members of the group might be used as mannequins. The dresser should know exactly what effect is desired. Supply psychological objectives and obstacles, as well as the obvious physical ones. Remember the necessary element of urgency. Structure the exercise, giving it a beginning, a development leading to a climax, and a conclusion. All exercises accomplish their purpose more fully when they are followed by a discussion regarding the clarity and urgency of the objective, the precision of the physical actions, the strategy for overcoming the obstacles, the adaptations, and the effectiveness of the structure. Both participants should discuss how the nature of the transaction affected their strategies for performing their actions.

Nonverbal Group Improvisation

Many people still think that Stanislavski discussed his productions for months before allowing the actor to explore the physical environment. This may have been true before he developed the Method of Physical Actions, but as soon as Stanislavski discovered the psychophysical process of human behavior, he sent actors on stage after they had read the play and briefly discussed the plot and characters. According to Sonia Moore, "Stanislavski realized that the discussions at the table artificially divided the actor's physical and psychological behavior. 'I think that you have done enough work now to begin moving, improvising on the stage.'"[8]

The actor may obtain further practice in adaptation through exercises in nonverbal group improvisation, a further extension of the exercises you have already been doing. Improvising with a group involves more complicated and interesting problems, bringing you closer to your ultimate aim of a shared performance. You will begin, as always, with the given circumstances out of which you must create an active, attractive, and truthful objective. You will face an added complication because you cannot know what you will need to do until you know what the others are going to do. As they play their objectives, they will create obstacles for you. Because the final definition of the scene will depend on your transaction with the other performers, you will need to be ready to adjust moment by moment. And again, the actions you adjust must be truthful and logical; you must believe they are what you would really do if you were the character in the circumstances. As you begin to sense your effect on the actions of the other performers and as you adjust your actions to the obstacles they present, you will be on your way toward learning one of the most important lessons of the theatre: acting is communal, and successful performance depends utterly on the stimulation you receive from and give your fellow actors.

Set a time limit—at the beginning, ten to fifteen minutes for a group exercise. After it is over, the work should be carefully analyzed (preferably by a competent observer) so that actors are aware of the points at which they have or have not behaved logically and truthfully and at which their adjustments have fallen short of what could have been expected. Actors can help themselves and sometimes help others by recalling when they were making real contact, when their actions seemed true and spontaneous, and when they did not. The analysis should not be concerned with whether the scene would be entertaining or exciting to an audience. Improvisation is a means, not an end, and you will defeat its purpose if you think about results other than truthful behavior.

Your first attempts may be frustratingly unfruitful, for group improvisation is a technique that takes time to learn. But it is time well spent, and it is essential to your training.

Figure 3.2 John Rainone, Neil Servetnick, and Doug Jackson in *A Day in Hollywood, A Night in the Ukraine,* produced by Theatre Three in Dallas, TX. These actors are portraying The Marx Brothers, a group who defined their careers with their exceptional improvisational skills.

EXERCISES **1.** The first exercise involves "Two people who are not on speaking terms." Talk over the given circumstances with your partner. Define your objectives. Know your obstacles. Create a central conflict. Understand your relationship. Determine the five "W's." The point of this and all improvisations, however, is an investigation of the sixth question, "How?" In fact, the exploration of *tactics* and *adaptations* is the most important part of rehearsals for a scripted scene or play. For this first exercise, however, do not speak or pantomime. There should be no need to talk. As soon as there is an organic need to speak, the improvisation is complete.

2. For our first effort in group improvisation, we will concentrate on a silent exercise utilizing the entire class. "Shake hands with different people." Each of you decides on a relationship between yourself and each of your classmates. Do not share your perceived relationship with others, but you must decide, for example, that Emma is a princess, Robert is a person who has hurt you, Sarah is someone to whom you owe money, Lauren is your best friend. Do not rush. Remember, you have to see the people who are actually in the room with you, but treat them as those you have built in your imagination.

3. The next exercise involves "A group of people sitting at a bus station." Know who you are and where you are going. Although we establish immediate relationships with everyone with whom we come in contact, there again should be no reason to speak to one another in this exercise. You may also perform this exercise as a group of people:

- ✦ riding in an elevator
- ✦ lounging on the beach
- ✦ relaxing in a park
- ✦ waiting in line
- ✦ sitting in a doctor's office
- ✦ sitting in detention in high school

4. Next, we will set circumstances that permit communication through psychologically motivated physical actions and expressive sounds—*without the use of dialogue.* The first scene of Romeo and Juliet, in which the servants of the rival houses of Capulet and Montague confront each other in the public square, suggests the situation. Because the two families are ancient enemies, the servants feel compelled to challenge each other whenever they meet, although they may have forgotten (or perhaps never knew) the cause of the age-old hatred. The servants are uneducated, not dangerously armed, and not overly courageous. Their purpose is to insult and perpetrate minor physical assaults. In this exercise the objective is to be accomplished through physical actions (including gesture and facial expression) and vocalized sounds—no articulated words. The servants of one house should create obstacles for the others. Actors should strive to play their objectives as fully as possible. Remember, though, that the actions must always be logical and appropriate within the given circumstances. The scene should not become chaotic. Each action must be purposefully performed. The circumstances prescribe a number of obstacles to a realization of the objective: the natural timidity of the characters, the need for self-protection, and the need for a degree of furtiveness because these encounters in the public streets have been forbidden by law.

Let the beginning consist of the meeting in the street and some cautious advances by one or two of the servants, followed by hasty retreats. Let the middle develop the confrontation, as some of the servants, exhorted by others, become bolder in their actions and ultimately involve the whole group. Let the end consist of the arrival of someone of authority who breaks up the quarrel.

The group could decide to set the scene in circumstances other than those of Verona in the Italian Renaissance. In *West Side Story,* a modern musical based on *Romeo and Juliet,* the enemies were not "two houses both alike in dignity" but rival street gangs in New York. It would be valuable to work on the same situation in different sets of circumstances.

5. The next situation is taken from *Tales of the Lost Formicans,* by Constance Congdon. Similar to the above exercise with *Romeo and Juliet,* the group should communicate only through psychologically motivated physical actions and expressive sounds—*alien language.* The actor playing Jerry, a human, should not speak. In this scene, Aliens are gathered around Jerry, who is lying unconscious on a bench, taking notes. Jerry wakes up and opens his mouth to scream but can't make a sound. To calm his nerves, the Aliens massage his jaw and stroke him like children petting a dog. They proceed with the examination—it should satirize a field examination of a wild animal—all with the air of dispassionate scientists. One Alien finds various objects in Jerry's pockets and holds them up for other Aliens to see. They all laugh rhythmically. Another Alien produces an adult magazine, opens it to the centerfold, and moves it in front of Jerry, trying to arouse him. Another Alien unzips Jerry's fly, looks inside and waits for an erection. After a beat, an Alien takes out a Dustbuster and inserts in into Jerry's pants through his fly and turns it on briefly. Jerry reacts as the semen is sucked from him. With the examination complete, the Aliens tag Jerry's ear, zap him unconscious, and exit.[9]

Verbal Group Improvisation

The value of group improvisation lies in your learning to make real contact with other actors, to heed what they do and say, to adapt the playing of your objective to the need of the moment, and to work freely and logically within the imaginary circumstances. What you learn should carry over into everything you do because all good acting is to some degree improvisational. Even a scene that has been "set" demands constant adjustment—a living connection with fellow players. The choices you make in the adjustments must be credible and appropriate. The social situation of a house party places restrictions on both hosts and guests. Behaving logically within the circumstances is the beginning of truthful acting. Avoid choices that are sensational, that are calculated solely for dramatic effect, or that mindlessly repeat what you have seen other actors do or even what you have done in the past. Verbal group improvisation is best when your imagination leads you truthfully into spontaneous adjustments.

Verbal improvisation is decidedly different from nonverbal improvisation in that it requires the actors to create their own dialogue. You should always remember that words *are* physical verbal action. Just as you do not perform a physical action until the circumstances demand you to do so, you must not speak until the situation mandates it. Like all physical actions, verbal action is a means of expressing inner life. As you add dialogue to a scene, you must carefully consider the characters' inner lives and their relationship to the other characters and circumstances. Although the dialogue is not scripted, your words, your inflections, your syntax, your inner objects, your silences will directly affect your partner, and ultimately the audience, at least as much as your external physical actions. Just as we do in life, you are attempting to influence the actions, images, and emotions of others through words in your fictitious improvisational scenes.

As in life, you must listen with full animation. You must respond to the other character's words through your psychophysical being. If your partner on stage is attempting to cheer you up through their verbal and physical actions, they are looking into your eyes for continuous feedback—transacting. They are watching your movements and gestures and interpreting your projected mood. Whatever your objectives, your partner must have counteractions to create obstacles. As with scripted scenes, you and your partners must create *communion* on stage. There must also be communion between the actors and audience, and the audience must completely *suspend their disbelief* for the entirety of the scene. In short, you must believe in your character, your given circumstances, your relationships, and your every action. Otherwise, your improvisation will fall short of its intended goal.

A final word of caution with your verbal improvisations. Do not try to impress your classmates with your quick wit! Contrary to some people's belief, verbal improvisation is not synonymous with comedy improvisation such as you would see

Figure 3.3 A scene from the Utah Shakespearean Festival's production of *The Pirates of Penzance*. Note the absurd and yet truthful animation with these "Keystone Cops."

on the hugely popular television show, *Whose Line Is It Anyway?* or on stage at Second City in Chicago or Los Angeles. Improvisations such as these must complement your formal acting technique training. These improvisations, more often than not, will be dramatic in nature. Your characters, situations, and actions must be completely three dimensional. By pandering to the audience and by attempting to transform every improvisation into a comedy sketch, you will succeed in creating only the shell of a human being.

EXERCISE   **1.** These first verbal improvisations involve two people. Build the situation. Think of the analogous emotion that you have experienced in life. When you are on stage, think of the physical behavior that will be expressive of what you have built in your mind. The objectives listed below are intended for one of the actors; however, the partner must create his or her own objective and counteractions.

- ✦ To humiliate
- ✦ To enlighten
- ✦ To encourage
- ✦ To provoke
- ✦ To deceive
- ✦ To challenge
- ✦ To motivate
- ✦ To tempt
- ✦ To persuade
- ✦ To seduce
- ✦ To coerce
- ✦ To con
- ✦ Find your own action verbs that motivate immediate simple actions

---

EXERCISE The following situations provide opportunities for verbal group improvisations. In each case additional circumstances must be supplied from either the play or the imaginations of the actors. All characters must clearly understand their objectives and attempt to realize them through actions appropriate to the circumstances.

1. In Tony Kushner's *A Bright Room Called Day,* five friends have gathered in Agnes' apartment in Berlin in 1932. They have consumed a considerable amount of alcohol as they celebrate the New Year. As the scene progresses, their conversation turns to Hitler and the war.

2. In *Catholic School Girls,* by Casey Kurtti, four first-grade girls—Elizabeth, Colleen, Wanda, and Maria Theresa—enter into the classroom. They are dressed in white uniform blouses, blue ties, white cotton slips, knee socks, and brown oxford shoes. They are carrying their uniform jumpers. They each stand by a student desk and begin to dress. They look around the classroom and at each other as they dress. Then Elizabeth raises her skirt to pull her blouse down neatly. All follow suit, straightening their blouses. When they are finished, Elizabeth shouts that she is ready. On this first day of school, the girls await the arrival of their teacher.

3. In *Fences,* by August Wilson, Troy Maxon tells his wife, Rose, that he is going to have a baby by another woman. Soon after he breaks the news, Gabe, Troy's brain-damaged brother, enters talking about various things. The two try to talk in between Gabe's babbling until Rose suggests that he go inside to make himself a sandwich. After he enters into the house, Troy and Rose continue their discussion.

4. In *Five Women Wearing the Same Dress,* by Alan Ball, four mostly unwilling bridesmaids lounge in a bedroom while the sounds of a rather raucous wedding reception can be heard outside. Frances, the youngest and most naïve of the lot, sits in front of a vanity, while Trisha and Georgeanne sit on either side of her performing a makeover. Trisha applies makeup; Georgeanne prepares to apply nail polish. Mindy is seated on the edge of the bed, holding a plate of food. All except Frances have made themselves comfortable by unzipping the backs of their dresses or removing their hats, shoes, etc. Most have cocktails and are at various levels of inebriation.

5. In *The Lesson,* by Eugène Ionesco, a mild-mannered professor and his newest female student prepare for her first lesson in his home. At the beginning of the scene, she is quite shy but then becomes progressively agitated and whiny as the scene goes on. She complains periodically of a toothache that also worsens as the action unfolds. As her pain increases, so does the intensity of the professor's lecture. Finally, he works himself up into a state of sexual frenzy bordering on hysteria. At the peak of his passion, he pulls out a knife and stabs the girl repeatedly while experiencing a sexual climax. Following the murder, he becomes immediately frightened and contrite. He confesses his latest crime to the housekeeper, who is not at all happy with his actions, treating him as a bad child.

6. In *The Rainmaker,* by N. Richard Nash, H. C. Curry and his two sons go to town to try to get the deputy sheriff, File, to pay a call on Lizzie (H. C.'s daughter), who is nearing that time when she will be thought of as an "old maid." They try to work the invitation into their conversation without being obvious about it.

7. In *The Royal Hunt of the Sun,* by Peter Shaffer, Spanish soldiers led by Pizarro climb the Andes in search of gold. Motivated by greed and by loyalty to the Spanish crown, the soldiers face exhaustion as they make "a stumbling, tortuous climb into the clouds, over ledges and chasms."

8. In *A Soldier's Play,* by Charles Fuller, a group of black soldiers return to their barracks after a baseball game. They are carrying their equipment, and they engage in the exuberant, loud, locker-room banter of young men in the army. A sergeant unexpectedly enters, and the raucousness of their conversation abruptly abates. (Actors of diverse racial and ethnic backgrounds could play this improvisation.)

Notes

1. Sonia Moore, *Training an Actor: The Stanislavski System in Class* (New York: Penguin Books, 1979), p. 139.

2. Robert Lewis, Method—Or Madness? (New York: Samuel French, 1958), p. 29.

3. Constantin Stanislavski, Elizabeth Reynolds Hapgood, trans., *An Actor Prepares* (New York: Theatre Arts Books, 1973), p. 117.

4. Kenneth Tynan, *Curtains* (New York: Atheneum, 1961), p. 77.

5. Uta Hagen, *A Challenge for the Actor* (New York: Macmillan Publishing Company, 1991), pp. 124–125.

6. Stanislavski, *An Actor Prepares,* p. 213.

7. Richard Schechner, *Public Domain* (Indianapolis and New York: Bobbs-Merrill, 1969), p. 157.

8. Moore, *Training an Actor,* pp. 190–191.

9. Constance Congdon, *Tales of the Lost Formicans and Other Plays* (New York: Theatre Communications Group, 1994), p. 52.

CHAPTER 4

Approaching the Creative State

S tanislavski referred to tension as the actor's "occupational disease." **Lee Strasberg** described muscular tension as the artist's greatest enemy and developed relaxation exercises to help the actor learn to identify and release unwanted anxiety. As long as physical tenseness exists on stage, you cannot focus on the delicate shadings of feeling or the spiritual life of your part. Consequently, before you attempt to create anything you must get your muscles in proper condition so that they do not impede your actions. No actor is ever entirely liberated from these enemies because they cannot simply be outgrown as one gains experience. All actors, therefore, must develop more-or-less conscious techniques of relaxing. The actor must strive to eliminate all tension not absolutely needed to execute a movement, say a line, or maintain a position. Economy of effort characterizes both good movement and good speech.

The ability to relax is necessary to the internal as well as the external aspects of acting, for the tense actor finds it impossible to focus on the subtle process of creation. Excessive tension inhibits freedom of action and clarity of objective, a point Stanislavski made clear by demonstrating that it is impossible to multiply thirty-seven times nine while holding up the corner of a piano. The actor's unwanted tension is often just as great as that required to lift a heavy weight, and playing a clear objective certainly demands as much mental acuity as solving a multiplication problem.

Linda Blase

Figure 4.1 A scene from the Dallas Theater Center's production of *Twelfth Night,* by William Shakespeare. Actors must release their excessive muscular tension in order to reach the creative state demanded in broad comedy.

The inability to relax shatters the actor's ability to perform a believable character. Watching a tense actor, the audience inevitably focuses on the resulting nervous mannerisms rather than on the actions of a fully developed three-dimensional character. These mannerisms belong to the actor, not to the character, so they destroy the believability of the scene.

In addition to learning proper relaxation technique, theatre artists around the world recognize that physical exercise to develop coordination and muscular control is an essential part of acting training. Indeed, most theatre programs require fencing and dancing to help the student develop poise and alertness. Most actors also value the regimen of some sort of athletic training such as gymnastics, yoga, t'ai chi ch'uan, or martial arts. Many actors also undergo training in stage combat, mime, and circus techniques. Anyone seriously interested in acting understands the need to develop a coordinated and responsive body.

Training the Body

In recent years, intensive efforts have been made to discover a genuinely effective program in body training for the actor. These efforts have produced significant changes both in concept and practice, together with an increasing emphasis on carefully directed work in stage movement. Several influential approaches to actor training were developed by such modern "pioneers" as Jerzy Grotowski, Peter Brook, Joseph Chaikin, and Arthur Lessac, great innovators who were oriented to physical training as a means of developing the actor's total instrument. Literally hundreds of teachers and "systems" have sprung from the work of one or another of these individuals, some of brief duration and others that have made genuine contributions to actor training throughout the world. All these people would agree with Grotowski that "the most elementary fault [of the actor], and that in most urgent need of correction, is the over-straining of the voice because one forgets to speak with the body."[1]

Practically, body training is designed to accomplish two basic, closely related objectives: proper body alignment and freedom from excess muscle tension. Accomplishment of these objectives enables the actor to move in any direction from a standing, sitting, or lying position with a minimum of effort and without a preparatory shifting of weight. Together they produce strong, efficient, unforced movement.

Proper alignment, occasionally called **centering,** is sometimes misunderstood to imply something that is static or artificially frozen. Many people believe that "correct" posture is synonymous with a stiff and artificial carriage. Correct alignment is our body's natural position. Look at babies who have just learned to sit up by themselves. Notice their relaxed and yet perfect posture. Poor alignment usually happens as a result of a lifetime of bad habits. As we age, we habitually distort and misshape our bodies. We slouch in our chairs; we slump our shoulders; we drag our feet; we hang our heads. As an actor, you must understand that each character is entirely different from you—both internally and externally. The manner in which they walk, sit, stand, and gesture is unique. Until we fully realize our own body alignment, our own habitual carriage, we will never go beyond ourselves as we adopt the physical body of our characters. Until we make a conscious effort to return our bodies to the alignment intended by nature, we remain blissfully ignorant, limiting our range as actors. Natural alignment is best achieved under the guidance of a skilled instructor; however, a description of the ideal will help you understand the work required to attain it.

We unconsciously achieve proper body alignment as we recline on a reasonably hard surface. From this prone position, we can eliminate excess tension, bringing our body weight naturally into correct relationship. As actors, we must transfer this relationship and this feeling of relaxation from a prone to an upright position.

When we do so, we will be *standing tall,* and the "tip at the back of the top of your head" will be the tallest point. The bottom line of your chin is parallel with the floor, as you relax your front neck muscles—a condition essential to ridding vocal tension. Your shoulders will be rounded forward to obtain the widest possible space between the shoulder blades. We should think of the shoulder blades as a double gate that is always kept open. Square-shouldered, closed-gate, military posture produces tensions and inhibits the body's natural expressiveness. Your abdominal muscles will be held firmly in place and the buttocks "tucked under," properly aligning the spine from top to bottom. When you stand in this position against a wall, little or no space will remain between the wall and the small of your back. Your arms swing freely from the shoulders, and your knees will be relaxed.

The second objective of body training—muscular relaxation—is a quality that characterizes all fine acting. The goal of relaxation is not dormancy. Instead, it should provide a state of alertness in which actors can attain their utmost capacity for accomplishing any activity. It bolsters their courage and increases their self-confidence. This condition has been variously called "blissful relaxation" (Morris Carnovsky) and the "potent state" (Moshe Feldenkrais). For our purposes, we shall refer to this state of concentrated relaxation as the *creative state,* a term coined by Stanislavski. Of this type of relaxation, Robert Benedetti wrote, "The kind of relaxation you want is a state in which you are most ready to react, like a cat in front of a mouse hole. Tensions that would inhibit movement are gone, and you are in a state of balance that leaves you free to react in any way required."[2]

Actors who have not attained a state of muscular freedom will often be told, "Just relax; take it easy." These words can easily produce the opposite of the desired effect by causing actors to become more aware of their tension and, consequently, to become more uptight. Unfortunately, no program will eliminate excess tension in a few easy lessons. You achieve the creative state through a lifelong regimen of exercise, relentless in its demand on your time and energy.

Although it will not eliminate the need for training and exercise, actors can help induce the creative state by **justifying** their actions and concentrating on performing them. These aspects of the actor's technique are exceptionally pertinent to the thrust of this book, so we will take them up here and in the following chapter.

Relaxing through Justification

Phrases frequently heard in describing actors' state of being are "They forget themselves on stage" or "They lose themselves in the part." On the contrary, actors must "find themselves" in their roles, and they must commune (not pander) with the audience. However, to enter into the creative state, actors must "forget

Figure 4.2 A scene from William Shakespeare's *The Winter's Tale* at Center Stage in Baltimore, MD. Focus and justification of actions allows these actors to remain in the creative state.

their limitations and inhibitions" by concentrating on their character's actions. "Forgetting yourself on stage" implies that you must enter into a trancelike state in which you are unaware of your surroundings and thus lose control of the situation. Actors can neither forget themselves nor the audience, and those who insist they do are either lying or insane.

Worrying about what audiences may think or about the responsibility of keeping them "entertained" produces instant tension. Like actors, athletes also cherish the approval of the spectators, but during the game they must concentrate solely on their assignment at hand. Athletes have one purpose: to win. They know that if they accomplish it by fair means, the spectators will be satisfied and overlook minor errors or shortcomings of form. Actors "win" by creating believable characters. To accomplish this, they must free themselves from worry over nonessentials. They must command their energies to serve their stage purpose freely and fully. They know that if they are totally absorbed in carrying out their character's action, their personal tension will disappear.

About Inhibitions

Social inhibitions can occasionally be another source of tension for an actor. In such cases, it may prove helpful to realize that social inhibitions take many forms and that they vary substantially from society to society, from era to era, and from individual to individual. In our society, for instance, men rarely touch one another except to shake hands or to engage in playful banter. But in other societies, such as Mexico or Italy, it is perfectly acceptable for men to kiss, embrace, and walk arm in arm in public. Even succeeding generations within the same culture have different sets of social inhibitions. Social inhibitions may have prevented our great-grandparents from wearing bikinis to the beach or shorts on a hot day. An important key to freeing inhibitions, then, is to understand them by assessing your character's society, customs, and traditions.

Still, the relationship between social inhibitions and the individual person remains complex. Why is it that some actors are less hindered by social inhibitions on stage than others are? Can an actor from a conservative background learn not to wince (either internally or externally) at using suggestive behavior or foul language on stage? What are the actor's rights and responsibilities in these delicate areas?

These questions have no easy answers. You must develop your own sense of ethics and turn down roles in which you feel yourself exploited. On the other hand, once you have accepted a role, you have a responsibility to behave truthfully from your character's point of view, even when his or her actions differ from your own personal choices. "What would I do *if* I were this character in this circumstance?" Also remember the comment from Chapter 1, "You must never judge your character; otherwise, you will never be able to sustain belief in your actions." If you believe in a play and in your role and concentrate on the reasons that characters behave the way they do, you soon will lose your inhibitions. They will slip away as you involve yourself in your character's simple objectives. Internal logic will prevail as you increase your empathy with the character.

It is realistic to expect that today's actor may have to decide whether playing a character in the nude is artistically justified. David Storey's *The Changing Room*, for example, takes place in the locker room of an English rugby team. At one time, all the players appear nude while changing from street clothing into their uniforms. The nudity is not central to the meaning of the play, but it is a necessary and rational part of the play's locale. Obviously, too much self-consciousness would work against an actor's ability to create the easygoing, uninhibited locker room banter. If an actor is not comfortable enough with his body to rehearse and perform the play in the nude, he obviously should not audition for the role.

Figure 4.3 Mark Brown (left) as Trinculo, Michael Fitzpatrick as Stephano, and David Ivers as Caliban in the Utah Shakespearean Festival's production of *The Tempest*. Removing excessive tension frees these actors to make large physical character choices in this comedic scene.

The Creative State

Let us now turn to a sequence of exercises designed to help you remove tensions and promote the **creative state.** Please realize that these exercises are a mere taste of the organized, rigorous physical-training regimen that serious acting students should undertake. We have also included a small number of vocal exercises, for training the voice and the body parallels one another. Again, however, we assume that serious acting students are taking speech classes simultaneously with courses in acting. We cannot emphasize too strongly that we agree completely with Kristin Linklater, Arthur Lessac, and others who believe that the creative impulse emanates from a synthesis of a sound, tension-free voice and a healthy, relaxed body. Excellent exercises may be found in both their writings, which are detailed in the Bibliography at the end of this book.

Incidentally, various combinations of the following exercises can serve as an excellent warm-up routine before classes, rehearsals, or performances. Just as athletes warm up before practicing or playing the game and pianists do finger-stretching and relaxation exercises before rehearsing or performing, actors must always prepare their tools and their mind for the work at hand. You should *never* commence a sustained period of practice or performance without warming up.

EXERCISES   The following exercises designed to help promote the creative state are sequential and move logically through eight basic phases: focusing, meditating, tensing and releasing, centering, shaking, stretching, moving, and vocalizing. They are divided into two basic categories: floor exercises (lying prone or sitting) and standing exercises. Remember, as you begin the following sequence, you must have enough room so your movements will not be restricted, and you should not wear clothing that will hamper your freedom.

1. Focusing: Sit comfortably on the floor with your hands to your side, your back straight, and your legs crossed. Select a small personal object that you have with you and that you like a great deal (e.g., a watch, a necklace, a key chain, a ring, a tube of lipstick, etc.). Place the object on the floor in front of you, and focus all your attention on this object as you inhale and exhale slowly and deeply for one to two minutes. Allow any thoughts that arise to play across your consciousness, and then simply return your awareness to the object in front of you. At the end of this exercise you should feel more peaceful and calmer.

2. Meditating: Lie down on the ground. Allow your arms to rest at your side. Extend your legs straight out along the floor away from your head and allow them to roll outward in a comfortable position. Pick a point on the ceiling, making that your focal point during this exercise. Concentrate on your breathing. Take a few easy breaths—inhaling through the nose and exhaling through the mouth. As you exhale, vocalize an elongated [a] sound. Continue this breathing pattern until instructed to do otherwise. Notice the movement of your chest and abdomen. Try to suppress all other thoughts, feelings, and sensations. If you feel your attention wandering, bring it back to your breathing. Now as you breathe in, channel your attention to different parts of your body (right leg, left leg, abdomen, chest, right arm, left arm). Take your time. Once you have completed this sequence, say the word "peace" as you inhale. As you exhale, say the word, "calm" aloud. Extend the pronunciation of the word so that it lasts the entire exhalation. "c – a – a – a – a – l – l – l – l – m – m – m – m." Repeating these words as you breathe will help you to concentrate. Now return to breathing without speaking. Remember to breathe in through the nose and out through the mouth. Meditation is focused on your breath for a good reason: the breath is life. Now raise your right hand and arm, holding it in an elevated position for fifteen seconds.

Notice if your forearm feels tight and tense or if the muscles are soft and pliable. Let your hand and arm drop to the ground and relax. Notice what happens to the muscles in your arms and hands as they transcend from a state of tension to relaxation. Repeat this process of elevation and relaxation with other parts of your body (left arm, pelvis, right leg, left leg, head).

3. Tensing and Releasing: Throughout each phase of relaxation exercises, you should frequently check yourself against excess tension. Most of us have tensions of which we are not aware, and relieving them is an ever-present problem, in life as well as on the stage. We go about our daily activities—walking, sitting, driving, even lying down—using more than the required energy. We should develop a habit of frequently checking ourselves in whatever we are doing to discover what muscles are unnecessarily tense and then proceed to relax them. We may often find we are holding onto a pencil as if it would jump out of our fingers, or we are walking with tense shoulders or standing with our knees locked, talking with a tight jaw, or reading with a frown.

   Routinely checking for tensions and relieving them yields several benefits. Although it may be impossible, on stage or off, to keep tensions from occurring, this habit will induce a state of more general relaxation. Our goal is to eliminate excess tensions at will—a capacity of great value to actors, who are always subject to nervous strain. Perhaps most important, finding tension helps actors discover their own nervous mannerisms. Different people reveal tensions in different ways, some by contracted muscles, others by random movements. Among the most common movements are shaking the head, pursing the lips, frowning, snapping the fingers, raising the shoulders. Make an inventory of your personal signs of tension, and focus on ridding yourself of them.

   To release excess tension, we begin by creating it deliberately and then letting it go. As each area is named below, isolate and tense the muscles associated with that part of the body for approximately fifteen seconds; however, you should keep the rest of your body relaxed. On the instructor's command, release the tension with a vocalized and elongated [a]. Feel the muscular movement as tension is released. We will work our way down the body from your head to your toes.

   A. Tense all your facial muscles inward toward the center of your face. Release.

   B. Press your tongue against the roof of your mouth. Release.

   C. Now work your way down your body in this order: neck, shoulders, right arm, right hand, left arm, left hand, upper chest and back, abdomen and lower back, groin and buttocks, right leg, left leg—your entire body.

D. Repeat the entire exercise again, but this time hold the tension in each area for only three seconds, remembering to keep everything free of tension until its turn in the sequence.

4. Centering:

    A. While still on your back from the previous exercise, make yourself as long as possible.

    B. Now make yourself as short as possible.

    C. Make yourself as wide as possible. Stretch as far as you can from side to side.

    D. Make yourself as narrow as possible without decreasing your length.

    E. Now roll to your side into a curled position. Roll the rest of the way over until your feet are on the floor. From this curled position, uncoil into a standing position by aligning (or stacking) your vertebrae one at a time, with your head being the last part to uncurl.

    F. From this standing position, gently lift from the lower part of your spine, again making yourself as tall as possible.

    G. Drop the upper half of your body forward like a rag doll. Your hands will probably brush against the floor. Let your knees bend slightly for balance and support.

    H. Locate the excess tension and gently move that part of your upper body. Allow the tension to drip out of your body.

    I. Alleviate the tension in your face by making a "motor boat" sound. Don't be afraid to drool on the floor.

    J. Gently swing from side to side three or four times.

    K. Rise to a standing position by again aligning (or stacking) your vertebrae one at a time.

    L. Drop from the waist and repeat.

5. Shaking: While standing in place, simply "shake" the tension out of the following areas of your body: wrists, right elbow, right arm, left elbow, left arm, right leg, left leg.

6. Stretching: Stretching prepares our bodies for physical activity. While it lowers blood pressure and improves blood flow to the heart, for the actor (and athletes), stretching increases muscle temperature, making them more pliable and adaptable to changes from the body's habitual use. The following is a sequence of stretching exercises that flow logically from one to the next, beginning in a prone position on the floor, then sitting upright, and finally from a standing position.

A. Stretch and Yawn.

    i. Lie comfortably on the floor, and stretch your entire body. Extend your limbs, drop your jaw and yawn.

    ii. Repeat and encourage a "real" yawn. Let the natural vocalized sound empty out of your body.

B. Spinal Stretch (Shoulder Press).

    i. Place your arms to your side. Relax the small of your back, and stretch your legs out parallel to each other.

    ii. Now lift your legs and hips by making a tripod with your elbows on the floor. Extend your legs toward the ceiling, making sure your toes are pointed. Hold for fifteen seconds.

    iii. Continue this movement, keeping the legs straight, until your toes touch the floor above your head.

    iv. Bend your knees, bringing them to your ears. Take a deep breath.

    v. Straighten your legs and again extend to a vertical position with your toes pointing toward the ceiling.

    vi. Slowly move your body back down through your spine until you are again lying flat on the floor. Take another deep breath.

    vii. Repeat the entire sequence.

C. Posterior Stretch.

    i. Bend your right leg and place both hands around your right knee. Pull the knee toward your left shoulder, keeping your head, shoulders, and right leg relaxed. Hold for fifteen seconds.

    ii. Repeat. This time, however, pull both your right knee and ankle toward your left shoulder.

    iii. Repeat the entire sequence with your left knee and ankle.

D. Lower Back Stretch (Diagonal Twist).

    i. Straighten your legs and place your arms straight out from your body.

    ii. Raise your right leg and rotate it over to the left at a ninety-degree angle and touch the floor with your right foot. Rotate your upper torso the other direction, looking to the right. Be certain your right hip is pointed up to the ceiling. Hold for fifteen seconds.

    iii. Repeat with the left leg.

    iv. Repeat the entire sequence two additional times.

E. Quadriceps Stretch.

    i. Roll over onto your stomach, and place your right hand under your forehead.

    ii. Press your hips firmly onto the floor and bring your left foot up toward your buttocks.

    iii. Clasp your left foot with your left hand, easing your foot closer to your buttocks. Hold for fifteen seconds.

    iv. Repeat with right leg.

  F. Abdominal and Lower Back Stretch.

    i. Remaining face down, lift your body off the ground so that only your forearms and toes support you. Your elbows should be on the ground and should be almost directly below your shoulders. Your forearms and hands should be resting on the ground, pointed straight ahead. Toes and feet should be shoulder width apart and your head in line with your spine.

    ii. Contract your posterior muscles gently. Hold for fifteen seconds.

    iii. Lift your right arm off the ground. Straighten and point it directly ahead. Hold for fifteen seconds and return to starting position.

    iv. Repeat with left arm.

    v. Lift your right leg off the ground, pointing it straight back. Hold for fifteen seconds and return to starting position.

    vi. Repeat with left leg.

    vii. Lift your right arm and left leg simultaneously, and hold them in position for fifteen seconds. Return to starting position.

    viii. Repeat with left arm and right leg.

  G. Front of Trunk Stretch (The Cobra).

    i. Remaining face down with your body stretched, bring your hands to the sides of your shoulders and ease your chest off the floor, keeping your hips firmly pressed onto the ground. Hold for fifteen seconds.

    ii. Repeat.

  H. Lower Back Stretch (The Cat).

    i. Assume a position on your hands and knees (like a cat).

    ii. Arch your back toward the ceiling.

    iii. Press your spine toward the ground.

    iv. Sit back on your heels, and reach forward with your arms.

    v. Repeat.

  I. Middle Eastern Prayer Stretch.

    i. Begin with your knees, face, and arms resting comfortably on the floor.

    ii. Inhale to the count of four as you rise to a kneeling position, sitting on your lower legs with your arms at your sides.

    iii. Exhale to the count of four as you put your hands on the floor behind you and push forward and up as far as you can with your pelvis.

    iv. Inhale to the count of four as you return to the sitting position.

    v. Exhale to the count of four as you return to the original Middle Eastern Prayer position (i.e., knees, face, and arms on the floor).

    vi. Repeat the sequence once using four counts for each movement.

    vii. Repeat the sequence twice using two counts for each movement.

J. Groin Stretch.

    i. Sit with tall posture.

    ii. Ease your feet toward your body, bringing the soles together and allowing your knees to come up and out to the side.

    iii. Resting your hands on your lower legs or ankles, ease both knees towards the ground. Hold for fifteen seconds.

    iv. Repeat.

K. Iliotibial Tract Stretch.

    i. Remaining in the seated position, stretch your legs out in front of you.

    ii. Bend the right knee, and place your right foot on the ground to the left side of the your left knee.

    iii. Turn your shoulders so that you are facing to the right.

    iv. Using your left arm against your right knee, ease yourself further round. Use your right arm on the floor for support. Hold for fifteen seconds.

    v. Repeat sequence to other side.

L. Hamstring Stretch.

    i. Again, start with your legs stretched in front of you, and place the sole of your left foot alongside your right knee.

    ii. Allow your left leg to lie relaxed on the ground.

    iii. Bend forward keeping your back straight. Hold for fifteen seconds.

    iv. Repeat with your other leg.

M. Lower Spine Stretch.

    i. From a squatted position on the floor, give yourself a wide base by placing your feet outside shoulder width.

    ii. Roll up your spine—one vertebra at a time—to a standing position and reach for the ceiling. Hold for fifteen seconds.

    iii. Bending at the waist and keeping your spine straight (known as "flat back"), reach forward, making certain to keep your head up and looking forward. Hold for fifteen seconds.

      iv. Relax the spine and hang from the waist down to the ground ("rag doll position").

      v. Repeat the sequence.

N. Chest Stretch.

      i. Standing tall with your wide base and knees slightly bent, hold your arms out to the side parallel with the ground and the palms of your hands facing forward.

      ii. Clasp your hands together behind your back and gently lift. Hold for fifteen seconds.

      iii. Return to the original position and repeat.

O. Upper Back Stretch.

      i. Maintaining the wide base, interlock your fingers and push your hands as far away from your chest as possible, allowing your upper back to relax. Hold for fifteen seconds.

      ii. Repeat.

P. Shoulder Stretch.

      i. Place your right arm parallel with the ground across the front of your chest.

      ii. Bend your left arm up and use the left forearm to ease the right arm closer to your chest. Hold for fifteen seconds.

      iii. Repeat with left arm.

Q. Shoulder and Triceps Stretch.

      i. Keeping your wide base, place both hands above your head, and then slide both your hands down the middle of your back. Hold for fifteen seconds.

      ii. Repeat.

R. Side Stretch.

      i. From your wide base position, again hold your arms out to your side parallel with the ground and the palms of your hands facing forward.

      ii. Keeping your arms straight, take your left arm up and over your head, reaching to the right. Take your right arm across your chest and reach to the left. Hold for fifteen seconds.

      iii. Repeat to other side, holding for fifteen seconds.

      iv. Repeat sequence.

7. Moving

    A. Walk / Run / Freeze: Everybody in class begins by walking. Do not employ this action for anybody else's benefit. Do not "act," and avoid walking in a circle. Note the way you carry yourself, the way your feet touch the ground, the way you move your arms. Where is your center? Do you lead with your chest? Your head? Your pelvis? Change directions. Modify your stride. See yourself in relation to everyone in the room. Throughout this sequence, you may interact with others as you walk. Have fun. When the impulse arises, run. Run fast (but in control). Now you are either walking or running. Follow some others in the class. Note the distinct way they carry themselves, and adapt your movement to theirs. Do not enlarge upon or mock their movement; instead, note the subtle differences. Break away in a different direction. Don't plan these actions. Be impulsive. Be erratic. Sometimes you are walking; sometimes you are running; sometimes you are following; sometimes you are not. Continue this pattern for a while noting your body's changes. Freeze. Do not move a muscle or look about the room. Note your position, your carriage. Where is your center? Resume moving. Sometimes you are walking; sometimes you are running; sometimes you are frozen; sometimes you are following; sometimes you are not.

B. Run/Freeze:

   i. Everyone in the room run at the same time. Freeze at the same time. There are no leaders. There are no followers. Everyone must work together.

   ii. Stand face to face with a single partner. Move at the same time; freeze at the same time. You do not have to mirror your partner. Your movements will be distinct with regards to both form and tempo-rhythm. But you must start and stop at exactly the same time. Vary the lengths of time you move and freeze. Explore various movements, using your entire body. Again, be erratic. No one is leading; no one is following.

   iii. Change partners. Stand face to face and move at different times. Person A moves while Person B remains frozen. Person A continues to move until Person B interrupts him with her movement. Person A freezes while Person B moves. Person B continues to move until Person A interrupts her. This pattern continues until instructed to stop. Your movements should not be empty forms, but rather they should reflect your state of mind.

C. Shaping/Reshaping: Again, change partners, and determine Partner A and Partner B. A makes an abstract shape (like a statue). B makes a different shape and places it in relation to A's shape. Once B has assumed a shape, A steps out of the original shape and reshapes in relation to B's shape, etc. Fill the negative space without touching. Move slowly and smoothly. Think creatively using your whole body. As you do this, consider the following suggestions with regard to your shapes.

    i. circular

    ii. twisted

    iii. angular

    iv. complex

    v. spacious

    vi. arched, etc.

Now consider the following images, and design your shapes/reshapes accordingly.

    i. a gentle breeze

    ii. an erupting volcano

    iii. mud

    iv. lightning

    v. melting ice

    vi. a river

    vii. falling leaves

    viii. rain

    ix. an ice storm, etc.

D. Walking with Purpose (Justifying Your Actions): Everybody in the class begins walking again. As you did in exercise 7A, avoid walking in circles. Note your carriage, your feet, your arms, your center. Now begin to walk with specific purpose. Walk (or crawl) as if you were:

    i. a baby learning to walk.

    ii. a teenager approaching someone of the opposite sex.

    iii. an elderly person crossing a busy intersection.

    iv. a hunter stalking a deer.

    v. a high-fashion model on the runway.

    vi. a burglar hugging the sides of the buildings in a dark alley.

    vii. a trapper on snowshoes.

    viii. a child crawling through a low tunnel.

    ix. a soldier crawling on your stomach under gunfire.

    x. a drum major or majorette.

    xi. a native balancing a can of water on your head.

E. Point to Point: All should stop wherever they are in the room. You are now at Point A. Do not move until you have determined Point B. This point should not be arbitrary or "in space." It should be a specific destination. Once Point B is determined, take the shortest, logical path to that spot. After you have arrived at Point B, determine Point C. Cross to that point, and so on. Continue this exercise, moving point to point, with the following variations.

  i. Cross with different tempo-rhythms. Be specific and justify your actions. For example, "you are late for an important meeting" or "you are an elementary student who has been sent to the principal's office."

  ii. Cross with the intent of completing a specific activity. For example, "you cross to the dictionary to look up a specific word" or you cross your backpack to retrieve your hairbrush and brush your hair."

8. Vocalizing:

   A. Massage your face with the palm of your hands and fingertips. Apply some pressure, paying particular attention to your jaw, your nasal-labial folds (your "laugh-lines"), and your forehead.

   B. Vocalize the sound "hummmmmmmmmm" five times.

   C. Shake your face back and forth. Your cheeks and lips should be loose.

   D. Wet your lips and stretch your mouth open as wide as possible.

   E. Make the sound of a motorboat—first without sound, then with monotone sound, and finally with sound that moves up and down the scales.

   F. Stick out your tongue as far as you can. With your tongue, touch the tip of your nose, your cheek on the right side, your chin, your cheek on the left side, etc.

   G. Anchor your tongue behind your bottom front teeth, and pulsate your tongue with a sigh, "aaaaaahhhhhh."

   H. Make the sound of a drum roll—first without sound, then with monotone sound, and finally with sound that moves up and down the scales.

   I. Repeat the sound [k] five times, projecting it to the back wall of your classroom or performance space.

   J. Repeat the sound [g] five times.

   K. Alternate between [k] and [g] five times.

   L. Repeat the sound [p] five times.

   M. Repeat the sound [b] five times.

   N. Alternate between [p] and [b] five times.

   O. Vocalize "hummmmmm maaaaaahhhhhh" five times, raising your pitch each subsequent time.

   P. Again, make the sound of a motor boat.

   Q. Vocalize "me me me me me me me me maaaaaahhhhhh" five times.

R. Again, massage your face with your palms and fingertips.

S. Vocalize "me me me me may may may may maaaaaahhhhhh" five times, making certain to drop the jaw as you say "maaaaaahhhhhh."

T. Repeat "me me me me may may may may maaaaaahhhhhh" five additional times, only now add an upward inflection at the end of the phrase.

U. Repeat the following tongue-twisters three to five times each.

    i. Red leather, yellow leather

    ii. Synonym, cinnamon, aluminum, linoleum

    iii. You know New York. You need New York. You know you need unique New York.

    iv. A proper cup of coffee in a copper coffee cup

    v. Whether the weather be cold, or whether the weather be hot, we'll weather the weather whatever the weather, whether we like it or not.

    vi. Peter Piper picked a peck of pickled peppers. A peck of pickled peppers did Peter Piper pick. If Peter Piper picked a peck of pickled peppers, how many pickled peppers did Peter Piper pick?

    vii. Father fries fish in a fish fryer.

    viii. She sells seashells by the seashore.

    ix. A big black bug bit a big black bear and made the big black bear bleed blood.

    x. Sixty-six sick chicks

    xi. Does this shop stock short socks with spots?

    xii. He thrust three thousand thistles through the thick of his thumb.

    xiii. Rubber baby buggy bumpers

    xiv. I slit a sheet. A sheet I slit. And on that slitted sheet I sit.

Notes

1. Jerzy Grotowski, *Towards a Poor Theatre* (New York: Simon & Schuster, 1968), p. 185.

2. Robert Benedetti, *The Actor at Work,* Sixth Edition (Englewood Cliffs, NJ: Prentice Hall, 1994), p. 11.

CHAPTER 5

Directing Your Attention

B y now you have learned that concentration helps actors to relax by properly channeling their energies toward the accomplishment of a specific goal. Concentration is also the principal means of commanding the audience's attention. The audience must see what the actors want them to see, hear what the actors want them to hear during every moment of performance. Otherwise, the spectators' focus may wander casually around the stage or stray to other points in the auditorium. Their minds may drift to personal situations that have nothing to do with the stage events. Even with dimmed auditorium lights, theatres are overflowing with distractions. Without supreme concentration, actors will have little chance of success, no matter what the other virtues of their performance may be.

Fortunately, the audience wants to follow the action; their attention corresponds with the actors' involvement in specific actions. *Attention demands attention.* However, concentration, like the "creative state," is easier to talk about than to do. Too many young actors resemble the fellow described by Stephen Leacock who jumped on his horse and rode off in all directions. Their attention is scattered to all points of the compass. Their minds wander from the stage to the audience to the wings to their next line to an upcoming scene to a past mistake, and so on. They do well to focus ten percent of their attention on anything related to the action, thus dissipating ninety percent of their mental energy.

Figure 5.1 LeRoy Mitchell as C.C. and Jeff Bowen as Buddy in Stetson University's production of *The Diviners,* by Jim Leonard, Jr. Directed by Kenn Stilson. The specific and intense focus of these actors demands the attention of the viewer.

Actors can make full use of their talent only by learning to focus their energies. *"Creativeness on the stage, whether during the preparation of a part or during its repeated performance, demands complete concentration of all his physical and inner nature, the participation of all his physical and inner faculties."*[1] Successful actors achieve maximum concentration. They find ways to control their attention despite the pressure of the audience, the distraction of backstage activities, and the mechanical demands of the role. The ability to concentrate, then, is an additional specific skill that actors must possess. Like most other acting skills, the technique for marshaling the forces of concentration and knowing where to direct one's attention can be attained only through hard work.

EXERCISE   Any activity that requires concentration, especially in the presence of distracting influences, is excellent discipline for actors. People training for the stage need to develop their power of attention through increasingly complicated exercises. *As with all exercises, however, their value is derived only when they are practiced regularly over a period of time. No exercise has served its purpose until it can be done satisfactorily with a minimum of effort.* Students of Stanislavski suggest the following kinds of activity for improving an ability to concentrate:

1. Read expository material in the presence of a group that constantly tries to interrupt and distract. Hold yourself responsible for remembering each detail you have read.

2. Solve mathematical problems under the same conditions.

3. Present a memorized passage of prose or poetry under the same conditions.

4. With a group sitting in a circle, one person says the first noun that comes to mind. The next person repeats the word and adds another word. The third person repeats those two words and adds another, and so on. Use only nouns, for they are easier to remember. Stay in the present. Do not try to think ahead. See in your mind what you have heard; associate the word with the person who said it; and add a noun suggested by the image of the words that preceded it so that a continuous logical story may develop. For example:

   ✦ cigarette

   ✦ cigarette, woman

   ✦ cigarette, woman, nightclub

   ✦ cigarette, woman, nightclub, peanuts, etc.

   The process continues around and around the circle until no one is able to repeat the entire series. Anyone who fails is eliminated.

5. Under similar circumstances, play a game of numbers. The numbers may be unrelated, or you may progress by having each person add three or seven, eleven or nineteen. The game can become quite challenging.

6. Do a sequence of "Mirror Exercises," in which two people stand opposite each other; one makes a movement, while the other mirrors them exactly without delay. The effect is that of synchronized swimming in which partners move at the exact same time.

   A. At first, do a "Movement Mirror" with abstract, nonrepresentational movements.

   B. Now change roles by switching who leads and who mirrors.

   C. Now you are both leaders and both mirrors. Work off your partner, and do not attempt to merely lead or follow.

   D. Go back to one leader and one mirror, but add realistic physical tasks such as sewing on a button, manicuring your nails, or applying makeup.

   E. Return to abstract, nonrepresentational movements with one person serving as the leader and the other person mirroring the first person's actions.

    F. Extend the above exercise into a "Sound and Movement Mirror," in which, along with the movements, the leader utters repetitive but constantly changing nonsensical sounds that are mirrored by the partner.

    G. Again, change leaders.

    H. Finally, you are both leaders and both mirrors with your "Sound and Movement Mirror."

7. Concentrate on coordination of arm movements. With the left arm fully extended, continue making a large circle in the air; with the right arm, continue making a square by extending it straight out from the shoulder, then up, and then to the side. Once coordination is established, reverse the arms, making the circle with the right arm and the square with the left.

8. Do a "Copy Exercise," in which one group performs a sequence of simple actions such as entering a room, removing a coat, getting something to eat, and sitting down to watch the big game on TV. Do not pantomime or perform any action that cannot be executed fully. Another group watches and then repeats the movements in exact detail and with the same tempo-rhythms.

Concentrating on Action

Stanislavski discovered that talented and trained actors always seem fully engaged in an action (or transaction). He referred to the actor's range of concentration as **circles of attention.** An actor must have a point of attention, and this point must not be in the audience. The more engaging the action, the more it will concentrate the attention. Stanislavski wrote, "In real life there are always plenty of objects that fix our attention, but conditions in the theatre are different, and interfere with an actor's living normal, so that an effort to fix attention becomes necessary." [2]

Stanislavski demonstrated his point to his students by turning off all the lights in his classroom, leaving it in complete darkness. He then turned on a small lamp, illuminating the center of a table where a number of small objects had been placed. With the students watching, he carefully examined each item. "Make a note immediately of your mood," he said. "It is solitude because you are divided from us by the 'small circle of attention.' During a performance, before an audience of thousands, you can always enclose yourself in this circle like a snail in its shell." He then expanded the area of illumination but concentrated his attention to performing the same score of actions. He called this the "medium circle of attention." Finally, he flooded the entire classroom with light—the "large circle of attention"—but again focused his attention to the same score of actions.

> When the lights are on you have an entirely different problem. As there is no obvious outline to your circle you are obliged to construct one

Figure 5.2 Corliss Preston as Jessica in the Utah Shakespearean Festival's production of *The Merchant of Venice*. The actor's ability to focus on the first circle of attention constitutes the difference between good acting and great acting.

mentally and not allow yourself to look beyond it. Your attention must now replace the light, holding you within certain limits, and this despite the drawing power of all sorts of objects now visible outside of it.[3]

Although they are aware of the medium and large circles of attention, the small circle of attention allows actors to focus ninety percent of their mental energy to the stage action; thus, the audience will more likely follow the story without distraction. Remember, "attention demands attention."

Much of this book has been devoted to the importance of action. In earlier exercises, you have been asked to write down—make a score of—the physical actions you would undertake if you were in the situation of an imaginary character. Actions are tangible and specific for both the actor and the audience, bringing a character to life and revealing the dramatic events of the play. Because actions are never divorced from specific desires, their advantage lies not just in the actions themselves but also in the meaning and feelings they have the power to evoke.

Good dramatists provide ample chances for actors to concentrate their attention on performing physical action. Sometimes the action is to satisfy a simple desire, and sometimes actors must find a logical pattern of action to satisfy their characters' pressing needs. Good actors and directors display great imagination in inventing physical action organic to the character and the situation.

EXERCISE   Plan and rehearse a score of physical actions for the following problems. Work on the exercise until you can repeat the score without any feeling of distraction from outside influences — the medium and large circles of attention — and until you are satisfied that every bit of your energy is concentrated on carrying out the action — the small circle of attention. Supply additional circumstances, giving yourself specific details that will lead you to believe your actions.

　　As always, write out your score, making certain that the scene has a logical beginning, middle, and end. Define your objective and obstacle(s) and perform your score with the greatest possible economy, discarding any details that do not help in achieving your goal.

1. You are searching for a lost article that is very important to you.
2. After breaking your mother's favorite antique, you attempt to cover your mistake by repairing the damage.
3. While folding your fiancée's laundry, you discover an article of clothing that does not belong to either of you.
4. Late on a cold winter night, you are standing on a street corner waiting for a bus.
5. Sitting alone in a bar, you discreetly attempt to attract the attention of a person you wish to meet.
6. Physically ill, you try to study for an important examination.
7. You are packing your suitcase in preparation for running away from home.
8. While dressing for an important dinner engagement, you discover a stain on your clothing.
9. Recovering from a serious illness, you take your first steps.

Concentrating on Other Actors

"The eye is the mirror of the soul," wrote Stanislavski. "The vacant eye is the mirror of the empty soul."[4] While on stage, your eyes should reflect the deep inner content of your soul. Therefore, you must build great inner resources to correspond to the life of a human soul in your characters. Each moment on stage, you must share these spiritual resources with the other actors in the play, what

Stanislavski referred to as **communion.** Similar to Richard Schechner's concept of transacting, communion is like an underground river, which flows continuously under the surface of both words and silences, forming an invisible bond between two human beings. The communion established by the process of transaction is one of the actor's surest sources of stimulation, leading to a rewarding theatre experience for the audience.

Drama is fundamentally about conflict, about characters attempting to force their will on others. The audience becomes interested in the ups and downs of the struggle, the suspense of which is resolved when finally the protagonist either succeeds or fails. Shakespeare's plays, as complex as they are, still center around elemental conflicts of will. *King Lear* begins with Lear's attempt to force his will on his daughters by requiring extravagant declarations of love from them. Othello's tragedy comes from Iago's determination to ruin his contentment, and *The Taming of the Shrew* is a straightforward clash between the robust wills of Katherina and Petruchio. In *The Winter's Tale,* Hermione's honor and her life depend on her ability to convince her husband he is wrong in suspecting her of being unfaithful. In Act II, Scene I of *Hamlet,* a frightened Ophelia explains to her father a recent encounter with young Prince Hamlet.

> He took me by the wrist and held me hard;
> Then goes he to the length of all his arm,
> And, with his other hand thus o'er his brow,
> He falls to such perusal of my face
> As he would draw it. Long stay'd he so.
> At last, a little shaking of mine arm,
> And thrice his head thus waving up and down,
> He rais'd a sigh so piteous and profound
> As it did seem to shatter all his bulk
> And end his being. That done, he lets me go,
> And with his head over his shoulder turn'd
> He seem'd to find his way without his eyes,
> For out o' doors he went without their help
> And to the last bended their light on me.

We sense, in these lines, the wordless communion between Hamlet and Ophelia.

Communion is accomplished through concentration. Actors concentrate on using actions and lines to get what their characters want from the other characters in the play. They seek to arouse honest feelings and stimulate genuine responses in the other actors. In this exciting way, the imaginary world of the play merges with the real life of the actor. Actors must constantly strive to influence the behavior of their fellow actors, for they need their real responses to build a believable characterization of their own.

EXERCISE   Using no words and limited facial expressions, gestures, and physical actions, create a circumstance in which an engaged couple have quarreled and are not speaking to one another. Seat them as far apart as possible. In the beginning, the young
woman pretends not to see him, but she does so in such a way as to attract his attention. He sits motionless, watching her with a pleading gaze trying to catch her
eye so that he might guess her feelings. The young man tries to feel her soul with
his invisible antennae, but the angry woman must attempt to withstand his attempts at communication.

To excite an audience, actors must excite one another. Stanislavski wrote: "Infect your partner! Infect the person you are concentrating on! Insinuate yourself
into his very soul, and you will find yourself the more infected for doing so. And
if you are infected everyone else will be even more infected."[5] A lion has the
power to stalk, attack, and seize its prey without distraction. You must have the
same power to seize with your eyes, ears, and senses. As an actor, if you must listen, listen intently. If you are to smell, smell hard. Do not simply gaze at another
person, but look into his or her soul. Infect that person.

Making an Action of Speech

Speaking is of great importance in the actor's transaction. Both in life and on
stage, we use words as a means of getting what we want, as a way of realizing our
objectives. We use words to ask, beg, demand, plead, explain, persuade, woo,
threaten—for countless purposes. Consideration of the particular problems of interpreting lines (an important part of the actor's job) comes later, but, at this point
in your training, you need to understand how to incorporate speech in the overall task of performing. A mere reading of the lines, no matter how intelligent or
how beautiful, is only a part of the actor's responsibility. No matter how glibly and
mellifluously delivered, all dialogue will appear superfluous, unless it is demanded
by the action of the play.

The basic function of stage speech is to help actors accomplish their goals. Actors have already been admonished to know what that purpose is at all times.
When they are called on to speak, they must also know how each word relates to
that purpose. They must have this relationship clear in their mind for every moment of the play, both during rehearsal and in performance. Acting is not only believing, it is also thinking! Concentrating on speaking smoothly or beautifully will
interfere with thinking about the action of the play. Actors must discover a genuine need to use the playwright's words and train themselves to keep their
thoughts alive as they speak them. They must particularly guard against the aban-
donment of live thinking during repetitious rehearsals.

T. Charles Erickson

Figure 5.3 From left: Helen Stenborg (E. M. Ashford, Dphil) comforts Kathleen Chalfant (Vivian Bearing) in Long Wharf Theatre's production of Margaret Edson's *Wit*.

It should be clear by now that, in terms of this book's methodology, *speech is an action.* Speaking is doing. In some primitive languages, the word for acting and speaking is the same. The actor's words are important tools for engaging in the transaction of the moment. Simply saying "good morning" has no justification on the stage (or in real life, for that matter) unless the speaker says these words to influence the listener in some way or other. The greeting may "infect" the listener with casual indifference, deep love, or intense hate. It may say any one of a dozen things, each intended to evoke a different response.

A transaction, of course, demands a two-way influence. You must concentrate not only on *affecting* others but also on *listening* to what is said, resisting or yielding to the desires of the speaker. A special ability to listen is often mentioned as one of the specific skills required of the actor. You must listen and respond to everything said at each rehearsal and performance as if it had never been heard before—Gillette's "illusion of the first time." This illusion is necessary for both you and the audience, no matter how long you have worked on a part—no matter how often you have rehearsed or performed it. For a talented and trained actor, each performance is a new and fresh transaction leading to an appropriate communion between actors and audience.

EXERCISE   A short dialogue from a scene we discussed in earlier chapters from the beginning of *When You Comin Back, Red Ryder?* gives both actors an excellent opportunity to speak with purpose. The scene, recall, is a diner on the desert in southern New Mexico in the late sixties. Stephen/Red has worked the night shift and is waiting for Angel to relieve him. She is five minutes late.

> ANGEL: Good mornin, Stephen. (*Stephen does not look at her, but glances at the clock and makes a strained sucking sound through his teeth—a habit he has throughout—and flips the newspaper back up to his face. Unperturbed, Angel proceeds behind the counter.*) I'm sorry I'm late. My mom and me, our daily fight was a little off schedule today. (*Stephen loudly shuffles the paper, sucks his teeth.*) I said I'm sorry, Stephen. God. I'm only six minutes late.
>
> STEPHEN: Only six minutes, huh? I got six minutes to just hang around this joint when my shift's up, right? This is really the kinda dump I'm gonna hang around in my spare time, ain't it?
>
> ANGEL: Stephen, that's a paper cup you got your coffee in. (*Stephen is entrenched behind his newspaper.*)
>
> STEPHEN: Clark can afford it, believe me.
>
> ANGEL: That's not the point, Stephen.
>
> STEPHEN: Oh no? You're gonna tell me the point though, right? Hold it— lemme get a pencil.
>
> ANGEL: The point is that if you're drinking your coffee here, you're supposed to use a glass cup, and if it's to go, you're supposed to get charged fifteen instead of ten and ya get one of those five cent paper cups to take it with you with. That's the point, Stephen.
>
> STEPHEN: Yeah, well I'm takin it with me, so where's the problem?

The objective of each of the characters is clear. Angel wants to gloss over her lateness. Stephen/Red wants to make her as miserable as possible. The playwright, Mark Medoff, is exceptionally aware of the importance of physical actions, and he supplies an excellent set of them for Stephen/Red. Angel, on the other hand, must devise her own from the given circumstances of arriving at work and settling in behind the counter.

Even though each character's objective emerges clearly from this scene, the actors should state it in each line in their own words. They might be stated as:

ANGEL: I must evoke a normal, friendly response from Stephen.

STEPHEN: I must make her admit that she's late.

ANGEL: I must gain his sympathy.

STEPHEN: I must punish her.

ANGEL: I must turn the tables on him.

STEPHEN: I must belittle her accusation.

ANGEL: I must not let him off the hook.

STEPHEN: I want to shut her up.

A few moments later, a dialogue between Stephen/Red and Angel does not provide so clear a reason for the lines:

ANGEL: I saw ya circle somethin in the gift book the other mornin.

STEPHEN: What *gift* book?

ANGEL: The Raleigh *coupon* gift book.

STEPHEN: Hey—com'ere. (*Angel advances close to him. He snatches the pencil from behind her ear and draws a circle on the newspaper.*) There. Now I just drew a circle on the newspaper. That means I'm gonna get me that car?

ANGEL: Come on, Stephen, tell me. What're ya gonna get?

STEPHEN: Christ, whudduyou care what I'm gonna get?

ANGEL: God, Stephen, I'm not the FBI or somebody. What are you so upset about? Just tell me what you're gonna get.

STEPHEN: (*Mumbling irascibly.*) Back pack.

How does Stephen want this information to affect Angel? What is Angel's purpose in asking him in the first place? Does she suspect that he wants to leave and fear that she will be left completely alone with no prospect of anybody her age to share her life? Does Stephen understand her fear and lead her on to make her suffer? Note that the playwright has provided fewer physical actions in the given circumstances. The actors must develop their own objectives, create imaginative physical actions to support them, and concentrate their attention on influencing the behavior of the other to complete the transaction demanded by the scene.

Of course, in developing a role completely, actors may be certain of the action of each line only after they understand the desires that motivate the character's total behavior. Understanding this motivating force is a problem we will engage with in Part 2, which considers the actor in relation to the play. At this time, you should continue to work on small scenes without assuming the responsibility of finding their total meaning in relationship to the rest of the play.

EXERCISE   Using the example given from *When You Comin Back, Red Ryder?* as a model, work improvisationally in the following situations. Influence your partner. Elicit specific responses. Your partner's job is to influence you. This means a transaction, a give-and-take that is the essence of a lively stage performance. It means that actors are sensitive to every detail of their partners' presence, that actors hear and understand what their partners are saying, that they are equally aware of each other.

Remember that these improvisations are free only within certain limitations. They require thoughtful preparation. Your simple objective—the response you want to provoke—should be determined and recorded in advance. You and your partner in the exercise should offer additional circumstances to supplement those briefly given here, and your behavior should be appropriate within those circumstances. The exercise, as always, should be scored and structured into its three parts, and the "key lines" should be used in the beginning unit. You might do well to determine in advance other key lines to be made part of the other units.

This kind of preparation gives you direction and purpose, and it does not eliminate spontaneity and immediate adaptations. It is like playing any game. You know the rules and the objectives, but you do not know what offensive actions your partner will attempt or what defenses he or she will use against your attacks.

1. In *Album,* by David Rimmer, Trish and Peggy are sixteen and best friends. Trish thinks Peggy has had her first sexual experience, and she wants her to tell her about it. The fact is, however, Peggy is also a virgin but wishes to hide the truth. Their key lines are:

TRISH: You look the same to me. Didya feel different after you did it?

PEGGY: Will you leave me alone?

2. In *Boy's Life,* by Howard Korder, Jack, a self-assured young man in his late twenties, is sitting on a bench opposite a playground in a city park smoking pot and pretending to watch his six-year-old son, Jason. Maggie, wearing running attire, has stopped to catch her breath before continuing in the organized race against apartheid. Attempting a seduction, Jack stands and crosses to her. Their key lines are:

JACK: I'm a cardiologist. (Pause.)

MAGGIE: Please go away.

3. In *The Boys Next Door,* by Tom Griffin, the good-natured but mentally marginal Sheila has been "dating" the retarded Norman and has greatly admired a large ring of keys Norman wears attached to his belt. For her birthday, Norman presents her with a box covered with stuck-on bows. She opens it, and inside is her very own ring of keys. Their key lines are:

SHEILA: Oh, Norman, keys.

NORMAN: Try them on.

4. In *A Coupla White Chicks Sitting Around Talking,* by John Ford Noonan, Maude comes in with great dismay to tell Hannah Mae that she has consummated an adulterous affair with Hannah Mae's husband. Much to her surprise, Hannah Mae takes the news very calmly. Their key lines are:

HANNAH MAE: The only thing I feel, Honey, is closer to you.

MAUDE: Get those hands off me! I already had his on me, I don't need yours.

5. In *Dutchman,* by LeRoi Jones, the scene is a subway car. A white woman, a stranger sitting beside a young black man, tries to tempt him erotically. Their key lines are:

LULA: (*Grabbing for his hands, which he draws away.*) Come on, Clay. Let's rub bellies on the train. . . . Get up, Clay. Dance with me, Clay.

CLAY: Lula! Sit down, now. Be cool.

6. In *In the Wine Time,* by Ed Bullins, Lou and Cliff are a young married couple sitting on the street in front of their house on a hot summer night. They are drinking wine, and their conversation alternates between bantering and wrangling. Their key lines are:

LOU: What should I do when I find lipstick on your shirt . . . shades I don't use? (Silence.) What should I say when I see you flirtin' with the young girls on the street and with my friends? (Silence.)

CLIFF: (Tired.) Light me a cigarette, will ya?

7. In Neil Simon's *Lost in Yonkers,* Bella tries to convince her brother, Louie, that the man she wishes to marry is a good man. They hope to open a restaurant, but they need five thousand dollars to begin operations. Louie, who is prone to volatile outbursts, tries to dissuade Bella from carrying through with her intentions. Their key lines are:

BELLA: It'll only cost five thousand dollars.

LOUIE: (Laughs) Five thousand dollars? Why not five million? And who's got the five grand? Him?

8. In *Our Town,* by Thornton Wilder, George and Emily are on opposite sides of Main Street in Grover's Corner. George has just been elected president of the junior class, and Emily has been elected secretary and treasurer. Emily is carrying an armful of "imaginary" schoolbooks. When George crosses to Emily, their key lines are:

GEORGE: Emily, why are you mad at me?

EMILY: I'm not mad at you.

9. In Tennessee William's *27 Wagons Full of Cotton,* Jake Meighan, a cotton-gin owner near Blue Mountain, MS, has left his shapely wife on the front porch with Silva Vicarro, superintendent of the Syndicate Plantation, which has just burned to the ground as a result of a suspicious fire. Suspecting that Jake

is the culprit, Vicarro attempts to seduce the information out of his naïve bride. Their key lines are:

FLORA: I'm not much good at—makin' conversation.

VICARRO: (*finally noticing her*) Now don't you bother to make conversation for my benefit, Mrs. Meighan. I'm the type that prefers a quiet understanding. (*Flora laughs uncertainly.*)

10. In *The Zoo Story,* by Edward Albee, two men quarrel violently over which one has the right to occupy a particular park bench. Their key lines are:

PETER: This is my bench, and you have no right to take it away from me.

JERRY: Fight for it, then. Defend yourself; defend your bench.

EXERCISE   Return to any of the situations in the previous group of exercises, and improvise them in gibberish, so neither will understand the words of the other. This kind of improvisation can be made a valuable part of your work, creating an increased awareness of the function of lines in accomplishing objectives. Too often actors speak their lines while concentrating too much on the words and not enough on their purpose. Overcome immediately any feeling of ridiculousness that may occur in speaking gibberish. If you concentrate on working with purpose, you will alleviate this feeling.

Notes

1. Constantin Stanislavski, *Stanislavski's Legacy,* ed. Elizabeth Reynolds Hapgood (New York: Theatre Arts Books, 1958), p. 174.

2. Constantin Stanislavski, *An Actor Prepares* (New York: Theatre Arts Books, 1948), p. 78.

3. Ibid., p. 79.

4. Ibid., p. 185.

5. Constantin Stanislavski, *Building a Character* (New York: Theatre Arts Books, 1949), p. 118.

CHAPTER 6

Seeing Things

The study of human nature is a major lifelong concern of the actor. The great actors of France have long been famous for their ability to dazzle an audience by means of their technical perfection and the incisiveness of their character portrayal. One of the greatest was Constant Coquelin, creator of the role of Cyrano de Bergerac. Coquelin wrote, "It is one of the necessary qualities of an actor to be able to seize and note at once anything that is capable of reproduction on the stage."[1]

"Seizing and noting," which we call **observation,** is another necessary skill. Although you have lived through an infinite number of experiences and emotions to help you create diverse characters from any period, you must constantly augment this experience by observing the world around you. You must perpetually enlarge your impressions of life, for these are the materials from which you create. You must make it a practice to seize and note, as Coquelin suggests, not only anything that can be reproduced on stage but also anything that reveals truth or provides understanding about what may be produced there.

The technique of observation begins with a conscious effort to develop fuller awareness of happenings around us, a fine-tuned sensitivity to what we see, hear, taste, feel, and smell. Uta Hagen tells a story of an argument between Albert Basserman's director and a designer about producing the special effect of an actual rainstorm on stage. After a brief discussion, Basserman interrupted with, "Pardon me, but when I enter, it will rain!" According to report, when Basserman entered, it did rain—without special effects.[2]

Jean Louis Barrault is fond of telling a story about Charles Dullin, a noted French director whose productions were always vital and vibrant. Dullin himself was marvelously childlike in his appreciation of everything in his environment. Once Dullin was asked, "How can you stare at the same scenery every day? You stare out of the train window as if seeing the scenery for the first time, even though you travel on this same train practically every day." "Because," he responded, "every night, before I go to sleep, I 'kill' the old Charles Dullin. Each morning, I am reborn." This was Dullin's method for maintaining his powers of observation: Each day he saw the world anew through the eyes of a child.

Our senses are so intensely bombarded by our comprehensive surroundings in the modern world that we tend to take most things for granted. We do not really look at people's faces, hear their voices, listen to sounds, or even taste the food for which we have paid dearly in an expensive restaurant. Emily in *Our Town,* by Thornton Wilder, movingly expresses this indifference. Returning from the dead to relive a childhood experience, she sees people going insensitively about their everyday tasks. She says of her family at breakfast: "They don't even take time to look at one another." You must learn to observe familiar things as if you had never seen them before, and you must remember the experience. Through remembered observation, you will build a stockpile of materials from which you can construct performances. But more important, you will enrich your life, and an enriched life will increase your chances of being an insightful actor.

Observation is both intellectual and sensory. The mind tells us the uses of things, classifies them, analyzes them in any one of a number of ways, and permits us to retain them in memory. Recognizing that a flower is a carnation and not a buttercup, is red and not yellow, and is a variety of the clove, pink, spicy-scented, double-blossomed carnation used for bouquets and buttonholes is an intellectual response. We perceive the flower, however, through the senses. Experiencing a carnation is not just knowing about it. It is seeing its color, smelling its fragrance, holding it, touching it. Fortunately our memory can retain sensory as well as intellectual experience, and sensory perception is the bedrock of the technique of observation. You must have the ability to recall not only your knowledge of the carnation but also the way it affected your senses.

The more extreme your sensory experience, the easier it will be to recall on stage. We all have surely stubbed our toes, burned our fingers, or cut ourselves on a sharp object. But how does the actor recall everyday experiences? How do you deal with putting on mascara with a dry brush, drinking tea as if it were brandy, getting drunk on a non-alcoholic beverage, burning your tongue on food that is room temperature, or nicking your face with a bladeless razor? How do you make yourself believe that you are hot and sweaty in a cold theatre, nauseated due to illness that does not exist, or, like Basserman, make it rain on a dry stage? The more sensitive you are to the real world, the more intensely you will respond to the stimulus that induces these everyday sensory experiences.

As an actor you must have the ability to produce a natural behavioral response to arrive at the essence of the experience. Just as you cannot "play" an emotion, you cannot entirely produce a sensory experience simply by thinking about it or isolating it from subsequent behavior. There are two ways in which you may make your on-stage sensory experiences truthful to yourself and to your audience.

First, you may give the quality of one object to the quality of another object. For example, you may drink water as if it were vodka. A cold stove may be treated as if it was hot, and a dry mascara brush may be treated as if the bristles were wet with makeup. Playwrights often require physical objects that actors cannot actually use on stage. Real firearms, medicine, alcohol, and illegal drugs obviously have no place on stage, for they pose a genuine danger to the actor or alter the actor's mode of thinking. Drinking beer on stage is not a morality question but rather a question of foolishness. Anything that poses a threat or affects the actor's ability to think or act with clarity has no place in the theatre. Even such everyday items as eye makeup, onions, and hot irons are precarious items for the actor to use while performing before hundreds of people. In the same regard, valuable antiques, jewelry, authentic paintings, and any object of extreme value also do not belong on stage. The actor must find similar, less dangerous or expensive, objects and bestow upon them the essential qualities of the actual item.

Second, to discover truthful environmental and human conditions, such as heat, rain, sleet, drunkenness, anxiety, and exhaustion, you must determine their precise cause and their particular effect on a specific part of the body. From there, you must find the correct physical adjustment necessary to overcome the condition. If, for example, you arrive at your "imaginary" beach and try to "feel" the intense heat of the sun by simply thinking about it, you will find it almost impossible to believe your reality. You can, however, believe an appropriate set of physical actions that result from the imagined conditions that surround you. Instead of isolating the condition of heat, you simply score your actions. Working within this score, you walk quickly to your spot in the "sand" and spread your towel to get off the hot ground. A ship catches your eye off in the distance. You squint as you stare at the boat. You shield your eyes and look up at the glaring sun. You rummage through your bag for your sunglasses and put them on. You grab a cold drink from the cooler, sit on your towel, and begin to apply suntan lotion. Your belief in the condition of heat results from your belief in your score of physical.

To believe your on-stage life, including the most trivial sensory conditions, you must either substitute the qualities of one object for that of another or perform the logical sequence of physical actions necessary to alleviate the imagined conditions. Only then can you produce the sensation at will.[3] To believe you are drinking a steaming cup of coffee when in fact it is room temperature, you perhaps stir it with a spoon and blow across the brim before carefully picking up the "hot" cup with your fingertips and taking a sip. On-stage exhaustion may perhaps be achieved by kicking off your shoes, putting on your slippers, pouring a drink, reclining on the sofa, turning on the television, sipping your drink, and shutting your eyes. What do you do to alleviate the environmental condition of rain? What is the sequence of actions you undertake to alleviate the human condition of grogginess when waking up from a deep sleep? What do you do to lessen the condition caused by a pungent odor, a sour lemon, a bitter pill, a dark room, or a slippery surface? Just as the Method of Physical Actions allows you to discover true emotion, an appropriate sequence of physical actions allows you to actually believe in the sensory experience.

EXERCISE   **1.** Create a scenario using three objects that cannot or should not appear on stage. Substitute similar objects and give them the essential qualities of the actual objects. Provide for yourself given circumstances. Establish your objective and obstacle(s). Score your actions and title your units. Remember, the sensory experiences are not the primary purpose of the scene but simply part of the given circumstances. You may use the objects listed below or create your own.

Object used on stage	Given the qualities of
inexpensive vase or glass	a valuable antique
cold iron	a hot iron
toy pistol or rifle	a real pistol or rifle
rubber or plastic knife	a sharp knife
doll	a newborn baby
empty jar and dry mascara brush	liquid mascara
print	a valuable oil painting
clove cigarettes	marijuana
plastic or cardboard crown	a real crown
empty jar and dry fingernail brush	a liquid nail polish
costume jewelry	valuable jewelry
rubber snake	a real snake
razor with no blade	a bladed razor
tea	hot coffee or brandy
candy	medicine
apple	an onion
silk flower	a rose
water	vodka or acid
canned peaches	oysters or eggs

2. Adapt your score of physical actions from the above exercise with one or more imaginary conditions. The manner in which you alleviate your conditions is part of your adaptations to achieving your objective. You may use the environmental or human conditions listed below or create your own.

Environmental Condition	Human Condition
summer evening	drunkenness
winter morning before daylight	nausea
sweltering summer afternoon	exhaustion
rainy day	high (drug induced)
snowy winter day	stress
crisp spring morning	depression
windy fall afternoon	headache
autumn evening	starvation
bright winter day	upset stomach
spring evening	vertigo
winter ice storm	broken bone

3. Perform the same sequence of actions, but add the element of time. As an actor, you must always have a specific idea about how much time you have and how much time the specific sequence of actions will take. Notice how the tempo-rhythm of the scene changes with the amount of time you have to complete your objective.

Increasing your awareness of what goes on around you and developing your **sense memory** are your first steps toward sharpening the technique of observation. Once you have command of the technique, you will find that it provides you with three essential kinds of information that can be used as raw material for building a character. They are:

1. Characteristics of human behavior (manners of walking, talking, gesturing, and so forth) that may be reproduced precisely on the stage

2. Other human characteristics, incidents, and situations that, when filtered through your imagination, may be adapted for use on the stage

3. Abstract qualities of animals, plants, and inanimate objects that can help stimulate your imagination about how characters *might* look or behave on the stage

In a description of her working methods, Helen Hayes gave examples of these uses of observation. After defining acting talent as "a peculiarly alert awareness of other people," she continued:

When I was preparing for my role of the duchess in Anouilh's *Time Remembered,* I had some difficulty capturing the spirit of the role, until . . . I heard some music written by Giles Farnaby for the virginal—you know, one of those sixteenth-century instruments. . . . That old duchess, I told myself, is like the music, light, dainty, period, pompous, tinkling. And, poor me, I'd been playing her like a bass drum. I had one scene in *Victoria Regina* that I played like one of my poodles. . . . I had a poodle that used to just sit, and he'd look almost intoxicated when I'd say, "Oh, Turvey, you are the most beautiful dog."

. . . and believe me every night for a thousand and some performances of that play, I saw that poodle. . . . There was a famous moment in *Coquette*—I didn't know what really true way to accept the news that my lover had been shot and was dead. . . . I remembered a picture on the front of one of the tabloids—the *News* or the *Mirror*—of a mother standing over her son's grave. He was a gangster, in Chicago, and this coffin was being lowered, and this woman was standing there and she was holding herself as if she'd had a terrible, terrible pain in her insides. And I knew that this was the complete, complete reaction to something like this.[4]

Explore these outcomes of observing through the following illustrations, explanations, and exercises.

Observing People

"Always and forever, when you are on the stage, you must play yourself," wrote Stanislavski. "But it will be in an infinite variety of combinations of objectives and given circumstances which you have prepared for your part, and which have been smelted in the furnace of your emotion memory."[5] The impartial observation of other people is most certainly an important part of actor training; however, this skill is most useful when you learn something about yourself in the process. The simple manifestation of external gestures and movement serve no purpose unless you discover that you have behaved in a similar fashion under different circumstances. You cannot get away from yourself on stage without it leading to *indicated* actions. Therefore, as you observe others, you must find a way to identify with their actions within your own person.

With that in mind, let's return to the hypothetical production of *Romeo and Juliet* for which we were rehearsing in previous chapters. Suppose you are now cast not as Juliet nor as Romeo but as Juliet's old Nurse. Let's see how observation can help in understanding, and ultimately in believing, this character. What kind of person is Juliet's Nurse? As you answer this question, remember to always look

Figure 6.1 Laurie Birmingham (left) as Abby Brewster and Leslie Brott as Martha Brewster in the Utah Shakespearean Festival's production of *Arsenic and Old Lace*. Actors must find themselves within their characters.

through the eyes of the character. You must consider the factual information. But then you must infer how "you" as the character perceive yourself. You may be unaware that others describe you as a fat, old, bawdy, opportunistic gossip, who lacks moral fiber and likes to put on airs. You may instead perceive yourself as a youthful—although slightly out-of-shape—fun-loving, good-natured, vivacious nursemaid, who has helped raise Juliet and who loves her with every fiber of her being.

Obviously this role is a considerable stretch for the young actor. The process of self-exploration will reveal the essence of your imagined character, but here is an acting problem for which your own resources will need to be reinforced. How can you create a three-dimensional vulgar and yet jovial older woman, when you are a gentle, warmly humorous, slightly introverted twenty-one-year-old undergraduate with limited life experiences?

One relatively simple answer would be to locate and carefully observe someone like this nurse. "Seize and note" the way she rolls from side to side when she walks, the way she pants after any physical exertion, and the way she moves her head and holds in her stomach when she laughs. Remember to look for mannerisms with which you can identify. Practice these adopted gestures and movements until you can make them your own. Once these external manifestations are true, you may be surprised to learn that you have also grasped many internal aspects of the character.

Unfortunately, you probably do not have among your friends even a reasonable facsimile of Juliet's Nurse. You will rarely play a character for whom you can find a counterpart living in the next block. Developing a character through observation usually consists of piecing together details supplied by a number of different persons and, very possibly, noted at widely different times. Observing the people with whom you have contact must be a continual process. The way your geology professor smacks her lips to express approval may be a mannerism exactly suited to the next role you will play. Using your newly heightened powers of observation, you may have noted that the way a casual acquaintance sips a soda reveals a great deal of his character. File this observation in your memory, for it may later provide the key to understanding a character you portray.

The material for bringing to life such a character as Juliet's Nurse will spring not only from observing people while you prepare the role but also from the reservoir of details you have retained from past observations. The specific mannerisms of a talkative landlady at whose house you roomed three years ago might help you to believe this same quality in the Nurse. Remembering the way a neighbor used to put on airs when she dressed up to go downtown might help you to create the behavior of the Nurse when Juliet sends her forth to find Romeo. And your memory of the way an uncle used to tease you when you were a child might help you to appreciate the pleasure the Nurse derives from nettling Juliet when she returns with Romeo's message.

EXERCISE   **1.** Each day during the next week, make a special effort to use your powers of observation. Start an observation notebook. Carefully note mannerisms, gestures, and ways of talking, walking, and eating that reveal character traits. Visit a busy railway station, hotel lobby, or some other place where you will have the opportunity to observe people of all ages. Practice reproducing details until you can do them accurately and until you feel you have captured some of the inner quality of the person. Again, remember to look for character traits with which you can relate to your own past and present external behavior. Attempt to discover their objectives by observing their physical actions.

     2. From one of the above observations, prepare a complete character autobiography, answering all the appropriate questions. Score the actions, and define your objective and obstacle(s). Rehearse and present a short scene with imagined circumstances leading to action that you believe would be truthful for the character you create from the observed raw material.

3. Observe a painting—an original, if you have access to a museum—that reveals character. Re-create with your own body the posture and the facial expression. Make the character move; imagine how he would walk, sit, and use his hands. If it is a period picture, read about the manners and customs of the period. Make him speak. Invent a scene in which you can bring the character to life in a sequence of actions.

4. Write down your observations of a room belonging to an acquaintance or, better yet, to someone you are meeting for the first time. Study the furniture. Speculate on the reasons for its choice and its arrangement. Observe the manner of the decoration. Are the colors carefully planned or haphazard? Is the room neat or disorderly? What feelings does the room evoke in you? What does it tell you about the person who occupies it?

Adapting Observations through the Imagination

In the preceding exercises, you were asked to remember or observe, and then repeat, actions you knew to be true of some person. To understand these actions fully, you no doubt had to supply circumstances that could account for why the people behaved as they did. Supplying such circumstances involves imagination, and a facile imagination is an invaluable acting tool. For every one observed human behavior that transfers directly to one of your characters, you will encounter a hundred observations that will serve only to stimulate your imagination. Therefore, you should seize every opportunity to exercise and expand your power of imagination, and one of the best ways to do so is by observing human behavior, then creating circumstances to justify it.

Stanislavski provided a striking illustration. Walking down the street one day, he observed a forlorn-looking woman wheeling a caged bird in a baby carriage. He knew, of course, nothing of the circumstances. Very probably the woman was moving into a new apartment. The carriage was a practical means of transporting her pet bird, and the exhausting job of moving probably accounted for her forlornness. Stanislavski's imagination, however, created circumstances that provided him with a richer understanding of human experience, and his memory recorded the incident to use sometime in developing a character.

He adapted the observed fact in this way: the woman was a widowed mother who a short time before had lost her two children. To dispel her grief, she had directed her affection to the bird, caring for it as if it were a child. Each afternoon she took it for an airing in the carriage exactly as she used to take the children.

Such a combination of observed fact and imaginary circumstances is one of the actor's primary sources of stimulation, and physical objectives in which they can believe spring from it. Think of the number of short scenes based on the incident of the woman and the birdcage you might improvise. Can you see her bathing the bird, feeding the bird, caressing it, talking to it, getting it ready to go for the ride? Many questions will immediately arise, for which your imagination must supply the answers:

+ How old is the woman?
+ What does she look like?
+ What kind of place does she live in?
+ Is she rich or poor?
+ What kind of bird does she have?
+ How long have the children been dead?
+ How did they die?
+ What is the bird's name?
+ Is the substitution of the bird only a temporary outlet, or does it indicate some permanent mental derangement?
+ What attitude does the woman have toward friends who see her behavior with the bird?

Having answered these and other questions, you can visualize a series of actions designed to bring this character and this situation to life. In performing them, you would concentrate on accomplishing these physical objectives so that the action would lead you to believe in the situation and the character. The belief in turn would produce the desired emotional state. Remember that observed and imaginary circumstances lead to external expression or action, and belief in your character's actions and the on stage stimuli leads to truthful internal feeling.

EXERCISE   Make careful observations of human behavior. When you see a situation that stimulates your imagination, supply circumstances you can use as the basis for an improvisation. Why, for example, might a sailor in a nightclub be dancing with a child's doll? Why might an old woman selling pencils on the street be reading a report of the New York Stock Exchange? Remember that the purpose of these imaginary circumstances is to provide a reason for action. Action means specific physical objectives that show behavior you can believe of the person observed. Work out the details carefully.

Rehearse the scene until each part seems right and logical. *Warning:* Do not attempt to substitute a "made-up" situation for the original observation. Without the observed fact, you have no way of knowing whether your imaginary circumstances are true. *Imagination must have a basis in reality.*

Observing Animals and Objects

The study of plants, animals, and inanimate objects as a means of understanding a character is a third way an actor may use the technique of observation. The process involves **abstraction,** a commonly misunderstood principle. *To* abstract means, literally, "to separate, to take away." The actor applies the principle of abstraction by observing an object for the purpose of taking away from it ("seizing and noting") qualities that will be useful in developing a character.

The qualities of elegance, glitter, and aloofness abstracted from the observation of a crystal chandelier might be important elements in coming to understand some of the characters in Restoration drama. Observing, then abstracting, the comfortableness, the homeliness, and the unpretentiousness of an old leather chair might provide insight into a character of a completely different kind. The qualities to be abstracted from a gnarled and weather-beaten tree could be an observed fact for developing yet another type of person.

Close observation of an eggplant might help in preparing to play Juliet's Nurse. Looking at this vegetable, one is impressed by its bulky form, its grossness, and its unvaried purple surface—a growth that has matured in size without acquiring character. On feeling it, one becomes aware of its bland smoothness, and, on cutting it open, one finds the inside to be a yellow-white mass—pliant and spongy—with no core at all.

If an eggplant could walk, it would waddle from side to side; it would have difficulty carrying its bulk; it would perspire, fan itself, and gasp for breath. Its bright purple color, symbolic of royalty and dignity, seems pretentious when everything else belies those qualities (the Nurse putting on airs before Romeo and his friends). Its smoothness suggests a good nature stemming from a lack of principles and its "corelessness" gives insight into the Nurse's lack of moral fiber, both amply suggested by her lines and actions.

People are often compared to animals. We say that a certain young girl is kittenish, that a certain person is as clumsy as a bear, that one man is foxy, another is wolfish, and that still another is a snake in the grass. These comparisons are examples of abstracting an animal's essential qualities and applying them to aspects of human behavior. An actor will find that creating such abstractions from animals is another worthwhile exercise in observation that can provide outstanding raw material for characterizations.

In the motion picture of *The Women,* adapted from the popular play by Clare Boothe, each character was introduced as a different kind of animal. The gossiping, sharp-tongued Sylvia Fowler was a cat. The spreading, complacent Edith Potter was a cow. The vicious, husband-snatching Crystal Allen was presented as a panther.

A more famous example of observing the qualities of animals and applying them to dramatic characters is found in Ben Jonson's *Volpone,* a vicious satire on

Figure 6.2 Laurie Vlasich Bulaoro in *Berlin to Broadway with Kurt Weill,* produced by Stage West in Ft. Worth, TX. Directed by Jerry Russell. In addition to physical form, note this actor's predator-like attitude.

greed. Each character is appropriately named after some beast of prey. Volpone, or the Fox, is a rich merchant whose ruling passion is greed. Like his namesake, he is also sly and has hit on a scheme of pretending he is dying so his equally rapacious friends will court his favor with extravagant gifts in the hope of being made his heirs. His friends include Corvino, or Little Crow, who offers Volpone his young wife; Corbaccio, or Old Crow, who sniffs at Volpone's body to make sure he is dead; and Voltore, or the Vulture, who is exactly what his name implies. Slyest of all is Mosca, or the Fly, who turns the tables on Volpone by trying to prove him legally dead. Actors performing these roles would certainly want to find true human behavior that could be abstracted imaginatively from observing the behavior of the animal associated with each character.

Returning once again to *Romeo and Juliet,* let's suppose this time you are cast as Juliet's cousin Tybalt. You need look no further than your script for inspiration, for Shakespeare himself has Tybalt compared to an animal three times! Mercutio first refers to him as "more than prince of cats." Later, in challenging him to a duel, Mercutio addresses him as "good king of cats," declaring that he means to take one of Tybalt's nine lives. And after Tybalt has mortally wounded him, Mercutio says he is a "dog, a rat, a mouse, a cat, to scratch a man to death." With this suggestion in the lines, it would be a poor actor who did not search for and exploit the catlike qualities that have motivated Mercutio's comparison.

How might you develop this approach to playing Tybalt? First of all, what is a cat like? The word *kitten* may connote playfulness and cuteness, but isn't the word *cat* generally associated with spitefulness, slyness, and malice? A quick trip to the dictionary will confirm this distinction: "The cat family (Felidae) includes besides the domestic cat the lion, tiger, leopard, puma, etc." When Mercutio calls Tybalt "king of cats," the context clearly shows he is not thinking of a household pet. More likely he is seeing a sleek black panther. Turning back to the script, an imaginative actor can now find several additional instances in which abstractions of the behavior of this species of cat might inform Tybalt's actions:

1. From his first entrance, when he *creeps up behind* Benvolio with the line, "Turn thee, Benvolio, look upon thy death," Tybalt is a *threatening, menacing figure.* Later, at the Capulet ball, he is *lurking* among the other guests threatening harm to Romeo. Still later, it is his determination to inflict harm that causes his own death and Romeo's consequent banishment.

2. Mercutio's description of Tybalt's manner of dueling indicates that he is an *expert* but *unsportsmanlike fighter.* He fights *viciously* and *inhumanly* by the "book of arithmetic," unwilling to give his opponent any advantage. He is willing to kill Mercutio "under Romeo's arm" as Romeo attempts to come between them.

3. His expertness in dueling would require *grace of movement* and *unusual muscular coordination.*

4. Mercutio's description indicates that Tybalt is an *extremely elegant creature* possessing a kind of haughtiness that does not sit comfortably among the others' old customs and manners.

An actor assigned to play Tybalt might well spend some of his time studying pictures or visiting a zoo to observe the characteristics and behavior of a panther. He could watch the panther's lurking stealth, its leanness, its elegant sleekness, its easy graceful movement, its latent strength and energy, and its inhuman green-yellow eyes. Through his imagination, he could visualize a person possessing these same qualities. That person, with these determinate internal and external characteristics, might be the starting point for creating a believable Tybalt.

An actress preparing for the role of Maggie in *Cat on a Hot Tin Roof,* by Tennessee Williams, might do well to study not the panther but the alley cat. Since Maggie is the "cat" of the title, once again the script provides the starting place for this exploration. Maggie struggles to wrench life out of her alcoholic husband with the cunning, persistence, and sensuality of a feline. She has scratched and clawed her way out of poverty, and she is determined to hang on to her marriage, with the tenacity of an alley cat struggling to stay alive in the streets. Hear Maggie purr when it becomes necessary. Her attempts to seduce her husband Brick and flatter Big Daddy are catlike. When Maggie walks, imagine her whole body in motion with feline grace. When she is spiteful, see her claws emerge from their sheath. The actress working on the part will note the human qualities in cats as well as the feline qualities in humans.

Equus, by Peter Shaffer, provides a more subtle example. This play deals with the psychiatric case history of Alan Strang, a seventeen-year-old who has blinded six horses with a metal spike. In the course of the play, the trauma peels away as he relives the experience. Because Alan has a love–hate relationship with horses, the actor might want to observe and catalog the characteristic behavior of these animals as he prepares to play the role. Some potentially usable abstractions might be nervousness; skittishness; restlessness (especially true of a young colt); gracefulness of motion; head carried high, moving from side to side to observe the world; wariness of trust; and rollicking playfulness. Experimenting with these qualities could be a useful springboard to the character.

The observation of animals and objects will become an important part of your arsenal of rehearsal techniques. After penetratingly observing an animal, bringing as many of the senses as you can into play, you should attempt to create, in so far as it is humanly possible, the physical and emotional attributes of the animal. If you enter into animal study freely and with an open mind, such stretching of the imagination should then allow you to create a human character who possesses many traits you observed in the animal.

Animal exercises can often put you in touch with feelings and emotions that have heretofore been strange to you. Of course, if animal study is to be useful in developing a specific character in a play, you will need to make certain that the animal traits can be justified by the script. No external characterization tool can substitute for careful study of the given circumstances of the text; therefore, animal improvisations should never be used until after you have selected images and actions for the basic makeup of your character. Once this step has been accomplished, applying the sensations that grow out of the study of pertinent animals and objects can help you discover the unique manner in which your character performs its actions.

EXERCISE Choose an animal or inanimate object for observation. Study it carefully. Remember that you can observe through all of your senses, not just through sight. In addition to how the object or animal looks, consider how it feels, how it smells, how heavy it is, and possibly how it tastes. List all of its characteristic qualities. Plan a short individual scene, either with or without lines, in which you impersonate a character with these qualities. Remember you will not be trying to make yourself believe you are a radish or an old shoe or a Shetland pony. You will have abstracted the essential qualities, and, through your imagination, you will visualize a person with the same characteristics. You will use your imagination to "supply circumstances" that would require the person to act in a true and revealing manner. Carrying out these actions will help you to believe you are a person with the same characteristics as your chosen animal or inanimate object. Suppose, for instance, you have chosen for observation a Scottish terrier puppy. Your list of its essential qualities might include the following: shaggy, cute, playful, friendly, lively, clumsy. He likes both attention and sympathy.

You might decide a child of ten or twelve years would have these qualities. Plan a series of actions that will lead you to believe you are a playful, friendly, and clumsy child. Place your character in various imaginary circumstances, such as:

✦ Receiving a present unexpectedly

✦ Being left alone and told not to go out of the house

✦ Falling from a tree and hurting his leg

Determine your behavior in each of these circumstances by observing the Scottish terrier.

Notes

1. Benoit Constant Coquelin, "Acting and Actors," *Harper's New Monthly Magazine,* May 1887, pp. 891–909.

2. Uta Hagen, *A Challenge for the Actor* (New York: Macmillan Publishing Company, 1991), p. 82.

3. Ibid., p. 170.

4. Lewis Funke and John E. Booth, *Actors Talk about Acting* (New York: Avon Books, 1961), Vol. I, pp. 57–58. Reprinted by permission of Random House.

5. Constantin Stanislavski, Elizabeth Reynolds Hapgood, trans., *An Actor Prepares* (New York: Theatre Arts Books, 1973), p. 167.

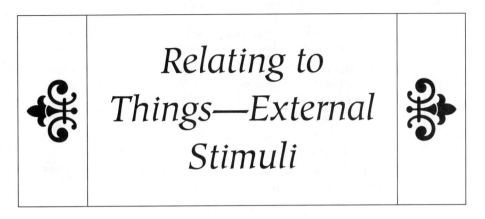

CHAPTER 7

Relating to Things—External Stimuli

arrying out a sequence of logical and truthful actions while pursuing an objective within a set of given circumstances is the foundation of effective acting. The actor's ultimate purpose, however, is not to perform the action itself but to reveal its significance. The final interest of the audience is not in the events of the play—important as they are—but in the underlying meaning of the characters' actions.

Think of the opening scene of Shakespeare's great tragedy, *King Lear.* When the aging monarch literally gives away his kingdom, his action must be clear to the audience, but the real import lies in the effect of his actions on him and the people surrounding him. Or consider *Faust,* Goethe's most famous drama, in which Faust, an old scholar, has sold his soul to the devil in return for a year of restored youth. One of the youthful pleasures he seeks is the seduction of the innocent Marguerite. To help achieve this aim, he leaves a casket of jewels where Marguerite is certain to find them. She does so in the company of Martha, her older and more experienced neighbor. Here is the material for a stunning scene, but it will be meaningful to the audience only if they understand the effect of the action on Marguerite and her neighbor.

The actor uses both external and internal sources as a basis for suffusing action with meaning. In this chapter, we learn about external sources and the technique of *relating to objects and to other actors.* Stanislavski wrote:

You must have something which will interest you in the object of your attention, and serve to set in motion your whole creative apparatus. . . . Imagined circumstances can transform the object itself and heighten the reaction of your emotions to it. . . . You must learn to transfigure an object from something which is coldly reasoned or intellectual in quality into something which is warmly *felt*.[1]

Return for a moment to the scene from *Faust*. It offers the actresses playing Marguerite and Martha a wonderful opportunity to engage in an intellectual and sensory observation of the jewels. They must experience the color, shape, and brilliance, the feel of them dripping through their hands, and the way they look hung about their necks and from their ears. Since the "prop" jewels will not be real, the actresses can—through remembered observation or *sense memory*—give the quality, the beauty and fire of the precious stones, to the counterfeit jewels.

They must not stop there, however. The actresses must also "transfigure" the jewels into something that is "warmly felt," to make emotional connections between themselves, their characters, and the objects. They (especially Martha) are overcome with the beauty of the stones. They desire them; they covet them. The jewels become a burning temptation, a successful lure in Faust's seduction. In the hands of professional actresses, this important object performs a key dramatic function in the total action of the scene. In both rehearsal and performance, the actresses will use their relationship with these objects to trigger their imaginations and to induce believable feelings.

The same object, of course, can evoke a variety of responses, depending on the character and the circumstances. Consider the relationship of a casket of jewels to a hungry beggar. What is the relationship of this object to a wealthy dowager contemplating a purchase, a customs inspector, or a jewel thief?

Good playwrights and directors are skillful and imaginative in supplying on stage objects that will help the actor find the truth of a scene. Such objects achieve their fullest meaning when, like the jewels in *Faust*, they are both logical and dramatically symbolic. Let us return to the scene in which King Lear carves up his realm for another example. Lear's throne, his crown, and the sword of state carried before him all symbolize the kingdom, which is his source of power and which he is now about to give away. The map depicting the newly divided kingdom visually represents the freedom from the cares of state Lear seeks in his old age; it is also a lure that entices his daughters to flatter his vanity by making boundless declarations of love before the assembled court. Shattered by Cordelia's refusal, Lear rashly changes his plan and violently tears the map. The actor who can personalize Lear's relation to these objects—transfigure them into something that is "warmly felt"—will find them to be a dependable source to stimulate believable actions, which, of course, leads to true emotions.

Relationships with characters are as important to the actor as relationships with on-stage objects. The first scene from *King Lear* requires the actor playing the title role to respond differently to each of the three daughters. Moreover, Lear's relation to Albany differs from his relation to Cornwall; his treatment of Burgundy differs from his treatment of the King of France. Each of these characters (and several others, as it is a large and complex scene) is at some time the object of the king's attention, and the actor playing Lear must make a specific and personal connection with them. He should use his experience and imagination to discover the king's feelings toward each of these people. He should also carefully observe the behavior of the others on stage and use their deportment to engender spontaneous responses (i.e., transactions).

Actors must also learn to relate to their characters' clothing and to the imaginary environment. The characters' clothing must be a part of their very existence. Actors must not treat their clothes as mere costumes that were recently hanging in the dressing room but rather as if the characters personally selected them. The actors' work with their characters' clothing will, in fact, communicate directly how the characters feel about themselves and their surroundings. In the same manner, actors must find ways to relate to various aspects of their environment. Like on-stage objects, the environment must be logical and symbolic and stimulate action. However, until actors define their relationship to their surroundings, it will simply be scenery with no significant meaning. A door, for example, is merely a decoration until the actor uses it. Only then will it be given definition in relationship to the character, the play, and the particular scene. All the techniques by which actors can instill an object with rich meanings can apply equally to their clothing and environment.

Many of the greatest moments in drama supply the actor with an opportunity to use the technique of relating to objects. From Shakespeare alone, think of Othello and the candle just before he murders Desdemona: "Put out the light, and then put out the light"; Hamlet and the skull, as he talks about the transitory nature of life: "Alas! poor Yorick. I knew him, Horatio . . ."; Lady Macbeth and her hands, which, in her deranged mind, she believes are covered with the blood of the murdered Duncan: "Out, damned spot! Out, I say!"; and Shylock and the knife he is sharpening on the sole of his shoe to cut out a pound of Antonio's flesh. Shylock's action motivates Bassanio's "Why dost thou whet thy knife so earnestly?"—a gentle reminder from Shakespeare that the actor playing Shylock should be concentrating on his physical action.

EXERCISE   For the beginning exercise in relating to objects, you will need a solid, nondescript article about eighteen inches long and about nine inches in breadth and thickness. A rolled-up coat secured with a string, a small pillow, or a block of wood will do nicely. Working in pairs or in groups and without saying what it is, one actor should decide on an identity for the nondescript article and establish a relation to it. Other actors should observe carefully so that, when the object is passed to them, they may establish the same identity and relation. They then should *change* the identity and relation and pass the object onto the next person, who will repeat this pattern before passing it to the next person.

At this time, we need to discuss briefly the actor's responsibility to the audience, a matter that we will take up in more detail later. Put simply, you must clearly communicate to the audience everything you do and why you are doing it.

To begin with, you can make something clear to the audience only if you have made it clear to yourself. Far too many student actors attempt an assignment with vague, general answers to the important "W" questions. As we said in Chapter 1, you must also project the character with an appropriate dimension, energy, and clarity that can communicate the meaning to an audience of a certain size occupying a certain space. If your actions cannot be seen or heard, you will lose your audience's attention. Many young actors get so involved in their actions that they forget to share it with the audience. Inaudible speech and actions are meaningless. To successfully communicate with an audience, even subtle behavior must be performed at a sufficient energy level, which will change with the size of the auditorium. Small actions that may be perfectly clear to an audience in a small experimental theatre may not communicate to an audience in a large proscenium house. Furthermore, student actors who believe that truth is found only in subtlety have a misconception about the nature of human beings. Human behavior is indeed sometimes subtle and understated; however, it is just as apt to be overenthusiastic and raucous. Large actions do not necessarily translate as indications. Honest human behavior is sometimes enormous. As long as you behave truthfully in imaginary circumstances, no matter how large your decisions, the audience will believe your actions.

Incidentally, everything the actor does should also be interesting. Attempting to accomplish this requisite, however, can lead the actor into the trap of producing out of place and illogical comedy, novelty, or sensationalism for its own sake rather than for the sake of illuminating the given circumstances. Shakespeare, in Hamlet's advice to the Players, wrote, ". . . o'erstep not the modesty of nature; for anything so overdone is from the purpose of playing. . . ." He later warned, ". . . for there be of them that will themselves laugh, to set on some quantity of barren spectators to laugh too, though in the meantime some necessary question of the play be then to be considered." The actor must recognize that human behavior is inherently interesting and is the theatre's heart and soul. Although the world of the play may be extraordinary, even absurd, audiences expect to see believable characters dealing with "real" problems. The way to generate interest in your exercises, as well as when performing a role, is to define the world, make the circumstances specific, and provide conflict by having an explicit objective that can be realized only by overcoming a definite obstacle. If you plan carefully and concentrate on each step necessary to carry out your plans, you have a solid foundation for a performance that will interest an audience.

EXERCISE   Working alone, score and present a logical sequence of actions that centers on one or more objects. You must supply given circumstances that will provide you with a specific relationship to the object(s). Make sure you have a specific objective and that you work against an obstacle. You should also consider the essential qualities of the object(s) and the human and environmental conditions discussed in Chapter 6. You may base your scenes around the suggested actions listed below or create your own. You are:

1. unwrapping a present.
2. preparing to bury a pet.
3. sharpening a knife.
4. counting a large sum of money.
5. looking at an album of family photographs.
6. taking medicine or drugs.
7. setting the table.
8. attempting to read a poorly drawn map.
9. repairing a valuable vase.
10. trying on clothing.
11. packing a box or suitcase.
12. folding a flag.

EXERCISE   Working alone or with one or more partners, use the given circumstances in one of the scenarios listed below as a basis for a scene. In this exercise, your primary task is to discover a specific relationship to the object or objects and to communicate that relationship by a score of psychophysical actions.

1. In *Appearances,* by Tina Howe, Ivy, a naïve young shopper, enters a messy dressing room with no stool to try on her selection of dresses. After her rather clumsy and unsuccessful attempts with a number of outfits, she decides to return to the first dress in the pile; she panics, however, when she can't immediately find it. Once the dress is located and back on her body, she looks in the mirror and strikes deliberately ugly poses.

2. In *Arms and the Man,* by George Bernard Shaw, the romantic Raina is in love with a soldier who is reported to have performed great deeds of heroism for

his country. Alone at night and thinking of "her hero," she takes up his portrait, caresses it, and returns it reverently to its place.

3. In *Buried Child,* by Sam Shepard, Vince realizes that his grandfather, Dodge, has quietly died. He covers his body with a blanket, smells some roses he is carrying, and then places the roses on his grandfather's chest.

4. In *Butterflies Are Free,* by Leonard Gershe, Don Baker is a good-looking young man who has just moved into an apartment in Greenwich Village. Although Don has been blind from birth, he accepts his blindness as more of an inconvenience than a handicap, and he is fiercely protective of his ability to care for himself. He tells Jill, his next-door neighbor, that part of the reason he does not bump into things around the apartment is because he has "memorized" his room. To prove it, he walks around the room calling off each item as he touches or points to it.

5. In *84 Charing Cross Road,* by Helene Hanff and adapted for the stage by James Roose-Evans, Helene is spring-cleaning her books. She loves them— they are her dearest friends. She pauses to touch a special favorite, sorts and rearranges volumes, and occasionally decides to throw one out, dropping it in a box. When she is through, she dumps the box of books in the hallway leading to her apartment.

6. In *Eleven–Zulu,* by Sean Clark, Jonsson is one of a group of six soldiers guarding a broken-down armored carrier in Vietnam. After being on a late-night watch for several hours, he looks through their dwindling case of C rations for something with fruit cocktail.

7. In Tennessee Williams' *The Glass Menagerie,* the gentleman caller, Jim O'Connor, is in the process of teaching Laura to dance when he bumps into a shelf containing her precious glass figurines. Her most special ornament, a unicorn, topples and breaks its horn. Laura cradles the figurine, as Jim apologizes. A tender moment ensues leading to a gentle kiss. Laura is faint with emotion when Jim informs her of his impending marriage and that he must leave. Laura hands Jim the broken unicorn as a parting gift.

8. In *Isn't It Romantic,* by Wendy Wasserstein, Janie rashly tells her new male friend Marty that she knows how to cook a chicken. He brings one for their dinner. While Marty is out of the room, she unwraps the chicken, holds it up by its wings, and examines it carefully without the slightest idea of what to do next. But, as she contemplates a relationship with Marty, she slowly cradles the chicken like a baby.

9. In *Key Exchange,* by Kevin Wade, Philip and Lisa have a tenuous romantic involvement. Lisa, who wishes to take it to the "next step," proposes they exchange keys to each other's apartment. Philip, who wishes to keep their

relationship casual, debates the importance and subsequent downside of her proposed key exchange.

10. In *Lost in Yonkers,* by Neil Simon, Louie, a henchman for the mob in World War II, demands that his two nephews, Jay and Arty, pick up the mysterious bag he has been carrying. Prior to this moment, they had been overly curious as to its contents. When Jay, the older of the two boys, refuses, Louie forces Arty to lift the bag. Louie drills the young boy as to its weight and what he believes to be the contents. After several tense moments, Jay intervenes and orders his uncle to stop the assault.

11. In *Mother Courage,* by Bertolt Brecht, Katrin is a young mute who follows the army with her mother. Her mother, however, has shielded her from any knowledge of men. Having observed the behavior of Yvette, her mother's friend who is also a prostitute, Katrin steals Yvette's plumed hat and red boots and practices walking about seductively. When an alarm sounds for an approaching enemy attack, she hides the articles of finery, contemplating further use of them.

12. In *No Place to Be Somebody,* by Charles Gordone, Johnny Williams has been given a copy of Sweets Crane's will. Sweets is an old man who befriended Johnny when he was a boy but with whom Johnny no longer wants to have association. Johnny does not read well and has difficulty figuring out that Sweets intends to leave him a good deal of property. In defiance, he throws the will on the floor.

13. In *On the Verge,* by Eric Overmyer, two women and a man are exploring some unnamed country at some undetermined time. One of them (Fanny) happens on an old-fashioned eggbeater, slightly rusty but in working order. She has no idea what it is.

14. In *Picasso at the Lapin Agile,* by Steve Martin, Pablo Picasso and Albert Einstein draw on bar napkins to compare their respective works. They then bicker over the meaning and significance of their hypotheses and theories and their effect on people.

15. In *Raised in Captivity,* by Nicky Silver, Hillary, a psychologist who recently blinded herself with a screwdriver, has asked Kip, a dentist turned painter who refuses to use any color except white, if she may feel his paintings. After reluctantly agreeing to grant her wishes, he is pleasantly surprised by her intuitive interpretations.

16. In *True West,* by Sam Shepard, two brothers clash while housesitting for their mother. The slobbish petty thief, Lee, tries to write a screenplay on his brother's typewriter. He pecks with one finger, makes many errors, tries to erase, rubs holes in the paper, gets the ribbon tangled up, and yanks it out of the machine in frustration.

Relating to Other Actors

When actors engage in transactions with other actors by trying to influence their behavior, they can hardly fail to establish a relationship. Both consciously and unconsciously, they will make logical physical and psychological adjustments to the other person, and such adjustments depend on an awareness of the other's presence and personality. Often the techniques for relating to objects are equally useful in accomplishing objectives that require you to relate to another actor. The actor uses these techniques to "transfigure" the other actor into something that is "warmly felt." The nature of the transfiguration depends, of course, on the given circumstances.

We are frequently faced, both in life and on the stage, with the problem of evoking the same responses from two or more people toward whom we feel quite differently or with whom we have dissimilar relationships. Again, the opening scene of *King Lear* provides a good example. Lear wants to influence his three daughters to shower him with love, but his relationship with each of them is not the same. He knows that Goneril is shrewd, cold, ambitious, and willing to do whatever is necessary to gain a share of the kingdom. Regan is a follower who wants what Goneril has and will do what Goneril does. Cordelia, on the other hand, is straightforward and honest; he expects her protestation of love to be genuine. Lear's vanity requires a public declaration of love from each of the three, but he uses a different strategy in each case to get it. Toward Goneril he could establish a kind of bargaining relationship: tell me you love me, and I'll give you a share of my kingdom. Since Regan's response is so predictable, he might approach her with indifference, perhaps even mingled with contempt. To bring about the proper impact of the scene, he will need to seek honest love from Cordelia, for he is depending on her for comfort in the loneliness of his advancing age.

These relationships are merely suggestions. The actor playing Lear establishes those that will work for him by (1) probing his imagination for an answer to the question: "If I were King Lear, what would I do in these circumstances to get Goneril, Regan, and Cordelia to behave as I want them to?" and (2) responding honestly to the immediate attempts of the actresses playing the daughters to influence his behavior. We pointed out earlier that actors' spontaneous responses to each other are the principal sources of vitality in any performance.

Opening the mind and body to these responses, sometimes called *playing off* or *working off* your partner(s), is a technique that aspiring actors should thoroughly explore and practice. Once mastered, this technique allows you to behave toward the other actors as if you believe they are the characters they play and simultaneously to make full use of your sensory and intellectual responses to each as a person. If, for example, the actor playing Lear tries to relate to nothing but a preconceived image of his daughters rather than "working off" his actual partners, he will quite simply be "alone" on stage with other actors. Acting requires

Figure 7.1 Steven Breese as Petruchio and Theda Reale as Katherina in Shakespeare in the Park's production of *The Taming of the Shrew* in Ft. Worth, TX. Directed by Kenn Stilson; costume design by Rhonda Weller-Stilson; scenic design by Patrick Atkinson. Communion between actors goes beyond the stage and engages the audience.

ensemble, and ensemble requires equal participation of everyone on stage. Thus comes the phrase, "There are no small roles, only small actors." Just as a lifeline connects mountain climbers to one another as they ascend great heights, every actor on stage is connected to their partners by a lifeline. If one person "falls," their partners must "save" them. Attempting to perform alone on stage with other people deprives the actor of the stimulation that comes from genuine relationships with fellow performers. The actor playing Lear must respond as fully as he can to the palpable qualities of the others with whom he is playing. If he were to play Lear again with different actresses performing the daughters, his performance would take on a new set of nuances, yet each performance would have equal truth and vitality.

EXERCISE   Perhaps the most ignored element of Stanislavski's system is the concept of **communion,** the spiritual intercourse between two actors on stage. Communion is a state of absolute connection with self, the other actors, and the audience. Sanford Meisner, one of the greatest acting teachers of the twentieth century, believed this loss of connection on stage is the biggest problem facing actors. Without this spiritual bond, the scene loses its power and has no chance to connect with the audience. According to Meisner, two actors could theoretically create three-dimensional characters, play the proper actions, discover true emotions, and still fail in the performance. The energy and tension in a scene come as a result of the interaction between characters. Drawing upon Stanislavski's idea of communion and Meisner's famed beginning acting classes at the Neighborhood Playhouse, perform the following sequence of exercises.

1. With the entire class, *really* look at one another. Don't pretend to look, but really observe each other. Look at one person's hair, another person's shoes, and yet another person's unsightly blemish. What do you notice? Say what you notice aloud to yourself. Don't worry about "being nice," as there is no place for "nice" on stage. Say what you really notice about the observable physical attributes of the people around you.

2. Now stand opposite one of your classmates. Decide who is Partner A and who is Partner B. A turns toward B and says aloud her first physical observation about B. For example, "Your hair is curly." B listens carefully and repeats back what he has heard. Then A repeats back what she has heard; B repeats back what he has heard, and so on. Continue this word repetition exercise until the instructor or observer tells you to stop. Repeat back exactly what you hear, not what you think you are supposed to have heard. Don't anticipate. Don't assume your partner will give you what you expect. For example, if your partner omits a word or accidentally inverts the sen-

tence, do not correct that response. Remember, you should repeat back exactly what you hear. On the other hand, there should be no pauses between phrases. There should be no *thinking* about your response. Also, do not try to be interesting, and do not purposefully do anything with the words. Simply listen and repeat. This exercise is extremely important, for it forces you to listen to one another. It also places your focus outside yourself and onto the other person. Therefore, self-consciousness, a common disease among actors, has little time to develop.

3. Now the exercise should evolve into what Meisner called "a truthful point of view." Partner A might say, "You have green eyes." Partner B, who has hazel eyes, may say without pause, "I do not have green eyes." or "I have hazel eyes." A says, "You have green eyes," because from her point of view B's eyes are green. B says, "I do not have green eyes," and so on. Let each partner start this exercise five times leading into repetition. Beware of pausing out of the human need to "be right." Simply repeat what you hear but from a truthful point of view and with what you know to be true.

4. Repeat Exercise 3. This time, however, the repetition should evolve into language. For example:

   A says, "Your hands are in your lap."

   B repeats, "My hands are in my lap."

   A says, "Your hands are in your lap."

   B repeats, "My hands are in my lap."

   A says, "Your hands are in your lap."

   B moves his hand to scratch his nose. Now he cannot truthfully say, "My hands are in my lap." Instead it changes to "I scratched my nose."

   A then repeats, "You scratched your nose," and so on.

   With this change in the repetition comes a remarkable development. Emotion has made an appearance. Sometime during this exercise, laughter may rise. Tears, rage, and scorn may appear. This simple exercise unleashes all kinds of unexpected energy. Keep in mind, however, that neither actor should take the lead by trying to push the dialogue a particular direction. The repetition should change only when it must.

5. Extend Exercise 4 by beginning with a personal question, and then begin the repetition with that question. Let your instincts dictate when you must change the repetition. This change must come only from a change in the behavior of your partner. Do not attempt to be outrageous. Do not try to impress your partner. Again, simply listen and react from a truthful point of view.[2]

Notes

1. Constantin Stanislavski, *An Actor's Handbook,* ed. Elizabeth Reynolds Hapgood (New York: Theatre Arts Books, 1963), p. 25.

2. Sanford Meisner and Dennis Longwell, *On Acting* (New York: Vintage, 1987), pp. 16–77.

CHAPTER 8

Relating to Things—Internal Stimuli

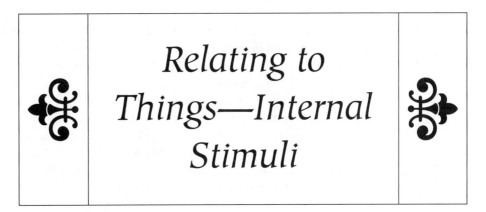

Everything on stage is a lie. The properties, the makeup, the costumes, the scenic environment, as well as the actor's emotions are not real. In life, we do not think about emotions such as love, hate, or anger as they are happening. Rather, these emotions occur naturally and subconsciously as a result of actual external stimuli. We think about the resulting emotions only as we later reflect on a particular event or circumstance. On stage, however, every action, every emotion must be controlled and conscious. Although characters may be insane, obsessive, uncontrollably violent, or drugged, actors must always remain in command of their emotional and physical being. That is one of the actor's paradoxes. Whereas emotions in life occur without thought, stage emotions result from deliberate choices and actions. Stanislavski wrote, "Through conscious means we reach the subconscious."[1]

Actors' inner resources consist of everything they have experienced. Every personal event, every movie, every book, every photograph, every time they explore the Internet, it goes into their memory bank and becomes an important resource from which to draw on stage. Stanislavski called his approach to the use of internal stimuli **affective memory,** which he later divided into **sense memory** and **emotional memory.** This technique was designed to produce controlled emotional reactions within actors that they could use to color their characters.

True emotions in life—what Stanislavski referred to as "primary emotions"—are extremely difficult to control. Our interpretation of emotions is also imprecise and vague, for we are never simply one emotion. At any given time, we may be happy, anxious, terrified, nauseous, and determined. But what is happy? What is anxious? Everyone interprets these emotions differently, and these isolated feelings meld together and change with the circumstances. They are almost impossible to define precisely and yet audiences ultimately judge the quality of the actors' performance by their ability to truthfully convey these emotions.

Stanislavski referred to stage emotions as "repeated emotions," and they differ greatly from primary emotions. If you love someone on stage, it is true love. A character's hatred, jealousy, and greed are as true to the actor as the eternal verities of life, but repeated emotions have a different quality than primary emotions. Stanislavski referred to these repeated emotions as a "poetic reflection" of the actor's primary emotions. Sonia Moore wrote, "No actor could survive long if he had to go through a true tragic shock every time he performs. And if an actor is honest, he will admit that an authentic emotion of suffering while performing gave him true joy."[2]

Repeated emotions do not arise from actual causes; they occur because actors have experienced **analogous emotions** in their own lives. We each have a lifetime of emotional experiences, and we all have the capacity to do anything within our physical realm. We have all experienced love, hate, jealousy, and greed, just as we have all felt incompetent, boastful, shy, and superior. We have faced every conceivable human emotion many times and under vastly different circumstances. According to scientific research, the nerves that repeatedly participate in the experience of each emotion become highly sensitive and responsive to that emotion. Therefore, through exercises, rehearsals, and performances, actors develop a conditioned reflex in which their emotions are stirred through the stage stimulus.

Unlike primary emotions, repeated emotions do not completely absorb us. When tragedy strikes in real life, we are completely immersed at that moment. We do not have the capacity to objectively consider our feelings. Years later, however, as we reflect upon the events and as other life encounters have penetrated our memories, we have the ability to objectify our experience. This is the actor's emotional state while living through the character's emotions for the "first" time. Actors live in the present—Stanislavski's state of "I am"—but they never completely forget they are in front of an audience. Their repeated emotions are absolutely sincere and truthful, but they are not real. There is a distance between these emotions and the actor. You must find your own personal emotions that are analogous to those of the character you are creating, remember your behavior, and use it for the character. "Then," according to Moore, "you will merge with the character, and it will be difficult to know what is yours and what is the character's, because you will also be revealing yourself."[3]

Finding appropriate analogous emotions are not an end in themselves, for they lead you to a more complete understanding of the character's desires, morals, fears, and distinct points of view regarding any person or issue in their world. Analogous emotions are not complete until they are transferred to your character and made synonymous with their circumstances. Analogous emotions help you believe in your given circumstances. They allow you to have faith in your relationships, and they help you to discover your character's behavior by justifying your every action.

Relating to Past Experiences

Fortunately, most of the time our memory serves us spontaneously, on stage as in life. Facts, figures, faces, stories, images we have known in the past—even sensory and emotional experiences—come back automatically as we need them. If actors perform logical actions; believe in the given circumstances; work toward objectives and against obstacles; and establish specific relationships with on-stage objects, clothing, environment, and other actors, their past experiences will likely be subconsciously serving them without thought. Their actions and relationships, coming directly from the imaginary circumstances of the play and from connection with the other actors, should automatically tap their inner resources and evoke the proper feeling. If, on occasion, the techniques of physical action, objectives, and relationships do not elicit the desired responses, actors may need to bring their past experience directly to bear on the situation.

Although theatre history provides much evidence that actors to some degree have always made conscious use of their experiences as a specific technique, Stanislavski first extensively explored this practice in the early twentieth century. However, his early experiments in emotional memory brought actors to a state of panic that actually affected their nervous systems. Thus, he concluded that the use of emotions as a principle means to discover truth on stage was very dangerous. When Stanislavski later discovered the Method of Physical Actions and made *it* the focal point of his system, he also revolutionized the use of emotional memory. He realized that emotional recall was an indirect process. As a reliable and safe approach to tap our emotional resources, we should focus, Stanislavski decided, on recalling the sensory experiences of the situation, and, most of all, we should remember our actions. With these admonitions in mind, we shall discuss emotional memory under five steps:

1. The original experience
2. Retaining the experience
3. Selecting an experience that relates to the problem
4. Recalling the sensory and physical details
5. Using the experience within the given circumstances

Figure 8.1 Joe Alberti as Jim and Holly Hickman as Valerie in Connor McPherson's *The Weir* at Stage West in Ft. Worth, TX. Directed by Jerry Russell. Actors must tap their own inner resources to fully connect with their character's inner images and feelings.

You ordinarily go through these steps without thinking about them, but a separate examination of each will help you when you need to make conscious use of the process.

The Original Experience "Time is an excellent filter for our remembered feelings," wrote Stanislavski. "Besides, it is a great artist. It not only purifies, it also transmutes even painfully realistic memories into poetry."[4] It is important for you to understand that the original experience must have occurred some time ago; some acting theorists insist that emotional memories must have occurred at least three years before their use on stage. Most of us do not have the ability to view recent events objectively. If, for example, you recently experienced the death of a parent, the rejection of a lover, or a false accusation by a close friend, you most likely will not have come to grips with your feelings as you think on these experiences. If you are overcome with emotions as you recall a particular memory, it is virtually impossible to use on stage. Over time, the memories of important events remain just as clear, but the distance allows you to view them with necessary objectivity. Childhood incidents, because they frequently remain in the mind with peculiar vividness, are often especially valuable. Regardless, any experience you use must be one you have felt deeply but have accepted emotionally.

Retaining the Experience Retaining the experience is partly a matter of natural memory and partly a matter of conscious effort. Most people are genuinely aware of what is going on around them and are likely to remember what has happened in the past. Any technique, however, that will aid the actor in retaining the details of an experience vividly in the mind is worth developing.

Here is what we mean. A story has it that the great French actor François Joseph Talma (1763–1826), a favorite of Napoleon and later of Louis XVIII, on hearing the news of his father's death, was shocked to the point of uttering a piercing cry. He immediately noted the nature of his grief, while commenting that the memory of it might be of use to him on stage. Such behavior might seem cold blooded, but there is no reason to doubt that Talma's sorrow was sincere. Good actors accumulate "inner resources" that may serve them once they can recall the experience objectively.

Selecting the Experience In deciding what experiences to recall, actors search their past for happenings most nearly parallel to those of their characters. They may be identical, or they may be far removed. John (Jack) Barrymore described how recall of a past experience helped him play the title role in *Peter Ibbetson,* a dramatization of George duMaurier's novel:

> An actor's performance, at best, is the way he happens to feel about a certain character. . . .

I'm a bit of Peter Ibbetson and a bit of Jack Barrymore. At least, I never utterly forget Jack Barrymore—or things he's thought or done—or had done to him.

I leave my dressing room to make Peter's first entrance. I am Jack Barrymore—Jack Barrymore smoking a cigarette. But before I make the entrance I have thrown away the cigarette and become more Ibbetson than Barrymore. By the time I am visible to the audience I am Ibbetson, quite.

That is, you see—I hope to make this clear—on my way to the entrance I have passed imaginary flunkies and given up my hat and coat. Peter would have had a hat and coat—naturally; and would have given them up. And he's a timid fellow. He gives up his imaginary hat and coat to these flunkies just as I, Jack Barrymore—and very timid then—once gave up my hat and coat to flunkies at a great ball given by Mrs. Astor.

Of course I don't always make Peter's entrance with the memory of a bashful boy at Mrs. Astor's ball. That would harden the memory—make it useless. You couldn't keep on conjuring up the same thing. You have to have different things to get the same emotion. . . .[5]

Barrymore's description is an example of recalling an experience close to the circumstance of the play. The entrance he mentions is Peter Ibbetson's arrival at a great ball given in honor of the Duchess of Towers. Peter, Barrymore's character, is a very timid fellow, painfully embarrassed in the presence of duchesses and liveried footmen.

More often than not actors—unlike Barrymore in the previous example—cannot find in their past so close an approximation to the experience of the character. Obviously, their personal experiences will not parallel those of every character they might be called on to play. Therefore, they must often resort to situations in which their feelings were similar to those of the character, although the circumstances that prompted the feelings may have been entirely different.

In playing Macbeth, for instance, an actor must be able to feel Macbeth's vaulting ambition to be king and his willingness to commit any crime to realize his desires. But the actor certainly will not find any experience in his past that parallels Macbeth's evil course of action. On the other hand, a young actor could probably recall a time when he was cast as a walk-on when he desperately wanted to play the lead. Might it have flashed across his mind that he wished the actor who was selected for the leading role would suffer a calamity that would render it impossible for him to perform it? If so, this experience—the momentary wish to realize an ambition at the expense of someone else—could enable him to come to grips with the terrible desire that drove Macbeth along his path of blood and crime.

Using experiences different from the given circumstances is called **substitution.** In the suicide in *Redemption,* Jacob Ben-Ami said he substituted the shocking experience of a cold shower for the impact of the bullet. His acting of this scene stunned many playgoers who were fortunate enough to see it. An actress might play some of Alma's scenes in *Summer and Smoke* by recalling a painful sunburn that caused her to tense and withdraw when anyone started to touch her.

Another situation that is likely to call for the technique of substitution is the potion scene (Act IV, Scene 3) from *Romeo and Juliet*. Secretly married to Romeo, Juliet has been promised by her parents to the Count of Paris. To get herself out of this entanglement, she is about to take a potion to make her appear dead. She then will be placed in the family tomb, and Romeo will rescue her. Juliet is about to do something the outcome of which is uncertain and fraught with dreadful possibilities, an action that will surely call for emotions starting with fear and mounting almost to hysteria. During the moments before this horrifying act, she imagines all the things that might happen to cause her plan to fail and is distracted. What if the potion does not work at all? What if it is a poison? What if she should wake before Romeo comes and find herself alone in the tomb with the remains of all her buried ancestors? If you are to play Juliet, you must make these fears personal and believable within the given circumstances.

What experience have you had that might enable you to realize Juliet's fear? Have you been in a situation, no matter how dissimilar in its actual circumstances, that induced a feeling akin to Juliet's? Have you ever been alone, preparing to take some step the uncertain consequences of which held possibilities of danger? Unhappiness? Pain? Discomfort? Did you ever prepare to run away from home? Contemplate an elopement? Did you ever prepare to go to the hospital for an operation? To go into the army? To go away to college? To move to a new town where you might be homesick? Have you ever felt trapped while exploring a cave? Perhaps you could recall an instance of fright from your childhood. Almost everybody has experienced something like this:

> When you were ten years old, you spent a weekend with an aunt who lived alone in a large house with no neighbors nearby. On the first evening, before you had become acquainted with your surroundings, your aunt was called to care for a sick friend. You boasted that you were used to staying alone, and because it was impractical to get a "sitter" on short notice, your aunt reluctantly left you to look after yourself for a couple of hours. You settled down in the living room, feeling grown up and independent, and looked happily at a picture book. Gradually you became uneasy. At home, you had activity and noise to calm you, but this place was terribly still. At home, lights all through the house made everything bright and cheerful. Here a lamp with a green shade in the living room and a lamp with a red globe in the hallway cast eerie shadows on unfamiliar surroundings.
>
> Suddenly you were overcome with fear. A noise on the porch started you thinking of thieves and kidnappers. You had no sooner quieted those

fears than a noise upstairs started you thinking of ghosts and haunted houses. It seemed impossible to stay in the house alone, but the outdoors was just as terrifying, and to reach the telephone you had to go down the hall and into the completely dark dining room.

If such an incident is your liveliest experience with fear, it will have to serve, and if you can recall it vividly, it will serve you well in preparing to play Juliet's potion scene.

Recalling the Details Concentrate on remembering the details of the experience rather than on the emotion itself. Begin by using sensory recall. In the last example, you should attempt to remember as much as you can about the room—the lights with their bright spots and especially the dark corners; the reflection of the light on the dark, polished surfaces of the furniture; the windows, shiny black in the darkness, reflecting the quiet gloom. Remember the chair you sat on, the objects on the table beside the chair, and the pictures you looked at. Recall the odors of the room—lilacs and furniture polish. Recall the stillness and the sounds you heard (or thought you heard).

When returning to such a situation as a source for your performance of the potion scene, you will need to develop a shortcut to the heart of the memory. By breaking the memory down into its individual components, you can usually recreate the sensation of the moment by concentrating on the aspect that provides you with the most vivid connection to the situation. You should be able to get to the sensation of fear by concentrating on a specific sound, a particular odor, or the way your body temperature changed, rather than by attempting to evoke the entire experience every time you need to use it. When you can place this odor, this sound, or this body temperature within the given circumstances of the potion scene, your use of emotional memory is complete.

If you are unfamiliar with this technique, you will be surprised (after you give it an honest trial) how many details you will be able to bring back and how much the memory of the way things felt and looked and smelled will help you recapture the essence of the entire experience.

As you are working with the experience during the rehearsal period, try to remember as much detail as possible about what you did in this situation. How did you deal with the cause of your fear—the frightening shadows? The sounds on the porch? The noise upstairs? Perhaps you first pretended you were not afraid. You may have tried to renew your interest in the pictures. Did you brave your way into one of the dark corners for another book? You tried then to reassure yourself by singing as loudly as possible. Gaining a little confidence, you may have gone timidly to the window to investigate the sounds on the porch. What happened physically, when you could not bring yourself to take a good look? Remembering the childhood situation at the level of physical action should give you a range of believable choices for performing Juliet's scene. Adapting them to the given circumstances of the scene you are playing should reinforce your emotional recall.

When you attempt to remember an incident, sit quietly relaxed, free of tensions that might interfere with the flow of memory and feeling. In a sense, this technique is an application to acting of Wordsworth's famous definition of poetry: "Emotion recollected in tranquility."

In each instance described, we have admonished you that the final step of the exercise is to make certain that anything you use from your remembered experience is believable within the given circumstances of the scene and your character. You will take yourself out of the play and away from your objective, unless you can use the feelings you have induced to help you play the actions and speak the lines of the character. *You must especially guard against reducing moments conceived by the imagination of a master dramatist to your own personal experiences, which may be drab and smaller in scope.* One of the strongest tendencies of a student actor is to "play everything too small." Don't forget that drama, for the most part, explores the greatest—and many times the largest—moments in the lives of its characters.

Unless your director schedules time during rehearsals for such exercises, you should carry on this process during your work on the role at home or during your preparation before rehearsal and performance. The mark of a prepared and competent actor is the ready ability to access responses during rehearsals and performances upon the demand of the script and the director.

EXERCISE | Remember a specific moment in your life when you strongly felt some emotion such as anger, hate, love, or fear. Reconstruct in your mind the detailed circumstances that caused you to experience this emotion. Perform an activity related to these circumstances until you can sense the emotion associating itself with the action.

It should be apparent that emotional memory is a technique better suited to the study and rehearsal periods than to performance. Used correctly, it sharpens your inner resources, especially those needed to perform scenes of intense emotion. Many teachers who use this tool in the classroom spend hours with individual students, attempting to stimulate the believable recall of an emotional experience. Others think this technique offers so much potential for self-indulgence and for "playing the emotion" rather than "playing the action" that they have turned away from emotional memory altogether.

If you are serious about becoming an actor, we urge you to spend the time it will take to develop this technique, to make it yours, and to be able to use it on command. If you find that believable, true emotions do not arise from selecting imaginative objectives and concentrating on the external elements of the physical actions you are performing, you will need a technique such as emotional memory to muster a complete mastery of the role. Another approach to emotional memory, which has stood the test of use by many great actors through the years, is the use of images.

Relating to Images

As human beings, we cannot speak without images. As you recall a place, illustrate an event, or describe a person with whom you had an encounter, images flow through your mind. Think of someone you recently met—perhaps someone you bumped into on campus. Describe his clothing. Her physique. His age. Was she from an urban area or a small town? Was he from a wealthy or a poor family? Did her body language suggest an air of confidence or was she shy and introverted? As you think of this person, images naturally appear in your head. You cannot block them out, as they are a natural function of the human brain. These **inner images** are not literal pictures; instead, they emerge as flashes of thought, pieces of the entire visual representation. To test this theory, try to describe an actual person, place, or event without imagery. It is impossible.

Remember, however, everything on stage is a lie. The images are not yours, but rather they belong to incomplete characters living in a fictitious world. Their world may closely resemble our humanity, or it may remind you of a nightmare. Theirs may be a world in which characters speak in verse or break into song when the moment arises. Regardless of the propinquity of their reality to our own, actors have the task of merging their own lives with their characters'. From an unfinished character, you must create a three-dimensional human being with a distinctive personal history. Everything about your creation must be unique—the character's desires, fears, goals, morals, values. Characters must dress, behave, gesture, speak, and carry themselves differently than anyone else. Their entire tempo-rhythm will belong only to them. Their thoughts, their speech, and their images must be as truthful and complete as our own.

The character's images, however, are false. They do not really exist. Additionally, many of the people, places, and events with which your character relates perhaps don't actually appear in the play. Some images are mentioned only in passing by the playwright. Regardless, it is your responsibility to realize the inner imagery of everything your character says and thinks. **Vladimir Nemirovich-Danchenko,** cofounder of the Moscow Art Theatre with Stanislavski in 1898, believed that actors' ability to create and communicate real inner images resulted from the completion of their **second plan.** The existence of characters on stage is only a small part of their whole life; the second plan includes their life before the play and after it. Like Stanislavski, Nemirovich-Danchenko believed the

Andy Hanson

Figure 8.2 Ronnie Claire Edwards and Leslie Ann Brown in William Gibson's *The Miracle Worker* at Theatre Three in Dallas, TX. Actors must see in their minds their characters' thoughts and images.

audience must be made aware of the whole inner life of the characters, their entire destiny, while they are on stage.

When inferior actors speak their lines, they rush over the dialogue. They see nothing in their minds. Their words have no thoughts; their images are dead. In life, our images are spontaneous, and we sometimes take them for granted. On stage, however, everything is conscious, including our imagery. As natural as inner images are in life, to the beginning actor, the process of communicating truthful images is extraordinarily difficult. But you must learn to clearly visualize your images so that your partners on stage see them as well. Only then will your speech and nonverbal gestures commune with the audience.

Sergei Eisenstein, the renowned Russian filmmaker and advocate of the "inner technique," described how an actor might use the practice of images when

preparing to play the part of a respected government employee on the point
of committing suicide, because he has lost a large amount of government money
at cards:

> I believe it would be almost impossible to find an actor of any training
> today who in this scene would start by trying to "act the feeling" of a
> man on the point of suicide. . . . We should compel the appropriate con-
> sciousness and the appropriate feeling to take possession of us. . . .
>
> How is this achieved? We have already said that it cannot be done
> with the "sweating and straining" method. Instead we pursue a path
> that should be used for all such situations.
>
> What we actually do is to compel our imagination to depict for us
> a number of concrete pictures or situations appropriate to our theme.
> The aggregation of the pictures so imagined evokes in us the required
> emotion, the feeling, understanding and actual experience that we are
> seeking. . . .
>
> Suppose that a characteristic feature of our embezzler be fear of pub-
> lic opinion. What will chiefly terrify him will not be so much the pangs
> of conscience, a consciousness of his guilt or the burden of his future
> imprisonment, as it will be "what will people say?"
>
> Our man finding himself in this position, will imagine first of all the
> terrible consequences of his act in these particular terms.
>
> It will be these imagined consequences and their combinations
> which will reduce the man to such a degree of despair that he will seek
> a desperate end.
>
> This is exactly how it takes place in life. Terror resulting from
> awareness of responsibility initiates his feverish pictures of the conse-
> quences. And this host of imagined pictures, reacting on the feelings, in-
> creases his terror, reducing the embezzler to the utmost limit of horror
> and despair.[6]

As Eisenstein pointed out, the mental process that would actually drive a person to suicide and the creative process that would stimulate a character to the
same action on the stage are very similar. A picture of the circumstances that led
him to such foolhardiness would be constantly in his mind, and he would be
driven to despair by the image of his associates casting him off when the crime was
discovered.

The technique of using images, then, begins with pictures of specific circumstances supplied voluntarily by the imagination. These pictures lead in turn to action, to belief, and to feeling. Again, we must recognize that feeling is the end and
not the means, that the actor is concerned with *causes*, not with *effects*. The actor
is like the interior decorator who wants to create a beautiful room. Decorators are

concerned with color and fabric, with line and form because they know they are the means to beauty; if properly controlled, they will produce a beautiful effect. But they also understand that trying merely to create beauty without a specific knowledge of how to use their materials would be futile.

In his "Introduction" to *Stanislavsky on the Art of the Stage,* David Magarshack describes the process of using images as an acting technique.

> The actor needs . . . an uninterrupted series of visual images which have some connection with the given circumstances. He needs, in short, an uninterrupted line not of plain but of illustrated given circumstances. Indeed, at every moment of his presence on the stage . . . the actor must be aware of what is taking place outside him on the stage (i.e., the external given circumstances created by the producer, stage-designer, and the other artists) or of what is taking place inside him, in his own imagination, that is, those visual images which illustrate the given circumstances of the life of his part. Out of all these things there is formed, sometimes outside and sometimes inside him, an uninterrupted and endless series of inner and outer visual images, or a kind of film. While his work goes on, the film is unwinding itself endlessly, reflecting on the screen of his inner vision the illustrated given circumstances of his part, among which he lives on the stage.[7]

Most of the time, however, inner images are incomplete. Instead, our images as we speak explode in our minds and change with the speed of light. Thinking is not based on verbally organized ideas. Whereas the storytelling aspect of writing and speech metaphorically resembles the unraveling of a film, as Magarshack describes in the previous paragraph, inner images are more akin to a contemporary teen watching television or logging onto the Internet. Many teens have short attention spans, preferring to "channel surf" or "surf the 'Net" rather than watching or reading an entire story. Rather than a logical and formalized unfolding internal visual narrative, the thought process, like "surfing," paints a fragmented depiction of your responses to external stimuli.

EXERCISE   **1.** These problems are for developing the habit of seeing definite images from word stimuli. For each of the following concrete words, visualize a detailed and specific picture. See yourself in the picture, and think what you would do if you were there. Let yourself respond. Remember that you can't *make* yourself feel but that you can *let* yourself feel. You can make this exercise more valuable by writing down what you see, or, if you can draw, by making a sketch of it. Describe your picture and your actions to the members of the group, making them see the images as vividly as you do.

party	beach (or forest)	vacation
dress	initiation (or ritual)	restaurant
bedroom	pet	celebrity
sister (or brother)	parent (or teacher)	home
wedding	date	rally
funeral	camp	antique
boyfriend (or girlfriend)	car	snow
concert	fire	team

2. Repeat the same process for the following abstract words. It is important that the actor learn to realize abstract concepts in meaningful concrete images that can stimulate responses.

serenity	disgrace	injustice
speed	desire	bigotry
love	fame	kindness
happiness	grief	glamour
poverty	cruelty	elegance
wealth	indifference	jealousy
mercy	beauty	power
embarrassment	infatuation	worship

EXERCISE   Opportunities abound in plays to use images. Present a solo improvisational scene using one of the problems described below. Illustrate the images through dialogue. The pictures should be definite, not vague and general. The images should also be from life experience, not from the theatre (that is, don't use an image of another actor in a similar circumstance). Reading the play from which the situation is taken will stimulate your imagination, but don't memorize the playwright's lines. Use your own words, and commit yourself to sharing your images with the group.

1. In *The Basic Training of Pavlo Hummel,* by David Rabe, Pavlo is a wide-eyed, totally inept soldier, born and raised in a middle-class environment. He wants to be thought of as a tough street kid, so he conjures up romantic pictures of stealing automobiles and being chased by the police.

2. In *Biloxi Blues,* by Neil Simon, a young soldier named Epstein has filched the notebook in which Eugene has been writing descriptions of all his army comrades. He opens it and reads the section about himself, discovering that Eugene believes Epstein is a homosexual. (*Note:* regardless of the situation in the play, actors may improvise this scene as if they are alone as they read or

that they are reading aloud to the entire barracks. They may also assume the given circumstance that Eugene's notion is either true or false.)

3. In *Boy's Life,* by Howard Korder, Phil tells the story of a girl for whom he would have "sliced his wrists" or "eaten garbage" but who recently dumped him for being "too needy."

4. In *A Delicate Balance,* by Edward Albee, Tobias recalls an instance several years in the past when a pet cat bit him, after which he took it to the veterinarian and had it killed.

5. In *Eleemosynary,* by Lee Blessing, Echo tells the story of her cutthroat, "take no prisoners" journey to victory in the National Spelling Bee Contest in Washington, D.C. Easily handling such words as "perspective," "glunch," and "palinode," she destroyed the confidence of her final competitor before winning with "eleemosynary."

6. In *Lu Ann Hampton Laverty Oberlander,* by Preston Jones, the teenaged Lu Ann sees a picture on the classroom wall of a European castle with a tiny door at its very top. The castle stimulates her to dream about getting out of the small, stifling, Texas town in which she lives.

7. In Charles Busch's *Psycho Beach Party,* a satire of the '60's beach movies, Chicklet reflects on how she got her name, her girlfriends' "kissy kissy" obsession with boys, and her all-consuming passion for surfing. (Charles Busch originated the role of Chicklet, but it may also be played by a female.)

8. In *A Raisin in the Sun,* by Lorraine Hansberry, Ruth, a young black woman, is preparing with her husband's family to move from crowded quarters into a large house in a white neighborhood. She anticipates the greater comfort their new home will provide as she packs bric-a-brac, accumulated over the years, into a carton. The objects provoke images from the past, and her anticipation evokes images of the future.

9. In *Suburbia,* by Eric Bogosian, Sooze tells the story of her mentally retarded brother, Mikey, with Down's syndrome who died by falling into an icy stream while looking for "the doughnut lady" ten years ago. As she recalls the event, she visualizes the condition of Mikey's body when they pulled him from the water later that spring.

10. In *To Gillian on Her 37th Birthday,* by Michael Brady, 16-year-old Rachel is standing outside scanning the late-summer night sky. As she traces the paths of falling stars with her finger, she slowly begins to visualize the face of her late mother, who would have been 37 that day, had she lived.

In the previous exercises, you have been "surfing" your mind for visual images and describing them vividly to the group. In the process, you have unwittingly used another helpful technique called the **inner monologue.** The inner monologue is a key aspect of the interpretative art of acting, as it is essential for transforming thought into speech. Stanislavski said that actors who do not use them on stage look like "prematurely born people." Like inner images, inner monologues occur naturally in life while we are listening, collecting our thoughts, or determining a course of action. Even though we are silent, we continue to debate and influence others in our minds and with our body language.

For that reason, the word "pause" is an improper term for actors. Pause indicates a momentary suspension in the action where nothing happens. The word "silence" is more appropriate, for our thought process and our attempt to transact with others never stops.

In reality, inner monologues like inner images occur with lightning speed and lack logical organization. Consequently, modern playwrights rarely compose inner monologues. The most common examples in which the classical dramatist creates inner monologues are soliloquies and asides that supply thoughts to be spoken to the audience. Hamlet's "To be, or not to be . . ." and Macbeth's "Tomorrow, and tomorrow, and tomorrow . . ." are examples of superb inner monologues. One of the greatest modern dramatists, Eugene O'Neill, experimented with the inner monologue in *Strange Interlude,* in which he wrote "thoughts" for the actors to speak between the lines of regular dialogue. Sonia Moore tells a story in which Nemirovich-Danchenko points out how, in literature,

> good novelists frequently introduce us to the innermost thoughts of
> the characters—the thoughts that bring them to their decisions and ac-
> tions. Mrs. Knebel mentions one of Chekhov's stories, "He Quarreled
> with His Wife," which consists almost entirely of the thoughts that go
> through a man's head after he has complained to his wife that the sup-
> per was not good. At almost the end of the story the husband speaks for
> the first time since his complaint. He says to his wife, "Stop crying, my
> little darling." This story shows what a great deal in inner monologue
> can lie behind one spoken sentence.[8]

Accomplished actors carefully plan their inner monologues, write them out, memorize them, and recall them at each rehearsal and performance, just as faithfully as they memorize and speak the playwright's lines. If you fail to write down your inner monologues, your thoughts will always be accidental. Thus, your work, which should be found through conscious and deliberate means, will always be unplanned and out of the your control. Always keep in mind, however, that what you write down does not necessarily have to appear in complete sentences. Therefore, your inner monologues may be simple phrases and fragments of thought. During rehearsals and performances, repeat in your mind your inner monologues through every silence. Only then will *pauses* disappear.

On the other hand, you must not have an inner monologue as you speak. You know why you are speaking, why you have selected these words. You project the meaning of the words, communicate the subtext, and see the inner images. Inner monologues occur only during silences in your own lines, as others speak on stage.

In telling the group the images you had in your mind in the previous exercises, you were, in a sense, speaking a formalized inner monologue using complete sentences. You were making the inner monologue an *outer* monologue and thus receiving an initiation into this useful technique. The next exercise will allow you to make further application of it using mostly fragmented thought, as it is in life.

EXERCISE   Create a score of physical actions and present a solo scene centering around an activity that you do not want anyone to know about, for example: opening someone's mail or searching someone's desk. For the purpose of practice, your inner monologue, which may be simple phrases and fragments of thought, you will speak as you are carrying out your score. You should make use of images and justify your actions. Be sure you have a strong objective and work against an obstacle.

Part 1 has offered you a basis for developing your own method of acting. It assumes that you establish, from the very beginning, a regimen of physical exercise and vocal study that will place these two tools totally and flexibly at your command. It has concentrated on developing your inner resources so you will be able to create a believable character to communicate with your body and your voice. Your inner technique consists of three stages: (1) discovering the physical actions required to perform the role; (2) creating objectives to go with each physical action that are believable and stimulating to the imagination; and (3) learning to respond to both external and internal stimuli provided by the given circumstances of the play. Along the way, we have also helped you discover an approach to the creative state, to direct your attention to the proper focus of the moment, and to learn to see things in the special, imaginative way an actor views the world. In Part 2, we shall learn how to mine the play for the raw materials of the role.

Notes

1. Constantin Stanislavski, Elizabeth Reynolds Hapgood, trans., *An Actor Prepares* (New York: Theatre Arts Books, 1973), p. 166.

2. Sonia Moore, *Training an Actor: The Stanislavski System in Class* (New York: Penguin Books, 1979), p. 65.

3. Ibid., p. 228.

4. Stanislavski, p. 163.

5. Ashton Stevens, *Actorviews* (Chicago: Covici-McGee, 1923), pp. 64, 66–67. Quoted in Toby Cole and Helen Krich Chinoy, eds., *Actors on Acting,* New Rev. Ed. (New York: Crown Publishers, 1970), p. 594.

6. Sergei Eisenstein, *The Film Sense,* trans. and ed., Jay Leyda (New York: Harcourt Brace Jovanovich, 1947), pp. 37–38.

7. David Magarshack, "Introduction," *Stanislavsky on the Art of the Stage* (New York: Hill and Wang, 1961), p. 38.

8. Moore, pp. 159–160.

PART II

The Actor and the Play

Chris Bennion

A scene from Seattle Repertory Theatre's
production of *King Hedley II*,
by August Wilson.

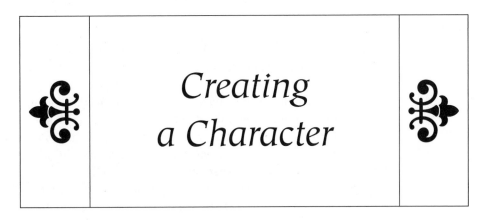

CHAPTER 9

Creating
a Character

Throughout Part 1, we concentrated on technique training that teaches you to use your intelligence, your life experience, your imagination, and your senses as raw material for creating a character. We frequently referred to the dramatist's given circumstances but clearly placed the initial emphasis on the actor. Many of the exercises in Part 1 derived from published plays, and we attempted to include enough of the circumstances to provide practice in developing logical and appropriate behavior within specific parameters. However, to fully create a three-dimensional character who behaves logically within the world of the play, you must learn how to read, uncover, and use the total circumstances of a script. The great Scandinavian playwright Henrik Ibsen frequently warned actors to read his plays "very carefully." You must think of yourself as a detective searching for clues found on every page of the text. You must rake the script with a "fine-toothed comb" as you sift through the evidence. A would-be actor who lacks the appropriate skills (or is perhaps too lazy) to analyze the play will succeed only in creating a characterization that is both incomplete and inconsistent.

Stage productions that contain living, vital characters result from a melding of the creative talents of the actor and the dramatist. Any argument over which of the two is more important is fruitless because they are completely interdependent. The actor relies on the character created by the dramatist to provide an essential, continuing stimulus and source of inspiration. On the other hand, without the actor to bring it to life, the dramatist's character will lie dormant on the pages of the script. The final creation is the result of a true collaboration—a marriage of sorts—between actor and dramatist. For instance, the audience will see neither Strindberg's Miss Julie nor the actresses' Miss Julie, but the actress *as* Strindberg's Miss Julie. Each character a playwright conceives has the potential to sustain a broad range of actions, and for a great character such as Hamlet, that number is practically unlimited. The character's final shape in a particular production will be colored both by the actions selected by the actor and by what the actor finds significant about his or her personal relationship to the part.

An actor's performance of a character consists of both an inner characterization and its outer form. To create the outer form—the way the character looks, moves, gestures, and speaks—the actor draws "from his own experience of life or that of his friends, from pictures, engravings, drawings, books, stories, novels, or from some simple incident—it makes no difference."[1] For you to perform a believable, three-dimensional characterization, you must also create the character's inner life. You accomplish this portion of your task by adopting the character's thoughts, emotions, and states of mind, drawing wherever possible on similar experiences in your own life. When you are working correctly, you make a direct connection between the character's external anatomy and your newly created inner being—the psychophysical union. That is your goal, and you must dedicate your study of the play and the role, as well as the designated period of rehearsals, to achieving it.

As we stated in Chapter 1, each character must spring from your own soul. You can create another person only by drawing on your own experiences, actual or vicarious. No matter how you may alter your outward appearance, no matter how you may change the sound of your voice (and this outer form is necessary to complete characterization), your ability to communicate the essential truth of your role depends upon your capacity to externalize your inner resources. Even though study and observation in the preparation of a specific part may greatly expand your own natural resources, what is essentially *you* remains the same from one character to another. Remember, however, *you* are infinite. Your soul has no bottom. Your imagination and personal history grant an unlimited source for diverse portrayals.

Thus, the actor's final product is a unique creation that cannot be duplicated. No two actors will relate in the same way to the same part because they have not had a lifetime of identical experiences. The characterizations of two actors performing the same role have the same father (the dramatist) but a different mother (the actor). David Magarshack extended this analogy:

> Every artistic stage character is a unique individual creation, like everything else in nature. In the process of its creation there is a "he," that is "the husband," namely the author of the play, and a "she," that is "the wife," namely the actor or actress. . . . There is "the child"—the created

part. There are in this process, besides, the moments of the first acquaintance between "him" and "her," their first friendship, their falling in love, their quarrels and differences, their reconciliations, and their union. . . . During these periods the producer, Stanislavsky points out, helps the process of the birth of the man-part by playing the role of matchmaker.[2]

To say that actors become creative artists in their own right in this process neither minimizes nor falsifies the creativity of the dramatist. *Kenneth Branagh's* Hamlet was different from *Mel Gibson's* Hamlet because each actor found meaning in *Shakespeare's* Hamlet in light of his own experience. In so doing, each was true to Shakespeare and to himself.

To this point in the book, we have concentrated on helping you learn how to be true to yourself as an actor. It is now time to consider how you can be true to the dramatist.

Penetrating the Script

While creating a characterization that is unique and personal, you must realize and readily accept the great responsibility you owe to the dramatist. Your first step toward fulfilling that obligation is to study the play until you have gleaned all evidence that discloses the dramatist's overall purpose for the character. Jerzy Grotowski explained that actors must allow the role to "penetrate" them. By definition, *penetrate* means to "enter by overcoming resistance," so Grotowski is admonishing the actors to yield freely to the physical and psychological demands of the part as they prepare to play it. Some teachers have suggested that actors "have an affair with the script," that they read it as if it were a sensual, "juicy" story. Thus, you must open your senses to the character, reading the script over and over, each time for a different purpose.

As you read the script, two basic questions guide your study: (1) What, overall, does the character want? and (2) What is she willing to do to get it? A certain character, for instance, may want more than anything else to be rich and may be willing to employ any means to satisfy his desire. He may be willing to forego all ordinary pleasures, even to sacrifice his health and the happiness of his family. He might break any law—legal or moral—that he found to be an obstacle. Another character may also want to be rich but might not be willing to obtain her wealth by gambling with the happiness and security of her family or by taking advantage of friends and associates. A certain character may want to find love, and might be willing to sacrifice everything, even her pride and virtue, to gain what she wants. Another with the same basic desire might be too proud to compromise her reputation. Still another might be too shy to let his desire be known.

If you know what your character wants and what she is willing to do to achieve it, you have the key to creating an honest performance. Answering these two questions provides you with the motivating force behind what your character does and says; thus, this task completely dominates your initial study of the play. Failure to understand the overall desire that motivates the character's behavior means a breakdown in understanding the dramatist's intention. This, in turn, means failure to interpret the play truthfully.

Studying a script is a process of analysis and synthesis, of taking apart and putting together. Actors analyze, or take apart, the characters, studying their behavior in relation to the other characters and to the play as a whole. Then, guided by their sensitivity and imagination, they reassemble the parts, organizing them to form an artistic creation.

Identifying the Motivating Force

In Chapter 3, we discussed the term **simple objective,** a character's quest at any given moment expressed and pursued by use of an action verb that motivates a sequence of simple actions. The **motivating force,** on the other hand, is "what your character wants" overall. Like the simple objective, you should state it in specific terms. Finding a name for the motivating force is an important step in creating a character. The name must designate a desire true to the author's overall intention, and, like the simple objective, it must also stimulate the actor to action. A motivating force that does not suggest action is worthless.

Stanislavski emphasized the importance of choosing the right name, recalling his analysis of the hero in Goldoni's *The Mistress of the Inn.* He wrote:

> We made the mistake of using "I wish to be a misogynist," and we found that the play refused to yield either humour or action. It was only when I discovered that the hero really loved women and wished only to be accounted a misogynist that I changed to "I wish to do my courting on the sly" and immediately the play came to life.[3]

Besides not being in accord with the dramatist's conception, "I wish to be a misogynist" was a weak choice because it was insufficiently specific. "I want to hate women" defines a general attitude but fails to suggest action. Such statements as "I want to avoid women" or "I want to take advantage of every opportunity to embarrass women" would have been better. For this character, however, they would still have been unacceptable because he did not hate women at all. And what splendid possibilities for action are suggested by "I want to do my courting on the sly."

A good motivating force, the character's overall desire, will be stated as a *specific statement that the character can attempt to satisfy through action.* Examples of unsatisfactory statements that cannot motivate specific action are:

+ I want to be unhappy.
+ I want to be popular.

David Cooper

Figure 9.1 "Mother, you have my father much offended . . . " Hamlet (Marco Barricelli) confronts his mother, Gertrude (Demetra Pittman) in the Oregon Shakespeare Festival's 2000 production of William Shakespeare's *Hamlet*. Directed by Libby Appel; scenic design by Richard L. Hay; costume design by Deborah M. Dryden; lighting design by Robert Peterson.

Examples of better statements are:

✦ For his indiscretions with my wife, *I want to ruin* my neighbor's reputation in the community.

✦ *I wish to make others laugh* in order *to divert attention* away from my own illness.

✦ *To exact revenge* upon my boss, *I must expose* his illegal activity.

The convention for naming the motivating force is the same as those for stating simple objectives. Begin the statement with "I want to," "I wish to," or "I must" and follow with an active verb expressing the overall desire of the character. Do not follow with the verb *to be* or a verb expressing feeling, because *being* and *feeling* are conditions, not actions, and consequently cannot be acted.

Another cardinal rule is that the statement must involve the actor with other characters. As we recognized earlier, a play is a conflict. Your motivating force must demand something of the other characters and bring you in conflict with them. And it is through conflict in motivating forces that the plot unfolds and characters are revealed.

Last, the character's motivating force must mean something personal to the actors. It must arouse in them a real desire to accomplish their aims. To *think* is not enough; the actors must truly *want*. Michael Chekhov explained that the actors must be "possessed" of their objective.[4]

Constructing "Your" Autobiography

Analysis, for the most part, is a solitary task. It begins with your first reading of the script and doesn't stop until the lights fade on the final performance. You must read, evaluate, analyze, and research everything that helps illuminate your character and her world. Using the script as your primary source, you must reflect on the character's personal history, present state of being, relationships, and self-perceptions. You must consider previous and present actions and the character's future expectations. Research may include pictures, paintings, music, poetry, textures, colors, books, articles, interviews, observations, or anything that may help you in the creative process. Whether writing on your computer or scribbling in a notebook as you lie in bed, you must write down all the information revealed in your script and from your research. You must fill the pages with information and discoveries about your character.

From the moment you have been cast in a role, you should consider everything from your character's point of view — "I" rather than he, she, or they. Remember, "you" are unique. "You" have your own history, ideas, attitudes, desires, and fears. "You" have a singular attitude regarding every social and moral issue "you" face. As you begin to take notes, don't necessarily worry about spelling and grammar. Write as your character would write — taking into consideration his level of education and mental capacity. "You" may be as completely subjective and biased as "you" wish with regard to everything in "your" world. Also keep in mind that although you may disagree with your character about his spiritual and moral views, his choices and significant life decisions, you must never judge your character. Otherwise, you (the actor) will never be able to sustain belief in "your" (the character's) actions. Writing your analysis in first person will help you eliminate the tendency to judge your character.

Your analysis for the most part is personal and private. The majority of it should be kept from your fellow actors, and much of the time you should refrain from discussing your most private thoughts with your director. This does not mean to abstain from openly talking about the given circumstances and many of the issues facing your character. Anything "you" would publicly accept, defend, or share with "your" family, friends, colleagues, and the general public is perfectly acceptable for discussion among your director and colleagues. However, you should avoid sharing "your" *private* thoughts and feelings, "your" secrets. This part of your analysis is solely for your eyes. Put it under lock and key as you would a personal diary. In life, mystery surrounds the most interesting people. We never really know even our closest friends (and sometimes we don't understand our own actions). We may think we know our parents, our siblings, our friends, our lover, but they will always contradict themselves. They do the opposite of what we expect. They relentlessly do things that are "out of character." Sometimes they harbor thoughts and feelings that stay hidden for years. Sometimes these feelings never surface. Human beings are "walking contradictions." They are mysterious. Therefore, as in life, the most fascinating acting is surrounded by mystery. We all have secrets, and our characters are no exceptions. Sharing too much of your analysis with others will destroy "your" mystery.

During the period of analysis and study, read the play "very carefully" many times. Take note of every hint, every clue that helps you bring your creation to life. You should consider:

+ What "you" do and don't do.

+ What "you" say and don't say (keeping in mind that characters sometimes exaggerate and lie).

+ What the other characters in the play say about "you" and do to "you" (always taking into consideration the other character's perceived purpose).

+ What actions are suggested in "your" lines.

+ What comments and descriptions the playwright offers in the stage directions (remembering that not all stage directions are appropriate for your interpretation and that many times they are simply a stage manager's notes from the first production).

From there, your analysis must advance into a detailed autobiographical investigation. The dramatist provides enough information for you to understand the motivating force and the essential traits of the character, but you must almost always supply an imaginary background to round out the essentials mined from the text. Begin by writing down what you perceive as logical and true. Your initial thoughts, however, will change — or evolve — as you go through the rehearsal process and as you merge with your character.

To be valid, a **character autobiography** should contain only details that logically extend from those provided by the dramatist, and, to be useful, it should contain only those particulars of specific behavior that can guide the actor's choice of objectives and relationships. In most of the great classic dramas, vital matters regarding the protagonist's present course of action depend on a full understanding of past events that are not fully explained in the text. Consider *Othello,* for instance. What relationship, before the beginning of the play, had existed among the characters that prompted the Moor to prefer Cassio rather than Iago as his principal officer and, at the same time, to trust Iago with knowledge of his personal affairs, of which he kept Cassio ignorant? What is Roderigo's background that he aspires to win Desdemona, has access to her only through Iago, and has the wealth to satisfy Iago's extravagant demands on his purse? Finding answers to such questions helps determine the behavior of a character.

Your character's autobiography will put you on closer terms with the character you are playing, and you should prepare one as a regular part of your analysis procedure. Write down "your" images, thoughts, and inner monologues. Some immature actors may see this as a limitation, but it is a means to freedom. Full knowledge of your character that comes through analysis gives you more choices in the rehearsal process. Conversely, failure to write down your character's thoughts results in vague decisions that are difficult to repeat with consistency. Discoveries will be pure accident, and you will stunt the growth of your character.

You may begin your character autobiography by asking "yourself" the questions listed below. Your answers to these questions will undoubtedly overlap. By the time you answer one query, you will have alluded to another one. This is expected. You should not attempt to isolate one from another. Remember to approach everything in first person from your character's point of view, as it is her autobiography.

Autobiographical Worksheet

1. **Who?**
    a. What is my personal history? (This should be a thorough investigation of your second plan, which is discussed in greater detail later in this chapter.)
    b. What is my present state of being?
    c. How do I perceive myself physically?
        i. Mentally?
        ii. Morally?
        iii. Socially?
        iv. Economically?
        v. Spiritually?
    d. What are my emotional relationships?
    e. What am I wearing?
2. **When?**
    a. What is the year?
    b. What is the date and time?

  c. What is the weather?

  d. How does "when?" affect my life?

3. Where?

  a. In what city am I?

  b. What are my immediate surroundings?

  c. How do the city and immediate surroundings affect my life?

  d. What are the social and spiritual customs and political tendencies of my family?

   i. Neighborhood?

   ii. Group?

   iii. Society?

4. What?

  a. What has just happened prior to the events in the script?

  b. What is happening presently?

  c. What is my attitude toward the unfolding events?

  d. How does my attitude differ from my family, friends, or society?

  e. What do I expect to happen in the future?

5. Why?

  a. How would I define the units of action?

  b. What is my simple objective for each unit?

  c. What noun names would I give each unit?

  d. What is my motivating force?

6. How?

  a. What stands in my way of achieving my goals?

  b. What is my "will" to get what I want?

Although the motivating force should be stated in a single phrase, the process of uncovering it is no simple task. Characters, like real human beings, are filled with psychological complexities. You must take pains to consider all the possibilities, finally stating the motivating force specifically and in terms that will stimulate you to action.

By now it must be apparent that discovering the motivating force is the key to getting into the part. Important as it is, actors frequently fail to understand the basic motivation clearly, to name it accurately, and to feel it fully. This failure stems from two causes: (1) many actors don't study the play with enough care and imagination, and (2) the motivating force—especially for a long and complex role—is frequently difficult to find.

You should not give up if you do not know the motivating force when you begin rehearsal; instead, keep searching throughout the creative process. During this stage, you can play specific actions and realize the character's simple objectives from scene to scene without knowing for certain how they relate to the motivating force. In fact, you may never be convinced that you have the absolute, final answer for some characters; however, the search must not be abandoned, because the effort itself is of great value. Because of the ongoing nature of this process, your statement of the motivating force you are working with at any particular moment is always hypothetical. You must continue to explore it, test it, and be willing to change it as your understanding of the character and the play increases.

As we stated previously, analyzing your role is mostly a solitary assignment. It is your homework. Analysis does continue during rehearsal, but there are boundaries. Stanislavski, in the early years of the Moscow Art Theatre, sat around a table with his actors for weeks discussing every aspect of the play. During this time, they uncovered a wealth of information about the characters and their environment; however, Stanislavski discovered that their table work actually impeded their progress, and the characters lost some of their mystery. Simply talking about the role stood in the way of discovery through the psychophysical process. Discussion is very important, but you must learn to do it in conjunction with the rehearsal process. As you—with the guidance of your director—determine physical *actions,* you are also forced to make psychological choices. Thus, as a serious actor, you must study the play, research "your" world, and answer many questions, but you must also understand that the analytical process is merely a means to discovering physical actions. *And the Method of Physical Actions is the only path to inspiration on stage.* Analysis is not an end in itself. Therefore, you must stop talking so much in rehearsals and work on action. Your character's biography—or rather "your" autobiography—is an extremely important part of the process that you work on primarily outside rehearsals and test and modify during rehearsals.

EXERCISE   Select a role from one of the plays listed in Appendix A at the back of this text or choose a character from another standard full-length script. Using the above worksheet as the basis for analysis, write a complete autobiography. State your initial idea of the character's motivating force in terms that are true to the dramatist's conception and that could stimulate you to action in playing the part.

Nurturing the Character

You are attempting to give birth to another person, a being filled with mystery and secrets, an individual who has a lifetime of emotional experiences and who is more complex than the most sophisticated computer. Without proper analysis, many actors simply do not have enough information to fully "penetrate" their characters. Thus, they play only the most primitive impressions. To fulfill their need for immediate gratification, these actors play the result rather than building their character one step at a time. Actors simply cannot grasp all the complexities of characterization at the beginning of the rehearsal and analytical process. As a fetus grows in the womb, the process of nurturing your character takes time to gestate. In an attempt to explain the piecemeal process of bringing a character to life, Stanislavski told the following story of a director talking to a group of actors.

> "Children!" said he laughingly, as the maid set a large turkey in front of him, "Imagine that this is not a turkey but a five act play, *The Inspector General.* Can you do away with it in a mouthful? No; you cannot make a single mouthful either of a whole turkey or a five act play. Therefore you must carve it, first, into large pieces, like this . . ." (cutting off the legs, wings, and soft parts of the roast and laying them on an empty plate).
>
> "There you have the first big divisions. But you cannot swallow even such chunks. Therefore you must cut them into smaller pieces, like this . . ." and he disjointed the bird still further.
>
> "Now pass your plate," said the director to the eldest child. "There's a big piece for you. That's the first scene. . . ."
>
> "Eugene," said the director to his second son, "here is the scene with the Postmaster. And now, Igor and Theodore, here is the scene between Bobchinski and Dobchinski. You two girls can do the piece between the Mayor's wife and daughter.
>
> "Swallow it," he ordered, and they threw themselves on their food, shoving enormous chunks into their mouths, and nearly choking themselves to death. Whereupon the director warned them to cut their pieces finer and finer still, if necessary.
>
> "What tough, dry meat," he exclaimed suddenly to his wife.
>
> "Give it taste," said one of the children, "by adding 'an invention of the imagination.'"
>
> "Or," said another, passing him the gravy, "with a sauce made of magic ifs. Allow the author to present his 'given circumstances . . .'"
>
> "This is good," he said. "Even this shoe leather almost seems to be meat. That's what you must do with the bits of your part, soak them more and more in the sauce of 'given circumstances.' The drier the part the more sauce you need.[5]

To begin the process of building your character, choose a fine cut (one sequence of actions) in which you can most readily believe. Think of it as the legs upon which your character will stand. Your sequence of actions need not be the first in which your character appears, and you shouldn't concern yourself with the level of importance of your selection. It is simply the chain of events with which you most identify with your character—one in which you can find an analogous

Figure 9.2 A scene from Oliver Goldsmith's *She Stoops to Conquer* at Center Stage in Baltimore, MD. Three-dimensional characters with strong motivating forces come as a result of thorough script analysis and a well-defined autobiography.

emotion, one that stimulates your imagination, or one in which you can readily become "possessed" with the objective. From there, you begin the gestation process that leads to the development of the entire imaginary human being.

Uncovering the Units of Action

As an actor, your basic responsibility is to find, one by one, the numerous simple objectives and actions that taken together constitute your role. Each is carried out to satisfy a singular desire of your character, and each has a precise relation to your character's total behavior. Stanislavski referred to the smallest whole division of a play—one in which there is a distinct beginning, middle, and end—as a **unit of action** (or "unit" for short). Many actors refer to units as *beats*. For our purposes, however, we shall return to Stanislavski's original phrase and refer to them as units with the understanding that they are synonymous with beats. Regardless, the transition between them is open to wide interpretation. Most new units are defined by a simple shift in the action—a "change of direction," so to speak. According to Charles Marowitz, it is "a section of time confined to a specific set of continuous actions, or perhaps the duration of a mood or an internal state. As soon as our actions graduate to the next unit of activity, we can be said to be in the next beat of the scene. . . . It is characterized by one overriding emotional colour."[6]

The actor and the director break down each scene into units so they can more precisely discuss the role and prepare its performance, in much the same way a conductor uses a "measure" to focus the attention of the individual members of the orchestra on a particular part of a score. The units of action are comparable to the measures of a musical score in another way: they are primarily useful as rehearsal aids and should never be evident to the audience. Harold Clurman explained the importance of uncovering units of action:

> The analysis of the play's beats, the characters' actions, can and should be made before the actual staging of the play is begun. The actors derive a basic direction from such analysis and from *the notation of the beats in their part-books,* a guiding line that is the foundation for their entire work in the play. Without such groundwork, we may get a display of "general emotion" but not the meaning of the play. . . . The actor's talent becomes evident in the manner in which he carries out these actions. But talent or not, they must be clearly presented for the play to become an intelligible, coherent whole.[7]

Stanislavski stressed the necessity of seeing the role as a series of units. As soon as one simple objective that fires a unit is satisfied, another desire arises that forms the basis for another unit. In earlier chapters, when we asked you to structure your work by clearly delineating a beginning, middle, and end, we were in effect dividing the exercise into units.

Every unit of action must be developed around a simple objective. Once an objective has been determined, it stands as the primary motivation until the character successfully achieves it or until the circumstances of the play force the character to move to a new unit and a new goal.

Once you have defined the simple objectives, you must give each unit a *noun name,* a single word that characterizes the whole section. For example, you may call a particular unit "Confrontation." The noun name will dictate certain behavior in your character and will define each unit. Only then will you *know* what the audience must understand. Defining each unit through a single word discloses its essence and propels the dramatic action forward.

Individual units must logically progress from one to another. Therefore, one noun name—the essence of that unit—will understandably lead to the next. Beginning with the noun name "Confrontation" it may follow that the second unit is entitled "Debate." This, in turn, leads to the following sequence of units: "Allies," "Battle," "Confession," "Retreat," and "Reparations." These named units form a logical progression that extends throughout the play. The movement from one unit to the next—the development of the inner life of your character—illustrates what Stanislavski referred to as the **through-line of action.** He compared the through-line of action to a traveler on a long journey. The traveler, while moving toward his destination, comes into contact with many new people and diverse situations; all the while he continues on his expedition toward his goal.

All actions should help disclose your character's motivating force to the audience. You should eliminate all of them not related to this purpose. The audience understands the play by following a series of logical and expressive units. You must facilitate this by communicating a believable and logical progression of actions, all of which grow from the given circumstances of your role.

Although the idea of truth remains constant, the given circumstances and the world of the play differ wildly with every production. The seeming illogic of some modern and contemporary plays—especially those identified as theatre of the absurd—is deceptive. The dramatist has written the play for a specific purpose and has given the characters some pattern of behavior. To express the absurdity they find in contemporary life, they may require from the actor a series of illogical actions. But by using speech and actions illogically, by introducing the fantastic and the ridiculous, their purpose is to express the absence of truth and meaning in modern society. As in the case of any drama, it is the actor's job to discover a motivating force that is truthful in the seemingly illogical pattern and to communicate it to the audience as clearly as possible.

Creating a character requires, more than anything else, the ability to follow a through-line of action. To do so, you must carefully perform each unit of action, always attempting to realize your objective and to relate each unit clearly to the one that follows it. A definite "terminal point" at the end of each unit and a firm "attack" at the beginning of each new unit give the play a sense of forward movement. There must also be clear cause-and-effect relationships between the units that illustrate the kind of analytical problem you will face in most plays, whether they be classic, modern, or contemporary.

EXERCISE   Return to the same character for whom you completed the Autobiographical Worksheet earlier in this chapter. Study the breakdown of the play carefully. Divide the role into units of action, state the simple objectives, and give a noun name for each unit. Make a score of physical actions, remembering that speech is action. Select one unit with which you can completely sustain your belief and that you can relate to your character's motivating force. Rehearse and present your scene for class discussion.

Characterization begins with discovering the character's motivating force and proceeds by breaking the role into small units of action, each with a clearly understood simple objective that moves the character toward accomplishing her overall goal. Discovering, enriching, and playing these units is a constant challenge throughout the rehearsals and performance. Few actors, even of the highest professional caliber (and after playing a role a great number of times), would claim they succeed in believing, with equal conviction, every unit. That, however, is the aim of all actors who seek to create art on stage, and they work to accomplish it at every rehearsal and performance. But they realize that failure to achieve complete belief at every moment does not indicate a bad actor any more than failure to return every ball indicates a bad tennis player. A good actor succeeds in believing a large proportion of what she does, just as a good tennis player succeeds in returning a large proportion of balls. The actor and the athlete both work to improve their techniques to increase the proportion of their successes.

Incorporating the Second Plan

When you write "your" autobiography, you are using your imagination to construct a history, a past life of the character. Although such work is necessary for creating a believable person who can live and act within the given circumstances of the play, you must concentrate your efforts on those moments in the character's life the playwright chooses to dramatize. The actor's second plan includes your character's life before the play and after it; however, it also incorporates the events that occur off stage during the course of the selected life. These events many times are extremely important to the development of the plot. You can make use of these actions by writing a narrative version of the entire story, curtain to curtain, from the point of view of your character, and by improvising actions that happen off stage.

EXERCISE   Using the same character you selected for the two earlier exercises in this chapter, write a narrative of your character's life that includes off-stage events during the actual time covered by the play. Select an important off-stage event in which your character is alone, break it into units, and present it as a scene.

Finding the Outer Form

Unless you have the ability to externalize your inner thoughts and feelings, you have no business on stage. Your external actions must influence the other actors and project into the audience. Most marginally talented actors have the ability to analyze and internalize a character. This, however, falls short of your goal. There must be communion with others. Otherwise, you would do just as well to stay home and "act" and "feel" for your own entertainment. If you fail to externalize

Figure 9.3 Dan Graul in an original dance theatre piece, entitled *Landscaping for Privacy,* at Southeast Missouri State University. Choreographed by Joséphine A. Zmolek and Paul Zmolek; costumes designed by Rhonda Weller-Stilson; lighting designed by C. Kenneth Cole.

your inner thoughts and feelings, you will never engage your psychophysical being. Your character will never project into the audience. They will not follow the action, and your presence on stage will be illogical. Action is your only means to external expression, your sole purpose on stage.

You externalize your character through posture, manner of movement, degree of mobility, gestures, physical abnormalities, and all nonverbal modes of expression. You communicate through your character's dialect, level of articulation, choice of words, and sentence structure. You reveal your character's inner being through animation and the unique tempo-rhythms of physical and verbal actions. Clothing, makeup, and hair cast a great deal of information about your character's self-perception. Personal objects (e.g., fans, pipes, canes, glasses, books, guns, etc.) become extensions of your imagined personality. Characters, as in life, are identified by their possessions. Everything the audience sees "you" do and hears "you" say, everything with which "you" connect, everyone with whom "you" relate projects something about your character. *Externalizing* a character is arguably your most important responsibility. The audience *suspends their disbelief* when they trust what they see and hear. Therefore, you must find outward forms that will help the audience believe your character.

Externals also greatly help actors sustain belief in their characters. They use their bodies as expressive instruments to project their inner being, and their external decisions reinforce their internal convictions. An especially erect posture, with chin held high and nostrils pinched, as if constantly trying to locate a slightly offensive odor, might aid an actress in characterizing the overpowering Lady Bracknell in Oscar Wilde's *The Importance of Being Earnest*. A mannerism of sucking his teeth might help an actor in believing the vulgarity of Mr. Burgess in George Bernard Shaw's *Candida*. Elia Kazan's notebook for *A Streetcar Named Desire* outlines effective externals for the crude, simple, naive, sensual character of Stanley Kowalski. He sucks a cigar. He annoyingly busies himself with other things while people are talking to him.

Dramas abound with opportunities for actors to use externals as a means of deepening and extending their characterizations. For instance, the actor playing Willy Loman in Arthur Miller's *Death of a Salesman* should examine the effect of carrying heavy sample bags on the physique of an elderly man. The rounded shoulders, the body leaning forward to balance the weight of the samples, the feet hurting from too much pressure, the eyes looking at the ground to search for obstacles—all these external manifestations can help create a truthful characterization of Willy's exhaustion.

Sir Laurence Olivier often used makeup to help find his character. For example, he once told of developing the right type of nose as a key to a role. From this center, he could create a whole physical presence. However, Olivier would have been the first to emphasize that the external approach must be used in conjunction with internal motivation to develop a complete characterization.

When using externals as a means to characterization, you must observe two cautions:

1. You must beware of clichés, the stereotyped mannerisms or properties that have been so frequently repeated they would occur immediately to even an unimaginative mind. For the audience, clichés no longer express individuality but only general types. They are the imitation of imitation, worn-out devices that can be executed mechanically. Consequently, they are powerless to aid in your belief in the character.

2. You must be sure that the externalization either results from or leads to a specific need you can relate to your character's motivating force.

The caution we registered about making externals serve the motivating force may be repeated with similar emphasis for all aspects of the characterization.

Everything you do, say, or wear on stage should help either create the motivating force or satisfy it. The more clearly you understand how a particular detail relates to your goal, the more significant it will be to you and your audience.

The motivating force is the unifying factor in selecting both internal and external details of characterization. All your decisions must relate to your character's motivating force; otherwise, they should be omitted. In fact, you should even avoid external character choices that are merely neutral; that is, details that perhaps do not hinder but bear no inherent relationship to your character. Neutral decisions are weak. They have no benefit and can distort the plot. Whether "you" smoke or not, whether "your" hair is long or short, whether "you" drink beer or coffee, whether "you" wear boxers or briefs, should all be determined by "your" motivating force. Every detail should make a positive contribution to the total characterization.

As an actor in production, you must focus only on your own character. That is the part you play. That is your contribution. Through individual analysis, you break down the entire script into units, complete with noun names and simple objectives. Connecting the units allows you to clearly see the through-line of action, which in turn leads to the naming of your character's motivating force. Keep in mind, however, that all this must naturally fit within the director's concept of the production, and you must have the ability to infect your partners and project your character into the audience.

You may identify your motivating force only if you have carefully completed your unit analysis along the way. Remember, however, the units are simply markers as you travel toward your destination. You cannot ignore the markers, for they lead the way. They are the fuel to be consumed on your journey. The markers also warn you of potential danger; they prevent you from wandering away from the path. However, you should not allow the markers to stand in your way. If you isolate the individual units and do not look at them as part of a connected whole, you will bog down in a multitude of shallow, unrelated details. They will merely confuse and frustrate you, as you lose sight of your destination. Analysis is your means to external freedom. It leads you to the path of discovery through the psychophysical process, as you work your way toward your character's motivating force.

Notes

1. Constantin Stanislavski, *Building a Character* (New York: Theatre Arts Books, 1949), p. 7.

2. David Magarshack, "Introduction," *Stanislavsky on the Art of the Stage* (New York: Hill and Wang, 1961), p. 77.

3. Constantin Stanislavski, *An Actor Prepares* (New York: Theatre Arts Books, 1936), p. 258.

4. Michael Chekhov, *To the Actor* (New York: Harper & Row, 1953), p. 69.

5. Stanislavski, *An Actor Prepares,* pp. 105–106.

6. Charles Marowitz, *The Act of Being* (New York: Taplinger, 1978), pp. 29–30.

7. Harold Clurman, "The Principles of Interpretation," in *Producing the Play,* ed. John Gassner (New York: Holt, Rinehart, 1941), p. 287. Italics ours.

CHAPTER 10

Expressing the Super-Objective

Creating a character is the actor's sole responsibility, but a single character is part of a much larger whole. Actors must relate their performance to the entire production. They must discover why the dramatist wrote the play, what she wanted it to say, and what emotional effect she wanted it to have on the audience. Ideally, the entire company will agree on the play's **super-objective,** and each actor will in turn build his particular role in relation to this concept.

In Chapter 9, we learned that actors must analyze their characters with considerable care to determine the motivating force behind their actions. In this chapter, we shall discover that a dramatist uses a group of characters, all motivated by different and often conflicting desires, for the purpose of expressing an overall meaning. Further, we shall be concerned with how each actor's role can help to realize the author's intention.

Several sources help actors prepare to learn about the play. They will want to know something of the playwright's life and of the circumstances under which the play was written. Knowing that *The Tempest* was probably Shakespeare's last play, and that in Prospero's farewell to his art—the practice of white magic—Shakespeare was saying farewell to his supreme artistry as a dramatist and a poet, might help an actor realize the calm, the dignity, and the finality of the overall tone of this play. An actor in Molière's plays may use the knowledge that this playwright had a young wife and that, in his several plays in which an old man is married to a young girl, his observations came from his own experience. Some of O'Neill's plays are almost completely autobiographical, and knowing about his relation with his parents and his older brother and about his life as a young man in New London, Connecticut, might well help actors select actions to illuminate O'Neill's characters and help them communicate the world of the play.

Good drama always reflects, if it does not deal directly with, the social, economic, and moral values of its time. It follows that actors need to learn about the prevailing social conditions at the time a play in which they are performing was written. An actor could hardly succeed in Congreve's *The Way of the World* without learning as much as possible about the amoral behavior of upper-class society in Restoration England. On a more modern note, it might help an actor preparing to perform in one of Bertolt Brecht's intriguing dramas to know that the enigmatic German playwright was ideologically a Communist and that most of his works protest against a capitalistic society. For the corpus of dramas written about the war in Vietnam, such as David Rabe's *The Basic Training of Pavlo Hummel* or Sean Clark's *Eleven–Zulu,* the actor needs to learn about the conditions in training camps, the prevailing moral values in the combat zones, and the breach that combat experience is likely to cause between returning soldiers and their families.

One of the fascinating aspects of being an actor is the constant need to understand what makes people from all walks of life "tick." Depending on the production in which they are working at the moment, they may have to learn about conditions among the coal miners in Pennsylvania or among sharecroppers in the South, or about the treatment of American Indians. They may have to learn about proper procedure in a courtroom, in a hospital, or on a battleship.

To understand and perform in period plays, the actor must find out about the clothes worn at the time. Actors must know not only how to wear them and move in them but also why a certain fashion prevailed. Why were stocks and farthingales worn in the Renaissance? Paniers and powdered wigs in the eighteenth century? How did Restoration gentlemen use a walking stick or Victorian ladies use a fan? Just as actors must fully understand the social, economic, and moral values of their characters' world, their understanding of fashion will make all period plays new and contemporary, clear and relevant to a contemporary audience.

Where do actors find answers to questions about the playwright's life and the historical context relating to the world of the play? First, they must be voracious readers, concentrating on both the fiction and nonfiction of the period during which the play takes place. They should study biographies of their playwright and of famous actors and other people from the period. Pictures from the period — paintings, engravings, and photos — are excellent sources for makeup and clothing, but they also indicate attitudes and atmosphere of the times. Good pictures arouse strong feelings, and good actors find ways to use the flavor of pictures in defining a believable character. For more recent periods, film and television, both fictive and documentary, provide excellent sources of behavior and social detail. To know too much about the play, the period, and the character is impossible.

The World Wide Web is another invaluable source of information for the actor. Most young people are extremely comfortable "surfing the 'Net." We must always keep in mind, however, that the Web is unregulated, and actors should be forewarned to use only legitimate sources. John Smith's undergraduate term paper from Anywhere University that he posted on the Web last night does not constitute a legitimate source. However, Web articles found in such sites as The History Channel, Biography Channel, The Learning Channel, The Discovery Channel, A&E, MSNBC, CBS, ABC, CNN, *The New York Times* Online, or any other long-standing journal, magazine, or newspaper represent an important means with which to research your character and period.

Indeed, the Web is an indispensable tool, but it is not the only tool. Many young actors naively believe that doing a quick search on sites such as Google, Yahoo!, Excite, or Ask Jeeves from the comfort of their dorm rooms is all the research they will need in creating a character or exploring a particular period. To them, the Web sometimes seems immeasurable and comprehensive, and the lazier the actor, the more infinite, all-powerful, and universal the Internet seems. Many of the most valuable resources can be found only in hard copy in such places as libraries and bookstores. You must supplement the legitimate work you have done on your computer. Therefore, get out of your chairs and go search "the stacks." You will be amazed.

With that said, knowledge of such matters as period and style is essential to a full understanding of the playwright's meaning. Consequently, actors find it doubly important to obtain this information; indeed, they cannot afford to ignore it. It helps them prepare to read more intelligently their chief source for interpreting the play—the script itself.

Finding the Super-Objective

Although the individual character autobiographies are mostly private, all actors in the performing company must agree on what a play is about, what meaning the dramatist had in mind, before the actors can fulfill their particular functions in the cooperative effort of a dramatic production. Stanislavski wrote about this necessity: "The main theme must be firmly fixed in the actor's mind throughout the performance. It gave birth to the writing of the play. It should also be the fountainhead of the actor's artistic creation." He called this main theme the *super-objective of the entire play:*

> In a play the whole stream of individual, minor objectives—all the
> imaginative thoughts, feelings, and actions of an actor—should con-

verge to carry out the *super-objective* of the plot. The common bond must be so strong that even the most insignificant detail, if it is not related to the *super-objective,* will stand out as superfluous or wrong.[1]

Harold Clurman stated emphatically that "no character of the play can be properly understood unless the play as a whole is understood." He recognized that understanding the play resolves itself into one central theme:

> What is the *basic action of the play?* What is the play about from the standpoint of the characters' principal conflict? . . . What is the play's core? . . . Saroyan's *My Heart's in the Highlands,* to its New York director, was the story of people eager to give things to one another — lovers all, in a sense. For me, Odets' *Night Music* had to do with the search for a home.[2]

Although finding the basic action is one of the director's most important tasks and sharing it with her cast is one of her most important responsibilities, the actor, if he is to be a creative artist in his own right, needs to understand the meaning of the play through his own efforts. Only then can they be certain that it is *theirs,* that it has possessed every fiber of their imagination. How do they discover this basic meaning, the wellspring of their characterization?

The meaning of a play cannot be determined solely from a study of its events. Story is rarely the unique feature of a dramatic work, for essentially the same story may be used to express a variety of meanings. People who are interested only in the "story" of a play are missing a good deal of its value, and a production that offers the audience nothing more than story is realizing only a part of its possibilities.

The story of *Hamlet,* as long and complex as it is, can be summarized in five sentences. Prince Hamlet has suffered the loss of his father only two months before his mother's marriage to his uncle. A ghost, whom he does not fully trust, informs the young prince that his uncle murdered his father. Unable to act until he discovers the truth, Hamlet "feigns" insanity as he furthers his investigation. Once he proves his premonition correct, the young prince exacts revenge on his father's murderer. In the end, all the principal characters die, leaving Fortinbras to "pick up the pieces." Simple, right? In fact, if this story is all the play offers, it cannot be distinguished from half the classic tragedies ever written.

Even a cursory reading of this most brilliant play will reveal the importance of a second dramatic element — character. Hamlet is an infinitely complex character, filled with frustration, wit, contradiction, and courage. Over the past four centuries, the most brilliant scholars have tried to understand his multifaceted relationships with his dead father, Gertrude, Ophelia, Claudius, and his comrades. These are complicated human beings — people, no matter their station in life, with whom we relate. We feel their joy, their pain, their desires, their frustrations, and their sense of revenge. We are engaged with their stories, but we bond with the individuals.

Story and character combine to form plot, and these two elements working in concert with each other allow the dramatist to make an observation on life. We have emphasized many times that revealing this super-objective is the actor's basic purpose on stage.

What observation did Shakespeare make in *Hamlet?* The play cannot be merely the story of a son's revenge. The story is not simply "a play dealing with the effect of a mother's guilt upon her son," as suggested by T. S. Eliot.[3] Such a story has little point unless it is directed toward some further end. What purpose does the action of the play serve? Of course, we become engaged by the story and empathize with the needs and emotions of the characters, but that does not relieve us from the responsibility of trying to determine the playwright's purpose, the super-objective. To be significant, any production must attempt to make clear the playwright's observations as interpreted by the artists associated with that particular performance.

Following this reasoning, the super-objective in *Hamlet,* according to Edward Gordon Craig, is the story of "man's search for the truth."[4] Sophocles' *Oedipus Rex,* on the other hand, attempts to show us an arrogant, blind, and godless "search for wisdom." Euripides' *The Bacchae* tells the story of the consequence of disobedience to the gods through the basic conflict between Pentheus and Dionysus. Thus, the super-objective may be stated as "the necessity for obedience to the gods."

Regardless of the play on which you are working, once you discover the super-objective, you must be unwavering in your commitment to this major purpose. All the events leading to the play's climax must serve this end. Your single and steadfast goal will be to clearly communicate this meaning to the spectators, for the through-line of action is complete only after the audience absorbs its significance.

The next step in interpreting the script is for the actors (and the director) to determine the basic action that grows out of its meaning, for it is this action that provides the play's dramatic conflict and through which playwrights make clear their message. Harold Clurman referred to this overarching action that embodies the meaning as the **spine.** It serves as a constant guide to the director and the actors, because it is the unifying factor for the super-objective of the entire play. To illustrate this concept, we shall examine *Romeo and Juliet,* relating the spine to the super-objective.

The play opens with a violent outbreak of the rivalry between the Montagues and the Capulets. Starting with a comic quarrel between the servants of the two houses, it next involves Benvolio and Tybalt (the younger generation), and finally the old men themselves, old Capulet calling for his sword and old Montague calling Capulet a villain. They are restrained from combat only by the jibes and pleadings of their wives. Only when the prince of Verona arrives does this unseemly brawl come to an end. It is a nasty fight, and it disgusts us with its violence and its pointlessness.

In subsequent scenes we see the Capulets and the Montagues not as enemies but as parents. We see they are not ogres but concerned parents, the Montagues with finding the cause of Romeo's depression and the Capulets with finding a suitable husband for Juliet. We wonder about this mixture of filial concern and violent hatred; that we first see Romeo and Juliet in relation to their parents is significant to understanding the play.

The conflict develops rapidly. In quick succession we see the meeting of the lovers, the balcony scene (death to Romeo if he should be discovered), the marriage, the killing of Mercutio and Tybalt, Romeo's banishment, and the death of the lovers in the tomb. We glory in the greatness of their love, but we loathe the senseless "canker'd hate" that brought about their tragedy. We are filled with wonder at their sacrifice and grateful that the ancient rivalry has ended. But how unnecessary! The parents are left with golden statues instead of living children, and they are faced with a realization of the awful price Romeo and Juliet have paid.

What is Shakespeare attempting to say with this story? What is the play's super-objective? It can probably be stated in some embodiment of the old bromide, "love conquers all." If we communicate it clearly, the audience should be sickened by the hatred between the families and rejoice for the love that overcame such bitterness. We want them to know that cankered hate brings tragedy and suffering and that it must ultimately yield to the force of love. The play's spine—the basic action that embodies the meaning we have just interpreted—could be stated as "to overcome all obstacles in the path of love." A production that uses this spine to guide the actors and the director throughout rehearsals and performance could provide an unforgettable experience for the audience.

To further demonstrate the concept of the spine and its relation to the super-objective, we shall look quickly at two additional classical plays. In Aristophanes' wildly popular comedy, *Lysistrata,* we may reveal the super-objective, "a feminine consciousness in a world dominated by men is the only means to solving major conflicts" by unveiling the play's spine, "sexual ritual has the power to domesticate the primitive energy found in war." In the world of *Lysistrata,* the "happy idea" is that women are on top. If mothers ran the world, he is saying, war would not exist. The late medieval play, *Everyman,* embodies the anxieties of its age, a time when people seemed more preoccupied with death and the afterlife than with life itself. In this play, however, the author, who remains anonymous, was attempting to show a successful journey to death that parallels what a successful journey through life should be (the spine). Therefore, the super-objective is not "how to die well" but rather "how to live well." "For after death amends may no man make."

Beginning actors sometimes have a mistaken notion that careful analysis destroys spontaneity. This attitude is difficult to defend. Acting, like any other art, is a conscious process. Spontaneity is fruitful only after careful study directs it toward the accomplishment of a purpose. The resistance to analysis may be especially strong in the case of comedy, where it is natural for the actor to assume that the purpose is simply to "be funny." Actually, a dramatist's basic intention is no different in comedy than in the so-called serious types of drama; the difference, if any, lies in the treatment. Successful actors accept without question the responsibility to know the meaning and spine of every play they undertake.

Assuming a Dual Personality

In discharging their responsibility of communicating the play to an audience, actors assume a dual personality. Figuratively, they split themselves into two parts. One part is the actor in the character, and up to now this has been our primary concern. The other part remains outside the character as a **commentator;** continually pointing out the significance of each action in relation to the total meaning of what the character is doing and saying.

The actor should never "lose himself in the part." George Bernard Shaw's maxim is frequently quoted: "The one thing not forgivable in an actor is being the part instead of playing it." Shaw would have stated the case more accurately if he had said: "In addition to being the part, the actor must also play it"; then his statement would warn against losing oneself yet recognize the necessity of the divided personality.

Let us state the actors' twofold function again. They must create the character, yet to make their creation fully express the dramatist's observation, they must also find a way to tell the audience what the dramatist (and, very possibly, what they themselves) thinks and feels about the character's behavior. This subtle finishing touch to developing a characterization often marks the difference between a work of art and merely playing a role. All great actors find a way to provide this *comment* without detracting in the least from the believability of their performance. *If such comment is handled well, it allows the audience to glimpse inside the mind of both the actor and the playwright.*

The actor-as-commentator must help the audience understand her character's basic impulses. The actor must guide the audience in forming an opinion of her character. By this means, actors lead the audience to an understanding of the super-objective of the entire play. The comment may say that a character is weak but essentially good, that although it may not be possible to approve of their actions, they are entitled to sympathetic understanding. It may say that another character is vain and selfish, undeserving of sympathy, and that still another is living fully and happily according to sound principles.

The comment comes from the omniscience of the actor who knows the character better than the character knows himself. In life, people rarely psychoanalyze their neuroses, their obsessions, and their fears. People who we might describe as "misfits" certainly would not see themselves in that way. Most individuals whom we deem insane consider themselves to be normal. Hamlet, perhaps more than any other character in dramatic literature, attempts to analyze himself, but does he (the character) ever understand his actions as completely as the actor portraying the role? Do young Romeo and Juliet fully understand their emotions and actions? The actor, through analysis, must objectively recognize his character's inner and outer being and clearly communicate it to the audience by emphasizing certain details of behavior.

Actors must commit themselves to expressing the playwright's intention. To make the audience dislike a character whom the playwright intended to be received with sympathy would alter essential values. Obviously it would be very wrong in our interpretation of *Romeo and Juliet* for the long-standing feud to seem justified and the love between the two young people to be seen as a breach of family loyalty. As a result of their comment, the actors will set the beauty and rightness of their love in contrast with the ugliness and wrongness of the obstacles against it.

Aware of her dual personality, a part of the actor's preparation is to decide how her performance can best express the meaning of the play and whether her comment should be made obvious or subtly detectable. Remember that actors must always behave truthfully in imaginary circumstances. The idea of truth remains constant, but the world of the play drastically affects the actor's commentary and the relative size of her character and subsequent actions. The imaginary world of some plays is very similar to our own world—"the mirror up to nature." Other characters live in a nightmare, whereas some survive in a post-apocalyptic world where nothing exists outside their immediate surroundings. In some plays, it is perfectly logical for a character to break into song and dance, whereas many other plays create a world in which characters speak in verse. Regardless, once the singular reality has been clearly defined by the playwright, the director, and designers, it remains for the acting company to behave truthfully in that specific imaginary world.

In your analysis, you must be careful never to "pigeonhole" a play. As artists, we must not make sweeping statements regarding periods, playwrights, and genres. Is it correct to say that all classical Greek plays have the same structure? Do all the plays of Ben Jonson really resemble those of William Shakespeare? With close inspection, we may identify structural parallels; however, the differences greatly outweigh the similarities. Every extant Greek tragedy is unique, just as every Elizabethan play is distinct. In actuality, the process of categorizing periods and playwrights into genres is merely an academic exercise that many artists see as ludicrous. Every play has its own reality. Each production paints an entirely new world. The theatre belongs to the theatre. There is no one style, no one method of interpretation, and no one point of view. The legendary Max Reinhardt wrote, "It would be a theory as barbaric as it is incompatible with the principles of theatrical art, to measure with the same yardstick, to press into the same mold, the wonderful wealth of the world's literature."[5] To label a playwright's approach may stifle the creative process. Every play must have its own voice. All art must have its own distinct style.

Nevertheless, actors must understand the basic structural differences between dramatic genres—academic as these labels are. Because student actors are as likely to be working with an Elizabethan tragedy as with a modern comedy, we must at least discern some of the overall and rather general demands they are likely to encounter.

The approach to the internal and external preparation of a role is essentially the same for all plays, no matter the period and no matter the genre with which it has been "lumped." Performance choices will definitely vary, depending on the extent to which the audience is allowed to be aware of the actor-as-commentator and the extent to which the actors are allowed to show their awareness of the audience. When a production labels itself as realistic or illusionistic, it is more than likely based on the tradition of the proscenium theatre, which presupposes an invisible "fourth side" through which the audience sees the actors but through which the actor must not seem to see the audience. When viewing plays produced in this tradition, audiences should have the impression that they are privileged to observe the action on stage, but that it would go on in the same way whether they were there or not. This concept of theatre is called *representational,* because the actor is attempting to represent action as it happens in life. Actors make no direct contact with their observers because to do so would destroy the illusion. Any adjustments they make to the presence of the audience (speaking in a voice loud enough to be heard, holding their lines for the laughs, and performing actions so everyone may see them) must seem "natural" or lifelike; they must be clearly motivated by the desires of the character they are playing.

It is in this kind of theatre that another one of the actor's paradoxes is most readily apparent. He must forget the audience, yet he must always keep them in mind. He must develop a technique that allows him to immerse himself in the imaginary world of the play and, at the same time, consciously adapt to the audience that is outside this invented world. The actor makes direct contact with the other actors while he makes indirect contact with the audience, and his connection—or communion—with both is reciprocal. His relationship to the spectators is always a challenge, because the real essence of theatre is what happens between the actor and the audience.

In earlier periods and in an increasing number of contemporary plays, the approach is sometimes more *presentational,* or nonillusionistic. Instead of representing events as they would happen in life, actors frankly accept the contrived circumstances under which the plays are given. Actors present the play directly to the audience without attempting to conceal the theatrical devices they are using.

The ultimate in presentationalism is the traditional Chinese theatre, in which both the performers and their audience recognize that the conditions of the theatre are not real and consequently find no necessity for creating an illusion of reality. An actor astride a pole suffices as a general on horseback. The property person sits at the side in full view and provides hand props as the actor needs them. The magic of the Chinese theatre comes from the formal manner in which it presents truthful observations of life without attempting to represent life. Chinese actors distinguish to a much greater extent than we do the difference between *truth* and *actuality*.

In some respects the classic plays—the plays of Sophocles and Shakespeare and Sheridan and Molière—are closer to the Chinese theatre than to the more modern illusionistic stage. They are presentational, in that they do not attempt to represent life in a realistic environment. They are not as theatrical as the Chinese plays are with their visible property people, but they permit the actor a greater frankness in recognizing the presence of the audience. Soliloquies may allow the actors to speak their characters' thoughts directly to the house, and "asides" may allow them to comment freely on the action of the play, although it is important to note that both are done *in character*. Some modern plays provide an interesting mixture of representational and presentational theatre. As an example, consider the following stage direction from Robert Patrick's play, *Kennedy's Children:*

> Wanda leans back wearily, checks the time on her travel alarm, puts her pencil down, and begins to speak. As with all the characters in the play, it is her thoughts we are hearing, and we have come in not at the beginning, but in the flow of an endless stream of revery. In no way does any character ever acknowledge the fact that another is speaking.[6]

Her actions, her attention to detail, are clearly taken directly from the realistic, representational, theatre. Speaking her thoughts is just as clearly a presentational technique.

One of the most exciting aspects of the contemporary theatre is that it has opened the door to plays and performances that establish almost every conceivable relationship, both social and physical, between the actor and the audience. One example is improvisational theatre, in which the actors create their own play, often attempting to include the audience in the improvisation. Other similar approaches are often termed *environmental theatre* or *alternative theatre*. Augusto Boal, an infectiously enthusiastic teacher and director from Brazil who is committed to this approach to performance, describes it as: "*theatre* in [the] most archaic application of the word. In this usage, all human beings are Actors (they act!) and Spectators (they observe!). They are Spect-Actors."[7]

Performers in this kind of theatre often advocate a social cause they strongly believe in and just as often do not create characters. Their technique is to reach the audience directly in their own persons, a method frequently called nonacting. Physical relationships are equally varied; performers often come into the aisles and walk between the rows of spectators, talking to them directly on a person-to-person basis. Other times they work in large open rooms, "found spaces," in which the differentiation between the space used for performance and the space used for the audience is blurred if not totally erased. Because a major objective is to break down any barrier between actor and audience, this concept minimizes the duality of the actor.

Summary

Every script and every production demands differences in acting, but they rarely are mutually exclusive. In improvisational and "nonacted" theatre, some sequences always present an opportunity for actors to behave in accordance with imaginary circumstances. In the most realistic play, on the other hand, the actors are always to some degree visible within the characters, and the audience responds to the actors as performers as well as to the behavior of the characters they have created. In addition, the actors play their roles to express the total meaning of the play; that is, they shape their characters to point out this meaning. We have termed this "shaping," this relationship the actors establish with the audience while commenting. Sometimes the actors figuratively hold up the characters to the audience for them to ridicule and enjoy. They themselves enjoy the ridiculousness of the characters, and they have a keen sense of sharing their enjoyment. Sometimes the comment is subtle, in which case the audience is never consciously aware of it. Sometimes the comment is obvious.

The idea of the actor's dual personality may seem hopelessly complicated and obtuse, but in reality it is not. *Good actors completely understand the world of the play; they incorporate the appropriate level of commentary into their characters and behave truthfully in their imaginary reality.* Regardless of the level of comment, the dramatic genre, or the production's individual style, the actors' job remains the same: to convince the audience that they are who they pretend to be, that what they are doing and saying is what they ought to be doing and saying, and that how they are doing and saying it is in keeping with the play and the demands of the production. Acting is believing. When the actor believes, the audience believes.

EXERCISE   **1.** Return to one of the plays you studied in a previous chapter, and determine the spine and super-objective of entire play. State the meaning briefly and clearly.

           2. List your character's traits that are important to the total meaning, and decide to what extent you might need to comment on them to make that meaning clear.

Notes

1. Constantin Stanislavski, *An Actor Prepares* (New York: Theatre Arts Books, 1936), pp. 256–258.

2. Harold Clurman, "The Principles of Interpretation," in *Producing the Play,* ed. John Gassner (New York: Holt, Rinehart, 1941), p. 277.

3. John Dover Wilson, "Mr. T. S. Eliot's Theory of Hamlet," in *What Happens in Hamlet* (Cambridge: University Press, 1970), p. 305.

4. Harold Clurman, "The Principles of Interpretation," p. 277.

5. Max Reinhardt, "*Regie* Book of *The Miracle*," *Max Reinhardt and His Theatre,* ed. Oliver M. Sayler (New York: Brentano's, 1924), pp. 64–65.

6. Robert Patrick, *Kennedy's Children* (New York: Random House, 1973), p. 5.

7. Augusto Boal, *Games for Actors and Non-Actors,* trans. Adrian Jackson (London and New York: Routledge, 1992), p. xxx. Italics in the original.

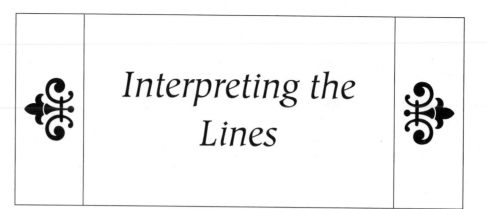

CHAPTER 11

Interpreting the Lines

Interpretation of the lines begins with your first reading of the script and doesn't stop until the lights fade on the final performance. One of your prime responsibilities is to communicate the dramatist's lines to the audience. Line interpretation coincides with your exploration and discovery of your character's motivating force and the super-objective of the entire play. At the same time you are "discovering the physical actions," you must dissect each line of the play, exploring every possible meaning.

The basis for effective interpretation is a good voice. The effectiveness and range of actors largely depends on their ability to use their voices and shape their speech. Vocal training greatly improves the actor's effectiveness. We have stated before that one of our basic assumptions is that all serious actors will undertake organized voice training at the same time they are studying the principles of acting proclaimed by this book.

The past few decades have seen a tremendous increase in the number of master voice teachers specializing in the problems of the actor. Primarily through the influence of such seminal thinkers and teachers as Arthur Lessac, Edith Skinner, and Kristin Linklater, the training of the actor's voice (as well as his body) is considered a continual and fundamental priority in good acting programs everywhere. These teachers have shown that, assuming the absence of physiological defects, no voice is so poor that it will not respond to proper training and that no voice is so fine that it could not be better if given the advantage of proper exercise. Whatever program of voice training actors undertake, they should try to accomplish several objectives. For instance, in training their voices, they should seek to acquire:

1. *Volume,* so the actors' voices may be heard without difficulty. On stage, even quiet, intimate scenes must be heard in the rear of the theatre. Jerzy Grotowski emphasized this objective: "Special attention should be paid to the carrying power of the voice so that the spectator not only hears the voice of the actor perfectly, but is also penetrated by it as if it were stereophonic."[1]

2. *Relaxation,* so their voices will not tire unduly during a long performance and so they will not involuntarily raise their pitch during climactic scenes. Relaxation means that the column of air carrying the sound flows freely and is not constricted by tension in the throat or the jaw. Voice tension creates undesirable empathic responses in the audience, impairs the actors' expressiveness, and can cause permanent damage to their vocal mechanisms.

3. *Quality* that is pleasant to hear and capable of expressing varying emotional states. A voice that is pleasant to hear is one of the actor's most prized attributes and is to a large extent a matter of resonance.

4. *Flexibility,* so their voices are capable of a variety of volumes, qualities, and pitches. A good voice is capable of adapting to a large range of demands with maximum ease.

5. *Energy,* so the voice commands attention and makes others want to listen. It is especially important to guard against a habit (common among young actors) of "fading out"—letting the energy diminish—at the ends of grammatical units. In speaking, as in golf or tennis, one must learn to "follow through."

Speech training should improve:

1. *Articulation,* so the actor can be readily understood, even in passages requiring rapid speech. Although not all characters are articulate, all actors must be. Good articulation, achieved primarily through careful attention to forming the consonants, is essential to clear speech. A story is told of a very great British actress who evaluated the work of an aspiring student with the comment, "Poor dear, no consonants."

2. *Pronunciation* that is free from slovenliness and provincial influences. This objective is becoming increasingly important. Television and motion pictures that reach audiences all over the country cannot use actors whose speech identifies them with a particular region, unless regional speech is essential to the character they are playing. Absolute absence of colloquial speech is necessary for classic plays, which emphasize the universality of the characters, not their individual idiosyncrasies.

3. *Artful control of tempo and rate* to convey satisfactorily the psychological and physiological connotations of human discourse. Perhaps no other factor of speech relates so closely to the actors' sensitivity to the complexities of their material. Tempo also is established by proper cue pickup so the performance moves at a pace appropriate to that of the audience's comprehension.

Most of the notable vocal training techniques we have recommended quite rightly focus on these aspects of voice and speech. Interpreting the character's lines falls more in the realm of acting technique; therefore, we shall consider that subject at this point in our overview. The art of interpretation, meaning what the actor expresses and why, is a necessary part of the study of acting, no matter what vocal training technique one uses.

In earlier chapters we noted that characters speak for the same reason that they act—to satisfy some basic desire. The question always in the actors' minds as they seek to interpret their lines is "Why do the characters say what they say at this particular moment?"

Exploring the Subtext

"Words are pig shit," declared Antonin Artaud. *You cannot act words. Words have no meaning.* When Polonius asks, "What do you read, my lord?" Hamlet responds with, "Words, words, words." **Subtext** gives meaning to your words. Stanislavski often proclaimed, "Without subtext, there is no theatre." Just as *subtext of behavior* defines the characters' actions, *subtext of words* underlies their every sound. Subtext influences everything on stage. It is the reason we go to the theatre. Subtext makes your words distinct. It colors your meaning, making it unique and unrepeatable. Every sound you utter must have a specific internal justification. Subtext allows you to transform a phrase into a verbal action by supplying this justification.

To find the subtext of words, you must discover a character's motivation beneath her lines. In seeking this motivation, you must consider (1) how a line helps your character accomplish her simple objective and (2) how a line relates to its context, especially to the preceding line. A line that does not help your character accomplish her purpose will be one of those details that Stanislavski said will stand out as "superfluous or wrong." A line that is not related to its context will baffle the audience because it will seem pointless and illogical.

The real significance of a line rarely is in the meaning of the words themselves or in the literal information they convey. Such a simple dialogue as

A: What time is it?

B: Eleven.

has no dramatic significance until the meaning beneath the lines is known. Why does one character ask the time? What is in the other character's mind when he answers?

These words can convey a number of different meanings, depending on the circumstances under which they are spoken. If Character A were on death row awaiting execution, the lines might mean

A: How much longer?

B: 'Bout an hour.

If the characters were listening to a dull and seemingly endless lecture, the lines might mean

A: Shoot me. I'm in hell.

B: It's almost over.

If the characters were "making out" in the back of a car, the lines might mean

A: I gotta go home.

B: It's early.

Or if the characters were preparing an important presentation, the meaning might be

A: We still okay?

B: Oh, my god. We missed our appointment.

As an actor, you must know and think your character's subtext, as it flows like an underground river just beneath the surface. Sometimes the text and subtext coincide or agree; however, you must always search for conflict between them. Conflict between what the character thinks and what he says creates drama. Stanislavski believed, "Contradiction between the text and the subtext makes the word unexpected, vivid, and significant."[2] As illustrated above, with any given line, there exists an opposite meaning, an undercurrent. Always playing the literal translation of a word is dull. Look for alternatives. Search for opposites. Human beings do not always say what they think. They tell "little white lies." They exaggerate. They deceive. Subtext clarifies the story for the audience; however, keeping them off guard by exploring opposites keeps them interested. It deepens their experience. Contradiction also helps engage other characters in strong transactions. Remember what we said about mystery and secrets. It is through unpredictable subtext that you must attempt to affect the behavior of other characters in the scene and to add color and meaning to your performance.

Your success in communicating your personal interpretation of a role lies to a very considerable extent in your choice of subtext. You must speak the text that the dramatist has written, but the subtext is your own contribution. It demonstrates your insight into the role and sensitivity to the play. Subtext is grounded in the motivating force and in the simple objectives of the units, both of which have been explored in the last few chapters. In fact, subtext is the vehicle through which imagination and interpretation connect with performance.

An example of how subtext affects meaning (in this case not just of a single speech but of an entire play) is Katharina's famous "advice" at the end of *The Taming of the Shrew,* in which she describes the responsibilities of a dutiful wife. Katharina is a headstrong, willful woman who has been "tamed" by and wed to Petruchio. He wants to complete the taming by having Katharina show her obedience at the wedding banquet. With one choice of subtext, the speech makes it plain that he has brought Katharina to submission. With another choice, we know she is not tamed at all but has learned to carry on the battle of the sexes in a more subtle way. For this second choice, Petruchio's response—his inner monologue while she is speaking—also has a significant effect on the total meaning. If he does not understand her subtext but takes the words for their surface value, the tables will have been turned completely, and it will now be Katharina who will dominate their relationship. If, on the other hand, he understands her subtext, even though the other characters do not, he and Katharina will clearly have a lively marriage.

In *The Zoo Story,* by Edward Albee, the confrontation between Jerry and Peter over a park bench leads to Jerry's suicide. The opening moment of the play demonstrates how important a clear subtext is to its successful performance. As the play begins, Peter is seated on a bench reading a book. Jerry's objective in his opening line, "I've been to the zoo. I said I've been to the zoo. *MISTER, I'VE BEEN TO THE ZOO!"* is more than "to become louder until he notices me." That would distort the author's purpose and create a willful, self-centered hoodlum who might frighten Peter immediately and cause him to leave. Instead, the actor playing Jerry wants to keep Peter there, so his subtext must include the pain and desperation of a person at the end of his rope. What Jerry thinks is as important as what he says.

Stanley's subtext in the scene with Lulu from *The Birthday Party,* by Harold Pinter, prepares the audience for the visit by the mysterious Goldberg and McCann. If his reason for refusing to leave the house is not specific and substantial, the word games with Lulu and his offer to take her anywhere will lose all importance. The actor must know that Stanley is in danger and that his options of hiding in the house or running away are ways of avoiding a dreaded confrontation. The net result of the scene would be mere mental gymnastics without the underpinning of fear, which can be established only through subtext.

In *Cat on a Hot Tin Roof,* Maggie is determined to have a child by Brick. The child is an economic necessity, but a Maggie whose subtext is based only on her own survival becomes a shrew, which is not the playwright's intention. Maggie is also full of positive life force, and her desire to achieve security is reinforced by her honest caring for Brick. If the actress misses this love, the pain of Brick's rejection would be hollow and unmoving. If we are to care for Maggie, the subtext has to contain the love along with the ambition.

People go to the theatre to "hear" the subtext; they can read the text in greater comfort at home.

EXERCISE   A helpful exercise is to find different subtexts for the same line and to speak the subtext immediately after you have said the text. You can create your own simple lines, but here are two examples to get you started:

> Don't go. (I command you to stay.)
> Don't go. (Please stay if you care anything about me.)
> Don't go. (It's not safe for you to go out now.)
> Don't go. (I warn you, you'll be sorry if you leave me.)

> I love you. (But not in the way you want me to.)
> I love you. (If you force me to say it, I will.)
> I love you. (How can you treat me this way?)
> I love you. (I don't ever want you to doubt it.)

Find at least two possible subtexts for each of the following lines. Speak each line, followed by your first choice of subtext. Then speak it without the second choice, making clear its different meaning. Have a partner or the entire class check your success.

I hate your guts.	Thanks.
You're beautiful.	You're late.
Fine.	Baby.
Get out.	Liar.
You shouldn't have.	Wow.
Sorry.	Kiss me.
Don't cry.	You're insane.

The above examples should make it clear that finding the subtext of a line is not the same as paraphrasing it or restating the words of the author in the words of the actor. Paraphrasing may be necessary when surface meaning is not immediately clear; indeed, you may find it especially worthwhile to restate in your own words the lines of a verse play. But the paraphrase will not tell you what is beneath the line and how it relates to the dramatic action and to the character's motivating force. Finding the subtext begins with understanding the character's purpose in saying the line.

Finding the Verbal Action

The interpretation of words is **verbal action.** You must use the words, expressing your inner life and attitude through every utterance. Verbal action is stronger than physical action. It is the drive, the purpose, behind every line. It is the means by which you communicate your inner relationship with yourself, your partners, and your world. The inner images stirred by your words can make an entire audience jump with fright or howl with excitement. Verbal action is the path with which to accomplish your objectives.

In the above example, when A asks, "What time is it?" meaning "How much longer?" the verbal action is to hold back the time. When the character means "Shoot me. I'm in hell." the verbal action is to get out of a dull lecture or to make the time go faster. And when A means "I gotta go home." or "We still okay?" the inherent action is to sound an alert.

To summarize, then, the significance of a line is not on the surface but beneath it; the real meaning is found in the subtext, for it provides the justification, motivation, and interpretation behind the role. When you speak a line, you must think simultaneously of the words you are saying, their subtext, and their inherent verbal action.

Let us illustrate this crucial point with examples from Oscar Wilde's famous satire on snobbery, *The Importance of Being Earnest.* When the haughty Lady Bracknell speaks slightingly of the family background of Cecily Cardew, Cecily's guardian, Jack Worthing, replies,

> Miss Cardew is the granddaughter of the late Mr. Thomas Cardew of
> 149 Belgrave Square, S.W.; Gervase Park, Dorking, Surrey; and the
> Sporran, Fifeshire, N.B.

To give the addresses of Mr. Thomas Cardew's three residences is not Jack's purpose. Rather, the subtext is

> My ward is a person of excellent family connections that may be quite
> as acceptable in English society as are your own, Lady Bracknell!

The verbal action is to put Lady Bracknell in her place.

Earlier, Jack has been informed that Lady Bracknell hardly approves of him either. He says, "May I ask why not?" His subtext is, "I am sure I don't see why she doesn't approve of me. I am every bit as good as she is." His verbal action is to assert his equality.

Linda Blase

Figure 11.1 A scene from *Crumbs from the Table of Joy* at the Dallas Theater Center. Words and silences are frequently stronger than physical action.

The choice of the subtext determines to a considerable degree the overall effect of a line—whether it will be comic, pathetic, or melodramatic. These lines from *The Importance of Being Earnest* are, of course, comic. Their subtexts must help point up the ridiculous seriousness with which the characters take themselves.

Relating the Lines to the Motivating Force

The subtext and the verbal action, both significant in interpreting a line, do not by themselves disclose its significance. You determine this by relating the meaning to your motivating force. By understanding how each line serves to help the character get what she wants, you will have a better chance of making the motivating force clear to the audience.

Although, in any circumstances, the character may be motivated in one of several ways, you must make a clear and unequivocal commitment to a motivating force before you can give a line its full value. Recall the situation in which A is on death row. The actor might decide that the condemned person feels only the primal urge to live, that he is hoping for a reprieve from the governor, or even hoping blindly for a miracle. With such a motivating force, his asking for the time will be essentially a cry for help. He might also decide that the person has accepted his death as inevitable, in which case his motivating force might be "to seek redemption," and his line might be a plea for more time in which "to make atonement." Another interpretation might be that even at the point of death, the person was filled with the same bitterness that led him to commit the crime and was determined to give no one the satisfaction of seeing any sign of remorse. In this case, the line would strengthen his motivating force "to refrain from making any repentance." In any case, once your motivating force has been decided, you must stick to it and follow it wherever it takes you as you interpret the lines.

Confusion often arises from the use of a variety of terms to describe the actor's relationship to the role and the relationship of the role to the whole play. For clarity, let us review the definitions of those terms as we use them:

1. *Motivating force* is the character's long-range goal. It gives the character a sufficient reason to pursue the course of action demanded by the play.

2. *Super-objective* is the theme or basic line of the play and is synonymous with its *spine*. In this context it is a directional term. The motivating force of each role (sometimes referred to as the character's super-objective) must be compatible with the super-objective of the entire play.

3. The *through-line of action* is the progressive movement from one *unit* of the play to the next. It assumes a series of consistent and logical actions, a pattern of behavior that is the route an actor takes to her character's motivating force. The attempt to fulfill the objectives of the character against a series of

obstacles moves the play to a conclusion, and the through-line of action is the thread that links all the character's actions.

Relating the Lines to the Super-Objective

You also must know how your lines serve the super-objective and how they aid in communicating the play's central idea to the audience. This problem has been anticipated in such previous steps as (1) finding the character's motivating force—a process in which the lines were an important consideration, (2) relating this fundamental desire to the meaning of the play as a whole, and (3) finding the subtext and the verbal action, which, as we have seen, emerge only after the lines have been related to the motivating force.

After completing these steps, you will likely understand how the dramatist intended each line to aid in expressing their meaning. For example, knowing that the playwright, Jean-Paul Sartre, believed that all people are "trapped in their feeling of shame and guilt" and that he used this theme in many of his works will aid in development of each character in his classic play, *No Exit*. Sonia Moore illustrates this example.

> Like many other modern playwrights, Sartre is preoccupied with people's inability to have healthy relationships. His heroes are lonely; they need each other but are unable to approach and reach each other. Sartre's idea is that a man is always surrounded by a wall as if he were in prison. People torture themselves with constant guilt feelings and they are also tortured by the condemnation they see in the eyes of others. . . . Their attempts to break loose from this hell are really an attempt to regain their feeling of innocence. But they cannot. Dissatisfaction with oneself makes it impossible to relate to people. The hell in the play represents the world in which a man must live whether he wants to or not. Sartre believes that a man must create for himself the values to live by. It is what a man does that defines him. By creating his own values, he creates himself, or as Sartre says, finds an exit. Sartre believes that man chooses his values and makes himself.[3]

Before you can begin creating your individual role in Sartre's play, you must understand the character's feelings of isolation, feelings of guilt, his burning desire to escape, and his frustration when he discovers the futility of his actions. You will fully understand your character only if you understand the author's meaning of the entire script.

Every unit of action must be carefully examined in the context of the super-objective interpreted by each particular production. No element of the production is excused from this basic demand. The actor's task is to hold to this interpretation with an unyielding grip and to make everything she says or does flow from some variation on the theme. Actors must turn the interpretation into action, and subtext is one of their major tools for doing so.

Once again, Oscar Wilde's *The Importance of Being Earnest* can serve as a contrasting example of the problem of relating the lines to the super-objective. This play is a satire on the snobbish upper classes at the close of the nineteenth century, who sought to relieve their boredom by concentrating on inconsequentials. Wilde saw the comic possibilities in the affectations of such people, and he ridiculed them good-naturedly in this farce. The plot has to do with two young ladies whose virtually sole requirement for a husband is that his name be Ernest, a requirement that compels both Jack and Algernon to arrange to be rechristened. The actors in this play must see that their lines serve Wilde's purpose of having fun at the expense of these people.

The following dialogue drips with Jack's boredom and underscores the eagerness with which Algernon engages in trivial pursuits.

ALGERNON: . . . may I dine with you tonight at Willis's?

JACK: I suppose so, if you want to.

ALGERNON: Yes, but you must be serious about it. I hate people who are not serious about meals. It is so shallow of them.

And later:

ALGERNON: . . . Now, my dear boy, if we want to get a good table at Willis's, we really must go and dress. Do you know it is nearly seven?

JACK: Oh! It always is nearly seven.

ALGERNON: Well, I'm hungry.

JACK: I never knew you when you weren't. . . .

ALGERNON: What shall we do after dinner? Go to a theatre?

JACK: Oh no! I loathe listening.

ALGERNON: Well, let us go to the Club?

JACK: Oh, no! I hate talking.

ALGERNON: Well, we might trot round to the Empire at ten?

JACK: Oh, no! I can't bear looking at things. It is so silly.

ALGERNON: Well, what shall we do?

JACK: Nothing!

ALGERNON: It is awfully hard work doing nothing. However, I don't mind hard work where there is no definite object of any kind.

Clearly, Algernon's verbal action stands in opposition with Jack's. Algernon's objective is "to relieve his boredom," while Jack's objective is "to remain inert."

Just as actors must search for contradictions and opposites with their own lines, they must also explore contrasts with other characters. Contrast leads to conflict, and conflict is the heart of drama.

Playwrights make their basic intention clearer and stronger by using contrasting elements. In such cases, the relationship of certain characters' lines to the total meaning is one of contrast with the central theme. The meaning is thus painted more sharply, just as colors appear brighter when contrasted with other colors.

Several examples of the use of contrasting elements appear in *Romeo and Juliet*. Remember that we found its theme to be the triumph of young love over "canker'd hate." Although Romeo and Juliet both meet a tragic death, their love is triumphant. Because of it, the Montagues and the Capulets end their ancient feud, and civil brawls no longer disturb the quiet of Verona's streets.

Triumphant love is expressed throughout the play in Juliet's and Romeo's lines:

> My bounty is as boundless as the sea,
> My love is as deep — the more I give to thee
> The more I have, for both are infinite.

and

> O my love! my wife!
> Death that has suck'd the honey of thy breath
> Hath had no power yet upon thy beauty.
> Thou art not conquer'd — Beauty's ensign yet
> Is crimson in thy lips and in thy cheeks,
> And Death's pale flag is not advanced there.

The final beauty of their love is moving and memorable because it stands out in relief against the hatred of old Montague and old Capulet, the Nurse's vulgarity, Mercutio's mockery, Tybalt's malice, and Lady Capulet's coldness. The lines of these characters are related to the total meaning through contrast, and it is important that the actors understand this relationship. For instance, Romeo's romantic love seems stronger because it rises above the jibes and cynicism of Mercutio's mocking lines. Tybalt's malicious lines put Romeo's newfound love to a test and bring about the duel that causes Romeo's banishment. Throughout the play, Juliet's warmth and generosity stand out against her mother's unyielding practicality. Lady Capulet rejects Juliet with:

> Talk not to me, for I'll not speak a word,
> Do as thou wilt, for I have done with thee.

These particular lines underscore the desperation of Juliet's predicament and propel her toward her final course of action.

Although the Nurse's character is vastly different from that of Lady Capulet, she serves a similar purpose in providing dramatic contrast—her bawdiness against Juliet's sweetness and purity. Her advice to marry the Count Paris for practical reasons, when Juliet is already secretly married to the banished Romeo, is revolting to a person of Juliet's innocence:

I think it best you marry'd with the County.
O, he's a lovely gentleman!
Romeo's a dishclout to him. An eagle, madam,
Hath not so green, so quick, so fair an eye
As Paris hath. Beshrew my very heart,
I think you're happy in this second match,
For it excels your first, or if't did not
Your first is dead—or 'twere as good he were,
As living here and you no use of him.

In such instances, relating the lines to the super-objective means making them provide dramatic contrasts. Knowing when this is so and how various relationships unfold demands a complete understanding of the play as a whole. No individual line can be interpreted without a complete command of the play's global meaning. Even difficult lines will yield to honest interpretation once this meaning has been mastered.

EXERCISE   Using one of the characters you have already studied, select a sequence of lines from one unit of action. Study it carefully. For each of your character's lines, determine

1. Its subtext

2. Its verbal action

3. Its relationship to the character's motivating force

4. Its relationship to the super-objective

Write out this information, as it will complete your score of physical actions.

Believing the Character's Manner of Speaking

The lines are composed of two elements, both of which are vital:

1. The content: what the lines say, including both text and subtext.

2. The form: the manner in which the content is expressed, including vocabulary, grammar, pronunciation, and articulation.

Mark Garvin

Figure 11.2 Jenny Bacon and Brandon Demery in *Compleat Female Stage Beauty,* by Jeffrey Hatcher, produced by Philadelphia Theatre Company—Philadelphia Premiere Fall 2000. No matter how different the character's manner of speech, the actor must personalize the language, making it his or her own.

We have explored how the actor detects the content of the lines, so we shall now consider the problem of believing the manner in which the character speaks.

Different speakers may express the same meaning in a variety of ways:

1. I hope it ain't gointa rain an' spoil the picnic we was plannin' fer so long.
2. I trust inclement weather will not mar the outing we have been anticipating for such a time.

These two lines are alike in content, and their surface meanings are identical. The subtext could be the same, and both lines could bear the same relation to the speaker's motivating force. But neither is expressed in a manner that the average actor would find "natural." The actor's problem is to understand the background of the character's speech so she can believe the manner of speaking in the same way she believes in the character's actions.

For the most part, the dramatist imposes the characters' manner of speech by choosing the vocabulary and the grammar, both of which should be accepted as given circumstances by the actor. Occasionally, as a part of the externalization of their characters, actors may introduce variations in pronunciation and articulation. For instance, they might play characters with a dialect, a stammer, or "baby talk." Like all good externalizations, such characteristics should support inner traits and help both the actor and the audience believe them. Baby talk, for example, might be helpful in characterizing a woman who had been pampered by her parents and whose motivating force is to get the same attention from her husband. Such decisions about the speech of the character are subject to the same intense scrutiny as are other character externals and are justified only if they enable the actor to realize the dramatist's intentions.

Actors study their characters' speech habits in the same way they study other traits provided by the dramatist: They try to find justification for them in the play. They also may need to supply, as they did when justifying actions, imaginary circumstances true to the playwright's conception that help explain why the characters speak the way they do (see Chapter 10).

If the characters' manner of speaking is similar to the actors' or if they have frequently heard others speak in a similar way, they will have little difficulty. The speech background of Trisha, Meredith, and Frances in *Five Women Wearing the Same Dress,* by Alan Ball, is so immediately comprehensible that it presents no problem to most young American actors. The entire play takes place in Meredith's bedroom, while her sister's wedding reception is in full swing outside. The following dialogue is typical.

> TRISHA: (*Looking at her reflection in the vanity mirror.*) God, would you look at me? I look terrible.
>
> MEREDITH: You look like a million bucks, as usual.
>
> TRISHA: I had to put about a gallon of white-out underneath my eyes this morning. (*She pulls a cosmetics bag from her purse and begins to skillfully retouch her make-up. . . .*) So Frances, did you enjoy the wedding?
>
> FRANCES: Yes, it was so beautiful.
>
> MEREDITH: It was ridiculous.
>
> FRANCES: Tracy's dress sure was something.
>
> MEREDITH: Yeah, it was a float.
>
> TRISHA: You've got to hand it to her, though, she carried it off. I could never wear anything like that with a straight face.
>
> MEREDITH: She didn't wear it. It wore *her.* If she has any sense at all, she'll put it on a mannequin and just roll around the reception and leave herself free to mingle.
>
> TRISHA: I shudder to think how much that thing cost.
>
> MEREDITH: Six.

TRISHA: (*Turns to her.*) That's obscene.

FRANCES: Six hundred dollars?

MEREDITH: Six *thousand.*

TRISHA: She talked me into designing her invitations for *free,* and then she made me go through *eight* revisions, and she spent six thousand dollars on her *dress?* That is totally obscene.[4]

On the other hand, the speech in Eugene O'Neill's *Desire Under the Elms* presents a problem. Simeon and Peter, both in their thirties, are square-shouldered, homely, bovine men of the earth who live on a New England farm in 1850.

SIMEON (*grudgingly*): Purty.

PETER: Ay-eh.

SIMEON (*suddenly*): Eighteen year ago.

PETER: What?

SIMEON: Jenn. My woman. She died.

PETER: I'd fergot.

SIMEON: I rec'lect—now an' agin. Makes it lonesome. She'd hair long's a hoss' tail—an' yeller like gold!

PETER: Waal—she's gone.[5]

The average actor will find it difficult to believe this manner of speaking in terms of his own experience. The actor may have no doubt that the speech is right for the character. He may understand the regional factors that have produced this unique, musical language. Still, he is aware that his own speech is quite different, and such a disparity is not always easy to reconcile.

Regional dialect is learned over a lifetime of improper reinforcement from family and friends. It is a difficult habit to break. Many actors struggle with hearing the subtle differences of articulation, vowel placement, and speech rhythms that differ from their own. Their early efforts are often mechanical and imitative. Actors must record and listen to themselves as they try to form the sounds in accordance with the dialogue on the printed page. Some playwrights are remarkably skillful in their use of phonetic spellings to indicate speech variations. Eugene O'Neill was a master of writing dialogue phonetically; George Bernard Shaw also represented Cockney English in this way. Actors, also, may listen to recordings or imitate actual models if they are fortunate enough to know someone whose speech is similar.

If this external approach is to serve its purpose, however, it must lead the actors to believe their characters' speech. And believing the speech should, in turn, increase their belief in the characters. In other words, as the actors become convinced they have developed a true manner of speaking, they will have a greater conviction in their total characterization. Diction—the way of expressing one-self—is one of the actor's principal resources in creating a character.

Trisha, Meredith, and Frances are average upper-middle-class young women who speak in a contemporary vernacular. Simeon and Peter, on the other hand, are modest folk who use their abilities to express their thoughts and feelings as best they can, as colorful as their speech often is. As you probably recall, we meet people in *The Importance of Being Earnest* with quite a different background. Algernon Moncrieff is, by his own admission, "immensely overeducated." He speaks not only to express his ideas but also to impress his hearers with his cleverness and his aptness of phrasing. We have known for some time that speech is an action; now we see that the manner of speaking can carry with it its own dramatic intention.

All the characters in *The Importance of Being Earnest* exhibit a kind of "speech embroidery" indicative of their elegance and earnest artificiality. The following lines of Gwendolen Fairfax are an example. She is talking to Cecily Cardew, whom she has learned is Jack Worthing's ward. Gwendolen and Jack have recently become engaged.

> GWENDOLEN: Oh! It is strange he never mentioned to me that he had a ward. How secretive of him! He grows more interesting hourly. I am not sure, however, that the news inspires me with feelings of unmixed delight. (*Rising and going to her.*) I am very fond of you, Cecily; I have liked you ever since I met you! But I am bound to state that now that I know that you are Mr. Worthing's ward, I cannot help expressing a wish you were—well, just a little older than you seem to be—and not quite so very alluring in appearance. In fact, if I may speak candidly—
>
> CECILY: Pray do! I think that whenever one has anything unpleasant to say, one should always be quite candid.
>
> GWENDOLEN: Well, to speak with perfect candour, Cecily, I wish that you were fully forty-two, and more than usually plain for your age. Ernest has a strong upright nature. He is the very soul of truth and honor. Disloyalty would be as impossible to him as deception. But even men of the noblest possible moral character are extremely susceptible to the influence of the physical charms of others. Modern, no less than Ancient History, supplies us with many most painful examples of what I refer to. If it were not so, indeed, History would be quite unreadable.

Taking command of these lines will provide quite a test for young American actors. Just learning to "say" them will not be enough. They must understand the ostentation and snobbery that produced such a vocabulary and structure. Only then can they begin to believe the speech and actions of the characters, and they must believe them before they can make an adequate comment on their ridiculousness.

Believing the characters' manner of speaking is a matter of understanding the influences in their background that have determined their way of speech, of justifying the characters' speech in terms of their background. The actor is constantly faced with such questions as

- Why does one character have such an extensive vocabulary, whereas another speaks almost entirely in words of one syllable?
- Why does one character speak in long, involved sentences, whereas another speaks in halting fragments?
- Why does one character speak with faultlessly correct grammar, whereas another says "he don't," "we was," and "I seen"?
- Why does one character say "you gentlemen," whereas another says "you guys"?
- Why does one character say "yeah," whereas another says "ay-eh," and yet another says "yes"?

EXERCISE   Choose a character whose manner of speaking varies from your own. Study the speech, and practice her lines until you believe you are truthfully reproducing the character's manner of speaking. If possible, use actual models, sound recordings, or phonetic transcriptions.

Motivating the Longer Speech

So far in this discussion of interpreting the lines, we have concentrated on the importance of motivation, of relating the lines to the characters' basic desires and understanding how each line helps the characters get what they want. For the most part, we have been thinking of lines no longer than a sentence or two. Long speeches frequently pose exceptionally difficult problems of interpretation. Usually, the best way to approach them is to break such speeches into small parts, find the subtext of each segment, and relate it to the character's motivating force. In other words, long, complicated speeches should be treated as if they were a series of shorter, more manageable lines. You should avoid the temptation to motivate all speeches as a single idea. Some long, complex speeches may contain several units.

When discovering and arranging the units of a longer speech for performance, remember that each section should have a clearly stated verbal action. In many long speeches, you can easily detect the familiar, classical, three-part structure—the beginning, the middle, and the end. Other speeches may have only two parts, and still others may have five, or seven. You should never divide a speech into so many units that you cannot keep its overall pattern in mind; otherwise, it will seem to the audience to lack structure or form. Sometimes, of course, speeches are broken off, either by the speaker or by another character, before they reach a structural ending.

A speech from *Golden Boy,* by Clifford Odets, will serve as an illustration. Joe Bonaparte, on the eve of his twenty-first birthday, is telling his father he wants to break away from the restraints of home so he may have "wonderful things from life." He thinks he can find what he wants by becoming a prize fighter. But Mr. Bonaparte, a humane and kindly man, wants Joe to find happiness as a violinist and has paid a lot of money for a fine violin that he plans to give Joe for his birthday. Others present in the scene are Frank, Joe's older brother who travels about a good deal, and Mr. Carp, a neighbor who owns an *Encyclopaedia Britannica.*

MR. BONAPARTE: Sit down, Joe—resta you'self.

JOE: Don't want to sit. Every birthday I ever had I sat around. Now'sa time for standing. Poppa, I have to tell you—I don't like myself, past, present, and future. Do you know there are men who have wonderful things from life? Do you think they're better than me? Do you think I like this feeling of no possessions? Of learning about the world from Carp's encyclopaedia? Frank don't know what it means—he travels around, sees the world! (*Turning to Frank*) You don't know what it means to sit around here and watch the months go ticking by! Do you think that's a life for a boy my age? Tomorrow's my birthday! I change my life! [6]

Joe's purpose in this speech is to make his father see that he is going to change his way of life and that the change will mean a difference in their relationship. His verbal action is to break away from his home and his father. He is excited and resentful, but the speech does not come easily and he cannot say it all at once. Once said, he also feels it necessary to defend his decision. Through all this, his relationship with his father creates a psychological obstacle to every verbal action in every unit.

The speech may be divided into three structural parts:

1. Verbal action: *to assert his independence from his father.*

   Don't want to sit. Every birthday I ever had I sat around. Now'sa time for standing.

2. Verbal action: *to defend his decision to break away from his father.* This is the middle part, the development leading to the climax. Joe gives several reasons for his decision, and he plays each reason with increasing intensity:

   Poppa, I have to tell you—I don't like myself, past, present, and future. Do you know there are men who have wonderful things from life? Do you think they're better than me? Do you think I like this feeling of no possessions? Of learning about the world from Carp's encyclopaedia? Frank don't know what it means—he travels around, sees the world! (*Turning to Frank*) You don't know what it means to sit around here and watch the months go ticking by! Do you think that's a life for a boy my age?

3. Verbal action: *to defy his family*. This is the climax of the speech.

Tomorrow's my birthday! I change my life!

EXERCISE | The following speeches provide material for practice in interpreting lines. Read the plays they have been selected from, because the significance of any speech lies in its relationship to the play. Determine the motivating force of the character. Break the speech into units. Find the verbal actions. Make a score of physical actions. Memorize the speech. As you rehearse it, look for the separate motivation for each unit, and relate its meaning to the objective of the speech as a whole. If the language is different from your own, study the speech background of the character.

1. Ardell in *The Basic Training of Pavlo Hummel*, by David Rabe[7]

(*A black soldier in Vietnam watches as Private Pavlo Hummel, a victim of a hand grenade, is placed on a stretcher by the body detail.*)

ARDELL: He don't die right off. Take him four days, thirty-eight minutes. And he don't say nothin' to nobody in all that time. No words; he just kinda lay up and look, and when he die, he bitin' on his lower lip, I don't know why. So they take him, they put him in a blue rubber bag, zip it up tight and haul it off to the morgue in the back of a quarterton where he get stuck naked into the refrigerator 'long with the other boys killed that day and the beer and cheese and tuna and stuff the guys who work at the morgue keep in the refrigerator except when it inspection time. The bag get washed, hung out to dry on a line out back a the morgue. (*Slight pause.*) Then . . . lemme see, well, finally he get shipped home and his mother cry a lot and his brother get so depressed he gotta go out and lay his chippie he so damned depressed about it all; and Joanna, she read his name in the paper, she let out this little gasp and say to her husband across the table, "Jesus, Jimmy, I used to go with that boy. Oh, damn that war, why can't we have peace? I think I'll call his mother." Ain't it some kinda world? (*And he is laughing.*) Soooooooo . . . that about it. That about all I got to say. Am I right, Pavlo? Did I tell you true? You got anything to say? Oh, man, I know you do, you say it out.

2. Juanita in *Blues for Mister Charlie*, by James Baldwin[8]

(*Juanita is a black student whose lover has been senselessly murdered by a white man.*)

JUANITA: (*Rises from bed; early Sunday morning.*) He lay beside me on that bed like a rock. As heavy as a rock—like he'd fallen—fallen from a high place—fallen so far and landed so heavy, he seemed almost to be sinking out of sight—with one knee pointing to heaven. My God. He covered me like that. He wasn't at all like I thought he was. He fell on—fell on me—like life and death. My God. His chest, his belly, the rising and the falling, the moans. How he clung, how he struggled—life and death! Life and death! Why did it all seem to me like tears? That he came to me, clung to me, plunged into me, sobbing, howling, bleeding, somewhere inside his chest, his belly, and it all came out, came pouring out, like tears! My God, the smell, the touch, the taste, the sound, of anguish! Richard! Why couldn't I have held you closer? Held you, held you, borne you, given you life again? Have made you be born again! Oh, Richard. The teeth that gleamed, oh! when you smiled, the spit flying when you cursed, the teeth stinging when you bit—your breath, your hands, your weight, my God, when you moved in me! Where shall I go now, what shall I do? . . . Mama was frightened. Frightened because little Juanita brought her first real lover to this house. I suppose God does for Mama what Richard did for me. Juanita! . . . Mama is afraid I'm pregnant. Mama is afraid of so much. I'm not afraid. I hope I'm pregnant. I *hope* I am! One more illegitimate black baby—that's right you jive mothers! And I am going to raise my baby to be a man. A *man,* you dig? . . . Did this happen to Mama sometime? Did she have a man sometime who vanished like smoke? And left her to get through this world as best she could? Is that why she married my father? . . . You're going crazy, Juanita. Oh, Lord, don't let me go mad. Let me be pregnant! Let me be pregnant!

3. Sparger in *Kennedy's Children,* by Robert Patrick[9]

(*Sparger is twenty-six, described by Patrick as being "languid, dressed with personal chic," an aspiring actor. This play takes place in a New York bar. All characters speak their "thoughts" without regard to other characters. It is a play of soliloquies, so to speak. Sparger has been drinking brandy.*)

SPARGER: (*Sloppy drunk*) The fact of the matter is, I *wasn't* always like this. Maybe people just weren't meant to live in the present. Meant? By whom? Who cares? Sure, I used to live in the present. According to science we all used to live underwater, too. But we adapted! We just haven't adapted to the present yet. Not till we grow asbestos filters in our nostrils. And learn to live on monosodium glutamate. And survive six inches of steel shoved up us in every other doorway. And ignore the pangs of dread and empathy and guilt that *paralyze* us whenever we see some human being, reduced to a lump of mucus, come wobbling towards us with his ragged, flaking hand held out, muttering and blubbering and slobbering, "Help me! Help me! Help me! For God's sake, somebody please help me!" Uh-oh. I'm thinking about things I don't want to think about. I'm too drunk too early. I'm trying to stay off drugs. I haven't got anything left to stop up the back of my brain, and I'm having a memory hemorrhage! I can't help it! I can't stop it! I'm remembering it all again! I'm remembering! I'm having an attack of the truth! It's coming at me, and it *is* me, the truth, the truth, I'm sitting here in a public place, seeping and sopping and soaking and reeking with truth. And the end—the end—the end of truth—is *death!* (*He runs off urgently to the mens' room.*)

4. Edmund in *Long Day's Journey into Night*, by Eugene O'Neill [10]

(*Even though he has tuberculosis and is soon to go to a sanatorium, Edmund has been walking late at night on the beach. He also has been drinking, and his father has just told him he should have more sense. Edmund is bitter because he blames his father for an intensely unhappy family situation.*)

EDMUND: To hell with sense! We're all crazy. What do we want with sense?
(*He quotes from Dowson sardonically.*)

"They are not long, the weeping and the laughter,
Love and desire and hate:
I think they have no portion in us after
We pass the gate.

They are not long, the days of wine and roses:
Out of a misty dream
Our path emerges for a while, then closes
Within a dream."

(*Staring before him.*) The fog was where I wanted to be. Halfway down the path you can't see this house. You'd never know it was here. Or any of the other places down the avenue. I couldn't see but a few feet ahead. I didn't meet a soul. Everything looked and sounded unreal. Nothing was what it is. That's what I wanted—to be alone with myself in another world where truth is untrue and life can hide from itself. Out beyond the harbor, where the road runs along the beach, I even lost the feeling of being on land. The fog and the sea seemed part of each other. It was like walking on the bottom of the sea. As if I had drowned long ago. As if I was a ghost belonging to the fog, and the fog was the ghost of the sea. It felt damned peaceful to be nothing more than a ghost within a ghost. (*He sees his father staring at him with mingled worry and irritated disapproval. He grins mockingly.*) Don't look at me as if I'd gone nutty. I'm talking sense. Who wants to see life as it is, if they can help it? It's the three Gorgons in one. You look in their faces and turn to stone. Or it's Pan. You see him and you die—that is, inside you—and have to go on living as a ghost.

5. Isabel in *My Children! My Africa!*, by Athol Fugard [11]

ISABEL: Oh I see. This is meant to be a "sad" good-bye is it? (*She is on the edge.*) I'm sorry if I'm hurting your feelings but I thought you wanted to see me because you had something to say about recent events in our little community . . . (*She takes a crumpled little piece of newspaper out of her pocket and opens it with unsteady hands.*) a certain unrest-related . . . I think that is the phrase they use . . . yes . . . here it is . . . (*Reading.*) ". . . unrest-related incident in which according to witnesses the defenseless teacher was attacked by a group of blacks who struck him over the head with an iron rod before setting him on fire." . . . the day after it happened I tried to get into the location. I wanted to find the witnesses who reported it so accurately and ask them: "Why didn't you stop it!" There was a police roadblock at the entrance and they wouldn't let me in. They thought I was crazy or something and "escorted" me back into the safekeeping of two now very frightened parents. There is nothing wrong with me! All I need is someone to tell me why he was killed. What madness drove those people to kill a man who had devoted his whole life to helping them? He was such a good man Thami! He was one of the most beautiful human beings I have ever known and his death is one of the ugliest things I have ever known.

6. Carol in *Oleanna*, by David Mamet [12]

(*Carol, a young woman of twenty, accuses her college professor of sexist, demeaning, and sexual assaults perpetrated on his students.*)

CAROL: How can you deny it. You did it to me. Here. You did . . . You confess. You love the power. To deviate. To invent, to transgress . . . to transgress whatever norms have been established for us. And you think it's charming to "question" in yourself this taste to mock and destroy. But you should question it. Professor. And you pick those things which you feel advance you: publication, tenure, and the steps to get them you call "harmless rituals." And you perform those steps. Although you say it is hypocrisy. But to the aspirations of your students. Of hardworking students, who come here, who slave to come here—you have no idea what it cost me to come to this school—you mock us. You call education "hazing," and from your so-protected, so-elitist seat you hold our confusion as a joke, and our hopes and efforts with it. Then you sit there and say "what have I done?" And ask me to understand that you have aspirations too. But I tell you. I tell You. That you are vile. And that you are exploitative. And if you possess one ounce of that inner honesty you describe in your book, you can look in yourself and see those things that I see. And you can find revulsion equal to my own. Good day.

7. Berniece in *The Piano Lesson,* by August Wilson [13]

(*Berniece, a thirty-five-year-old African-American with an eleven-year-old daughter and still in mourning for her husband after three years, denounces her brother's plans to sell the family's piano.*)

BERNIECE: You ain't taking that piano out of my house. (*She crosses to the piano.*) Look at this piano. Look at it. Mama Ola polished this piano with her tears for seventeen years. For seventeen years she rubbed on it till her hands bled. Then she rubbed the blood in . . . mixed it up with the rest of the blood on it. Every day that God breathed life into her body she rubbed and cleaned and polished and prayed over it. "Play something for me, Berniece. Play something for me, Berniece." Every day. "I cleaned it up for you, play something for me, Berniece." You always talking about your daddy but you ain't never stopped to look at what his foolishness cost your mama. Seventeen years' worth of cold nights and an empty bed. For what? For a piano? For a piece of wood? To get even with somebody? I look at you and you're all the same. You, Papa Boy Charles, Whining Boy, Doaker, Crawley . . . you're all alike. All this thieving and killing and thieving and killing. And what it ever lead to? More killing and more thieving. I ain't never seen it come to nothing. People getting burned up. People getting shot. People falling down their wells. It don't never stop.

8. Marie-Antoinette in *The Queen's Knight,* by Frank Cossa [14]

(*In October 1793, from her cell in Paris, the former Queen of France faces death.*)

QUEEN: I have been a prisoner of these people for four years. I watched them march to the gates of the palace and slaughter six hundred Swiss guards. I watched as all my friends were murdered or driven into exile. I watched them execute my husband who was their King. I watched them drag my children screaming from my arms so that after a year I don't know if they're alive or dead. I have lived in this room for seventy-six days. They allow me two dresses, no undergarments, no cloak, no blanket against the dampness that runs down the walls. There is never any firewood. There is always a guard outside my cell who must keep his eyes on me at all times. At all times. Some days ago the Princess de Lamballe, my last loyal friend, returned from a safe exile to be near me in my difficult time. She came here to visit me. The mob saw her and I watched them tear her to pieces. Her head was impaled on a stake and raised up to my window there. (*She points.*) One man made himself moustaches out of her private hair while the others, laughing and cheering, threw parts of her . . . her body up at me. You see, monsieur, for four years one horror has followed another. They have allowed me no comfort, no rest. They have spared me no cruelty, no shock, no terror. And you wish me to ask these people for . . . (*She turns, slowly again, to look at him.*) a favor?

9. Jeff in *Suburbia,* by Eric Bogosian [15]

(*Jeff, a 20-year-old in dark clothes of no particular style and messy hair, sits with a girl friend in darkness in front of a Seven-Eleven store philosophizing about his plight in life.*)

JEFF: Look at us. We all dress the same, we all talk the same, we all watch the same TV. No one's really different, even if they think they're different. "Oh boy, look at my tattoo!" You know? And that makes me free, because I can do anything if I really don't care what the result is. I don't need money. I don't care what the result is. I don't need money. I don't even need a future. I could knock out all my teeth with a hammer, so what? I could poke my eyes out. I'd still be alive. Strip naked and fart in the wind. At least I would know I was doing something real for two or three seconds. It's all about fear. And I'm not afraid anymore. Fuck it! (*Jeff starts disrobing.*) Because anything is possible. It is night on the planet earth and I am alive and someday I will be dead. Someday, I'll be bones in a box. But right now, I'm not. And anything is possible. And that's why I can go to New York with Sooze. Because each moment can be what it is. I'm on the train going there, I'm living there, I'm reading a newspaper, I'm walking down the street. There is no failure, there is no mistake. I just go and live there and what happens, happens. (*Down to his underwear.*) So at this moment, I am getting naked. And I am not afraid. FUCK FEAR! FUCK MONEY! I WILL GO TO NEW YORK AND I WILL LIVE IN A BOX. I WILL SING WITH THE BUMS. I WILL STARVE BUT I WILL NOT DIE. I WILL LIVE. I WILL TALK TO GOD!

10. Michael in *Two Rooms,* by Lee Blessing [16]

(*Blindfolded and sitting alone on a mat, Michael, who has been taken hostage by a militant group somewhere in Beirut, talks to his wife, Lanie, in his mind.*)

MICHAEL: (*A beat.*) War isn't a tear in the fabric of things, it is the fabric. If earth is our mother, our father is war. The chief priority we have on earth is to vie with each other for a place to stand. Does any of this make sense, Lainie? I'm trying to explain why this has happened to us. Americans fight all the time—lots of wars. But always far away. We haven't had to fight for the soil we stand on in a century. We've forgotten that level of sacrifice. These people haven't. Everyone in this country—Christian, Sunni Moslem, Shi'ite, Palestinian, Israeli—everyone is fighting for the ground. The ground itself. They stand here or nowhere. So it's easy for them to give up their lives. Small sacrifice. It's easy for them to kill, too. Small sacrifice. You know how being here, being swallowed up by it, makes me feel? Like I'm finally part of the real world. For the first time.

Lainie, something in me never felt . . . affected . . . until this happened. You know what it makes me think of? Shiloh. Vicksburg. The Wilderness. What those places must have been like: suffocating, endless, bleeding disaster. Stacking of bodies ten deep for a few feet of *our ground.* Don't you see? We're not different from these people, we've just forgotten. We think this urge doesn't exist anymore. We abstract everything, we objectify. We talk about global politics, how all this affects the balance of power. Do you know what a twenty-year-old Shi'ite thinks of the balance of power?

Notes

1. Jerzy Grotowski, *Towards a Poor Theatre* (New York: Simon & Schuster, 1968), p. 147.

2. Sonia Moore, *Stanislavski Revealed* (New York City: Applause Theatre Books, 1991), p. 125.

3. Sonia Moore, *Training an Actor: The Stanislavski System in Class* (New York: Penguin Books, 1979), pp. 238–239.

4. Alan Ball, *Five Women Wearing the Same Dress* (New York: Dramatists Play Service, Inc., 1993), p. 10.

5. Eugene O'Neill, *Desire Under the Elms* in *The Bedford Introduction to Drama,* 3rd ed., Lee A. Jacobus, ed. (Boston: Bedford Books, 1997), p. 938.

6. Clifford Odets, *Golden Boy* in *Six Plays of Clifford Odets* (New York: Grove Press, 1979), p. 252.

7. David Rabe, *The Basic Training of Pavlo Hummel and Sticks and Bones,* p. 99. Copyright © 1969, 1972, 1973 by David Rabe. Used by permission of Grove/Atlantic, Inc.

8. James Baldwin, *Blues for Mister Charlie.* Copyright © 1964 by James Baldwin. Copyright renewed. Published by Vintage books. Reprinted by arrangement with the James Baldwin Estate.

9. Robert Patrick, *Kennedy's Children,* pp. 26–27. Copyright © 1973 as an unpublished work by Robert Patrick. Copyright © 1976 by Robert Patrick. Reprinted by permission of Samuel French, Inc.

10. Eugene O'Neill, *Long Day's Journey into Night* (New Haven, CT: Yale University Press, 1956), pp. 130–131.

11. Athol Fugard, *My Children! My Africa!* (New York: Theatre Communication Group, Inc., 1989), p. 71.

12. David Mamet, *Oleanna* (New York: Dramatists Play Service, Inc., 1993), p. 33.

13. August Wilson, *The Piano Lesson* (New York: Dutton, 1990), p. 52.

14. Frank Cossa, *The Queen' Knight* in *Outstanding Stage Monologs and Scenes from the '90s,* Steven H. Gale, ed. (Colorado Springs: Meriwether, 2000), p. 15.

15. Eric Bogosian, *Suburbia* (New York: Dramatists Play Service, Inc., 1995), pp. 52–53.

16. Lee Blessing, *Two Rooms* (New York: Dramatists Play Service, Inc., 1990), pp. 20–21.

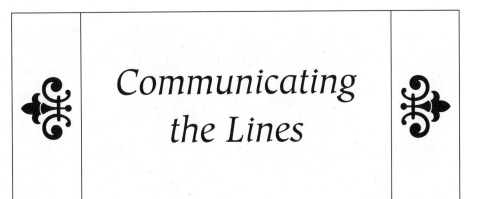

CHAPTER 12

Communicating the Lines

M any actors assume that if they understand the general meaning of a line and have an idea of its overall purpose, they will read the line correctly without further conscious effort. However faulty this assumption may be, it is reasonably understandable that many actors make this mistake when speaking straightforward prose dialogue. But many plays (all classics and a considerable number of contemporary works) are not written in simple prose. They nearly always use a range of rhetorical and poetic devices, and their vocabulary is frequently baffling. In these plays, actors must pay attention to both content and form if they are to communicate the full value of the dialogue to an audience.

To engage in a comprehensive study of the uses of rhetorical and poetic devices demands much more space and time than we can give it here. We must, however, explore the more common means playwrights use to make their dialogue effective. Understanding these strategies will stimulate you to examine the dramatist's lines more closely. Only by such careful scrutiny can you detect all subtlety of meaning and aptness of form. Because communication is the actor's primary responsibility and because language is a major means of communication, it goes without saying that successful actors constantly deepen their sensitivity to words and sharpen their ability to communicate their meaning.

Buddy Myers/Copyright by Allied Theatre Group

Figure 12.1 Clyde Ruffin as Prospero in *The Tempest* at Shakespeare in the Park in Ft. Worth, TX. Directed by Kenn Stilson; scenic design by Nelson Robinson; costume design by Dawn DeWitt; lighting design by Jeffrey Childs. Poetic and rhetorical language must be clearly communicated to the audience.

Understanding the Words

Actors must know the meanings of their words! This advice is so obvious you may resent having it said. Yet it is not uncommon for actors to go into rehearsals not only ignorant of what their lines mean but also ignorant of their ignorance. As an actor, you should own a good standard dictionary — or have immediate access to a computer dictionary — and use it frequently, even looking up words of which you think you know the meaning. You also need access to special sources: dictionaries of slang and colloquial speech are two prominent examples. For almost all period plays, you will also need a glossary and a well-annotated edition of the text.

You need to study such sources conscientiously to discover the meaning of the play's words. Let us return to *Romeo and Juliet* for an illustration. Juliet's first line in the balcony scene (Act II, Scene 2), spoken to herself after she has just met Romeo at the Capulet ball and fallen in love with him, is:

O Romeo, Romeo! wherefore art thou Romeo?

Without having a complete understanding of the words, actresses will inevitably misread the line by emphasizing *art* and thus making it mean "Where are you, Romeo?" with some such subtext as "I yearn to know where you are, what you are doing, whether you are longing for me as I am longing for you." But a simple check of the dictionary will disclose that *wherefore* does not mean *where;* it means *why. Wherefore* then becomes the emphatic word, and the correct subtext is "Why do you, whom I have come to love, have to be called Romeo, the son of our great enemy?" This reading leads logically to the next line:

Deny thy father, and refuse thy name;
Or, if thou wilt not, be but sworn my love,
And I'll no longer be a Capulet.

In analyzing the meaning of Juliet's first line, note also the absence of a comma between *thou* and *Romeo*—Romeo is not being addressed. Attention to punctuation helps greatly in finding the meaning of a speech.

Incidentally, Juliet uses *wherefore* in the same sense in expressing her alarm when Romeo reveals his presence in the Capulet orchard:

How cams't thou hither, tell me, and *wherefore?*

She means *how* did you manage to get in here and *why* did you come?

Several other usages in the same scene further illustrate the necessity of paying close attention to the meaning of the words. After Juliet has said her famous "that which we call a rose/ By any other name would smell as sweet," she continues:

So Romeo would, were he not Romeo call'd,
Retain that dear perfection which he *owes*
Without that title.

A few lines later, fearing Romeo will think she is too forward in declaring her love, she says:

In truth, fair Montague, I am too *fond.*

If your edition of the script has a good glossary, you will discover that *owes* in Shakespeare usually means *owns* and that *fond* usually means *foolish.* Juliet is not saying, "I love you too much," she is saying, "I am foolish to declare my love to someone I have known only an hour and whose family is an enemy to my family." This feeling is expressed more fully later in the lines:

I have no joy in this contract tonight:
It is too rash, too unadvis'd, too sudden;

Words that look familiar but that the dramatist uses with an unfamiliar meaning can be particularly deceiving.

Let us move to a related problem of interpretation. After Juliet has warned Romeo that he will be killed if any of her kinsmen find him in their orchard, he says:

My life were better ended by their hate,
Than death *prorogued,* wanting of thy love.

The word *prorogued* is not likely to be in the average student's vocabulary. It means *postponed* or *delayed.* Romeo is saying, "It is better to be killed at once by your kinsmen than to endure a living death without your love." To make this meaning clear, six words in the line must have some degree of emphasis:

My *life* were better *ended* by their *hate,*
Than *death prorogued,* wanting of thy *love.*

Selecting the word or words to emphasize is important when interpreting the lines. The selection is determined by the meaning of the words and by the context in which they are used. We will call these words the **operative words.** In this sense, *operative* means "exerting the force necessary to produce an appropriate effect," and we choose this term because it suggests the active influence that certain words have in communicating a meaning. Think of the simple sentence "I gave him the revolver." If we exclude the article, any one of the four words might be operative, depending on the meaning intended. Operative words are not, of course, chosen arbitrarily. Although different actors will make different choices, the choices the actors make should reveal their understanding of the playwright's text and their sensitivity to the uses of language.

Of course, vocabulary needs attention in all plays, not just verse plays from other periods. Actors from one ethnicity, social class, or geographical region may not be immediately familiar with the slang and syntax used by characters from another ethnicity, social class, or region. And most American actors will need help with the meaning of this Cockney dialogue in Edward Bond's *Early Morning:*

LEN: We'd bin stood there 'ours, and me guts starts t' rumble. 'Owever, I don't let on. But then she 'as t' say "I ain arf pecky."

JOYCE: Thass yer sense a consideration, ain it! I'd 'eard your gut.

LEN: I 'ad an empty gut many times, girl. That don't mean I'm on the danger list. But when you starts rabbitin' about bein' pecky I. . . . You're a rabbitin' ol' git! 'Ear that?[1]

In fact, practically every play demands close examination of its particular idiom. Michael Weller's *Moonchildren* depends heavily on the audience's familiarity with college slang of the 1960s; *Short Eyes,* by Miguel Piñero, makes heavy use of ethnic and prison slang (the term *short eyes* itself is prison slang for a child molester); and one would have to know a whole range of urban or "street" slang to extract nuances of meaning from many of the lines in plays representing that social class.

Handling the Sentence

An actor who is ignorant of the basic rules of grammar cannot possibly interpret and communicate a playwright's lines. No matter what the role or the play, you must have the ability to recognize subjects and predicates, modifying words, phrases, and clauses, and you must understand the principles of subordination and pronoun reference. Jerzy Grotowski wrote:

> The ability to handle sentences is important and necessary in acting. The sentence is an integral unit, emotional and logical, that can be sustained by a single expiratory and melodic wave. It is a whirlwind concentrated on an epicentrum [focal center] formed by the logical accent or accents. The vowels at this epicentrum should not be shortened but rather prolonged slightly in order to give them a special value, taking good care not to break up the unity of the sentence with unjustified pauses. . . .
>
> In poetry too, the sentence must be considered as a logical and emotional entity to be pronounced in one single respiratory wave. Several lines (one and a half, two, or more) often constitute the sentence.[2]

Understanding the sentence as a structural unit, recognizing the relationship and relative importance of its different parts, determining the operative words (or logical accents as Grotowski called them), and keeping the sentence moving toward its epicentrum is one of your principal concerns in dealing with the language of a play. Grotowski's warning against unjustified pauses should be heeded, because unnecessary pauses, whether for an intake of breath or for any other reason, obscure the relationship of the parts of the sentence and destroy its rhythmic flow. Doing the former blurs the meaning, and maintaining the latter is essential to the form. Good actors handle sentences so the words are constantly moving forward toward a focal point. The problem can be more complex than Grotowski suggests. In *The Tempest*, Prospero's "Farewell to His Art" (Act V, Scene 1) has a sentence that is seventeen-and-a-half lines long, and Juliet's potion speech (Act IV, Scene 3) has a sentence of eighteen lines. We provide some sentences, less complex than those just mentioned, that illustrate this problem.

In *Major Barbara*, by George Bernard Shaw, Lady Britomart answers the protest that she treats her grown-up offspring like children.

I have always made you my companions and friends, and allowed you
perfect freedom to do and say whatever you liked, so long as you liked
what I could *approve* of.[3]

Here is a sentence of thirty-one words that can be handled as a "single melodic
wave," culminating in the operative word *approve*. To select *approve* as the operative word does not mean that other words in the sentence do not have a degree of
importance and should not receive some manner of emphasis. But *approve* is a correct choice. It is logical because in Lady Britomart's mind her approval is more important than the freedom she claims to allow. It helps reveal her dominating character, and it highlights the comic contradiction of the line by suggesting that she
is blameworthy of the very charge she is denying.

The following line from Arthur Kopit's *Indians* presents a similar, but more
difficult, problem. John Grass, a young Indian, testifies before a group of senators
sent by the President of the United States, the Great Father, to investigate charges
of mistreatment. He talks about the futile and bungling attempts of a missionary
bishop to help the situation:

But when we told him we did not wish to be Christians but wished to
be like our fathers, and dance the sundance, and fight bravely against
the Shawnee and the Crow! And pray to the Great Spirits who made the
four winds, and the earth, and made man from the dust of this earth,
Bishop Marty *hit* us![4]

This is a group of fifty-nine words, punctuated as two sentences but constituting a single logical and emotional entity, always moving toward the operative
word *hit*. Grammatically, "Bishop Marty hit us" is the principal clause, and *hit* is
the main verb of the entire unit. Logically, it is John Grass's purpose to impress on
the senators the mistreatment the Indians have received, in spite of what (to them,
at least) has been a reasonable attitude. Emotionally, he feels very deeply about
the physical abuse they have suffered. Kopit's choice of the word *hit* is peculiarly
expressive of John Grass's uncomplicated earnestness and naiveté.

In *Blues for Mister Charlie,* by James Baldwin, a mature white man tells about
his love for a young African American woman:

I used to look at her, the way she moved, so beautiful and free, and I'd
wonder if at night, when she might be on her way home from some-
place, any of those boys at school had said *ugly things* to her.[5]

The speaker realized that at the school they attended, an African–American
girl's permitting any kind of relationship with a Caucasian boy subjected herself to
a good deal of cruel comment. In expressing this concern, the whole sentence must
move forward to *ugly things.* This speech also affords the actor a chance to observe
the principles of subordination, to pick out the main structure, the "skeleton," and
to relate the less important parts to it. Here is the skeleton of this sentence:

> I used to look at her . . . and I'd wonder if . . . any of those boys . . . had
> said ugly things to her.

The other parts must be made subordinate.

EXERCISE   Select a speech of at least twelve lines spoken by a character in a play on which
you are working. Look up all the words (with the exception, perhaps, of articles
and conjunctions) to make certain you understand the possible range of meanings
of the passage. If necessary, do a prosaic, line-by-line paraphrase—especially if
the speech is from a verse play. Find the operative words.

Remember, each sentence may have more than one operative word, but each
sentence should be unified into a single structure with its parts related to the
whole through the proper use of subordination. Memorize this speech, and rehearse it until you have control of both its meaning and its form.

Building a Progression

In the previous section, we stressed the importance of finding the operative words
and of directing the rest of the sentence toward them—if not like a whirlwind, as
Grotowski suggested, at least in some form of progression. We must feel when actors are speaking that their lines are "going somewhere," and following this progression keeps the audience listening. Even moments of silence (not to be confused with unnecessary pauses) must drive the dramatic action forward. Actors,
like travelers, must keep moving toward some predetermined destination, and
they must structure their dialogue with this direction in mind.

Besides the examples already cited, dramatists have other ways of giving direction and forward movement to their lines. The simplest is a series of two or
more parts, in which each part receives increasing emphasis as the series progresses. One of the best-known lines in dramatic literature, the beginning of
Antony's funeral oration for Julius Caesar, is such a series:

> Friends, Romans, countrymen, lend me your ears
>
> (ACT III, SCENE 2)

In *Romeo and Juliet* Shakespeare uses a similar construction when the Prince
of Verona breaks up the street brawl between the Montagues and the Capulets:

> Rebellious subjects, enemies to peace,
> Profaners of this neighbour-stained steel—
> Will they not hear? What ho! you men, you beasts. . . .
>
> (ACT I, SCENE 1)

In *The Lady's Not for Burning,* by Christopher Fry, Jennet has told how her father, an alchemist, once accidentally turned base metal into gold and how he died trying to rediscover the formula. The cynical Thomas Mendip answers that if he had been successful:

> . . . you
> Would be eulogized, lionized, probably
> Canonized for your divine mishap.[6]

Effective handling of progressions requires looking to the end of the series and building it to a climax.

Playwrights may also use a *ladder* device, in which the idea is "stepped up," like ascending the rungs of a ladder, by a careful progression of words. Starting at the bottom, one must look to the top rung. Claudius makes the following toast to Hamlet before the duel he has plotted between Hamlet and Laertes:

> And let the *kettle* to the *trumpet* speak,
> The *trumpet* to the *cannoneer* without,
> The *cannons* to the *heavens,* the *heavens* to the *earth:*
> "Now the king drinks to Hamlet!"
>
> (ACT V, SCENE 2)

Hamlet's mother is overcome with grief when he makes her aware of her guilty behavior:

> Be thou assur'd, if words be made of *breath,*
> And *breath* of *life,* I have no *life* to *breathe*
> What thou hast said to me.
>
> (ACT III, SCENE 4)

A delightfully complex example of this device occurs in *As You Like It* when Rosalind tells Orlando how Celia and Oliver fell in love:

> . . . For your brother and my sister no sooner *met,* but they *look'd;* no sooner *look'd,* but they *lov'd;* no sooner *lov'd,* but they *sigh'd;* no sooner *sigh'd,* but they ask'd one another the *reason;* no sooner knew the *reason,* but they sought the *remedy.* And in these degrees have they made a pair of stairs to marriage, which they will *climb incontinent,* or else *be* incontinent before marriage.
>
> (ACT V, SCENE 2)

Another way dramatists "progress" the lines is by piling, one on top of another, details that accumulate to create a total effect. This is called a *periodic* structure. Here, the term *periodic* means "consisting of a series of repeated stages," which well describes this method. The repeated stages build to a climax, with no trailing subordinate elements afterward to minimize their effectiveness. Again, this structure is easily recognized when read silently but requires careful handling when spoken. From the very beginning, the actor must look forward to the end and keep moving toward it. Shakespeare often used periodic structure, and a classic example is John of Gaunt's soaring description of England in *Richard II:*

This royal throne of kings, this scept'red isle,
This earth of majesty, this seat of Mars,
This other Eden, demiparadise,
This fortress built by Nature for herself
Against infection and the hand of war,
This happy breed of men, this little world,
This precious stone set in a silver sea,
Which serves it in the office of a wall
Or as a moat defensive to a house
Against the envy of less happier lands;
This blessed plot, this earth, this realm, this
England. . . .

    (ACT II, SCENE 1)

This great speech actually contains several more "stages" before the final climax. Speaking it well is a strong challenge for even the finest actor, but practicing it will prepare you to deliver simpler usages of this structure with ease.

And prepare you must, for all good playwrights use periodic structure, although not always so formally as the ringing example from *Richard II*. Sean O'Casey uses it in *Juno and the Paycock,* when Mrs. Madigan describes how "her man" used to court her:

"That'll scratch your lovely, little white neck," says he, ketchin' hould of
a danglin' bramble branch, holdin' clusters of the loveliest flowers you
ever seen, an' breakin' it off, so that his arm fell, accidental like, roun' me
waist, an' as I felt it tightenin', an tightenin', an tightenin', I thought me
buzzom was every minute goin' to burst out into a roystherin' song about
    "The little green leaves that were shakin' on the threes,
    The gallivantin' buttherflies, an' buzzin' o' the bees!"[7]

Arthur Kopit uses this same type of periodic structure for building a progression in *Indians* when Wild Bill Hickok is standing over the beautiful Teskanjavila:

Hickok, fastest shooter in the West, 'cept for Billy the Kid, who ain't as
accurate; Hickok, deadliest shooter in the West, 'cept for Doc Holliday,
who wields a sawed-off shotgun, which ain't fair; Hickok, shootinest
shooter in the West, 'cept for Jesse James, who's absolutely indiscrimi-
nate; this Hickok, strong as an eagle, tall as a mountain, swift as the
wind, fierce as a rattle-snake—a legend in his own time, or any other—
this Hickok stands now above an Indian maiden. . . .[8]

It is interesting to note how, for comic effect, Kopit has Teskanjavila ruin the climax of Hickok's splendid speech, forcing him to weaken the periodic structure by adding subordinate elements:

TESKANJAVILA: I'm not an Indian and I'm not a maiden!

HICKOK: Who's not an Indian and not a maiden, but looks pretty good anyhow. . . .

Thinking Antithetically

"Suit the action to the word, the word to the action." Particularly with the plays of William Shakespeare, you must look for **antitheses.** As the playwright himself wrote in *Richard II,* ". . . set the word itself against the word. . . ." John Barton, Associate Director of the Royal Shakespeare Company, said:

> We can easily overlook it because we don't use antithesis very much today, particularly in our everyday speech. Yet Shakespeare was deeply imbued with the sense of it. He *thought* antithetically. It was the way his sentences over and over found their shape and their meaning. . . . 'Antithesis' is in a way a bad word for something very practical. It sounds obscure and learned.[9]

Perhaps it would simply be better to use Shakespeare's description and set one word or phrase against another. This is yet another of the actor's paradoxes. Although you must constantly build your progressions toward culminating points, you must also refer to what has already been said. Every word must either *qualify* what has preceded it or change the direction of the action. "If we don't set up one word," added Barton, "we won't prepare for another to qualify it. And if the next word doesn't build on the first and move the sentence on, both the audience and the actor may lose their way."[10] In this manner, we think antithetically. Actors frequently do not understand antithetical construction and consequently choose to "operate" on a word or phrase that has already been emphasized, rather than to find the antithesis that will advance the idea. Hamlet's "To be, or not to be" is a simple antithetical phrase. However, the operative words found in the next sentence are less clear.

> Whether 'tis nobler in the mind to suffer
> The slings and arrows of outrageous fortune,
> Or to take arms against a sea of troubles,
> And by opposing end them?
>
> (ACT III, SCENE 1)

Figure 12.2 Donald Sage Mackay as Marcus Brutus in the Utah Shakespearean Festival's production of *Julius Caesar*. Particularly in the plays of William Shakespeare, actors must learn to think and speak antithetically.

"Sea of troubles" refers back to and, in this case, is synonymous with "outrageous fortune." The operative words that carry the idea forward thus are *take arms*.

Portia's famous mercy speech in *The Merchant of Venice* (Act IV, Scene 1) begins with an antithetical phrase. After all legal recourses to save Antonio's life have been fruitless, she declares that Shylock must be merciful. But he retorts with:

On what compulsion must I? tell me that.

And Portia answers

The quality of mercy is not strained,
It droppeth as the gentle rain from heaven
Upon the place beneath. . . .

Strained means *forced* or *compelled* and is used antithetically against Shylock's *compulsion*. If an actor does not use the antithetical phrasing to clarify subtext, the audience will not follow the progression. The use of antithesis looks backward; however, it is a primary means of driving the dramatic action forward.

Contrasting two words or phrases or emphasizing the possibility of two or more alternatives is another means of speaking antithetically. When you recognize this device in a line, it is almost impossible to read it without correctly emphasizing each of the different terms or alternatives. This mode of expression is apparent in such well-known sayings as "It is more blessed to *give* than to *receive*" or by the double-contrast in "To *err* is *human;* to *forgive, divine.*" A few examples, from both contemporary and classic plays, will further clarify this usage:

Respect what *other people see* and touch even if it's the opposite of what *you see* and touch! [11]

An investigation of *my* affairs would lead to an investigation of *his* affairs. . . .[12]

ALICE: Kurt, we're *leaving.*

EDGAR: You're *staying.*[13]

I pray you, father, *being* weak, *seem* so.[14]

I have *hope* to *live,* and am *prepar'd* to *die.*[15]

And let my *liver* rather *heat* with *wine*
Than my *heart cool* with mortifying *groans.*[16]

Let that fool *kill hisse'f.* Ain't no call for *you to he'p him.*[17]

OL' CAP'N: Who's been putting these integrationary ideas in my boy's head?
     Was it you—I'm asking you a question, dammit! Was it *you?*
IDELLA: Why don't you ask *him?*[18]

Sharing the Imagery

In Chapter 8 we discussed the technique of relating to images or pictures that actors supply from their imagination. Playwrights also make extensive use of images in their dialogue, and communicating these images to the audience through the dramatist's words is one of the actor's major tasks in handling language. Peter Brook explained:

The exchange of impressions through images is our basic language: at the moment when one man expresses an image at that same instant the other man meets him in belief. The shared association is the language—

if the association evokes nothing in the second person, if there is no instance of shared illusion, there is no exchange. . . . The vividness and the fullness of this momentary illusion depends on his [the speaker's] conviction and skill.[19]

Laurence Perrine defined imagery as "the representation through language of sense experience." And of course, sensory experience is one of the pleasures derived from going to the theatre. Perrine's definition continues:

The word *image* perhaps most often suggests a mental picture, something seen in the mind's eye—and visual imagery is the most frequently occurring kind. . . . But an image may also represent a sound; a smell; a taste; a tactile experience, such as hardness, wetness, or cold; an internal sensation, such as hunger, thirst, or nausea; or movement or tension in the muscles or joints.[20]

Images are either *literal* or *figurative,* although they both serve the same purpose of providing a vivid sensory experience. A figurative image expresses something in terms ordinarily used for expressing something else; thus, some comparison is either stated or implied. A literal image is a direct description couched in terms intended to stimulate a sensory response. "The russet dawn colors the eastern sky" and "She talks about her secret as she sleeps upon her pillow" are literal images. But in *Hamlet* and *Macbeth,* Shakespeare says in figurative language:

But look, the morn in russet mantle clad,
Walks o'er the dew of yon high eastward hill,

and

Infected minds
To their deaf pillows will discharge their secrets.

The terminology relating to imagery can be very complex; indeed, more than two hundred kinds of figurative speech have been identified. It is neither necessary nor desirable for you to become entangled in such subtlety. It is essential, however, that for both literal and figurative images you appreciate the sensory experience the playwright is expressing. For figurative language, you must also understand the aptness of the comparison. Most important of all, you must respond to imagery with all your senses before you can communicate it to an audience. Sam Shepard's description in *Red Cross* of swimming in the rain provides a rich example:

JIM: . . . Your body stays warm inside. It's just the outside that gets wet.
It's really neat. I mean you can dive under water and hold your breath.
You stay under for about five minutes. You stay down there and there's

Mark Garvin

Figure 12.3 Elizabeth Van
Dyke and Marcus Naylor in
No Niggers, No Jews, No Dogs,
by John Henry Redwood, produced by Philadelphia Theatre
Company—World Premiere
Winter 2001. The eyes are the
mirror of the soul, and truthful imagery shows itself most
vividly through the eyes of
the actor.

nothing but water all around you. Nothing but marine life. You stay
down as long as you can until your lungs start to ache. They feel like
they're going to burst open. Then just at the point where you can't stand
it any more you force yourself to the top. You explode out of the water
gasping for air, and all this rain hits you in the face. You ought to try it.[21]

Shakespeare is an imagist par excellence. Consider this example from *Macbeth:*

Now does he feel
His secret murders sticking on his hands.

and from *King Lear:*

> Thou art a bile,
> A plague-sore, an embossed carbuncle,
> In my corrupted blood.

Imagery has particular power to affect the emotions of both the actor and his audience. Consider Constance's moving lament for her lost son in *King John:*

> Grief fills the room up of my absent child,
> Lies in his bed, walks up and down with me,
> Puts on his pretty looks, repeats his words,
> Remembers me of all his gracious parts,
> Stuffs out his vacant garments with his form.

Imagery can be beautiful, as in Romeo's rhapsody when he first sees Juliet:

> O, she doth teach the torches to burn bright.
> It seems she hangs upon the cheek of night
> As a rich jewel in an Ethiop's ear.

It can be folksy, as in O'Casey's *The Shadow of a Gunman:*

> MRS. HENDERSON: I'm afraid he'll never make a fortune out of what he's sellin'. . . . Every time he comes to our place I buy a package o' hairpins from him to give him a little encouragement. I 'clare to God I have as many pins now as ud make a wire mattress for a double bed.[22]

It can be earthy, as in Davis's *Purlie Victorious:*

> OL' CAP'N: You don't know, boy, what a strong stomach it takes to stomach you. Just look at you sitting there—all slopped over like something the horses dropped; steam, stink and all![23]

EXERCISE Work on several of the following speeches, exploring the language and using it fully to communicate the meaning. Do whatever research is necessary to understand the words, the structures, and the images.

1. Michael in *Dancing at Lughnasa*, by Brian Friel[24]

(*Michael is speaking to the audience.*)

MICHAEL: In that memory, too, the air is nostalgic with the music of the thirties. It drifts in from somewhere far away—a mirage of sound—a dream music that is both heard and imagined; that seems to be both itself and its own echo, a sound so alluring and so mesmeric that the afternoon is bewitched, maybe haunted, by it. And what is so strange about the memory is that everybody seems to be floating on those sweet sounds, moving rhythmically, languorously, in complete isolation; responding more to the mood of the music than to its beat. When I remember it, I think of it as dancing. Dancing with eyes half closed because to open them would break the spell. Dancing as if language had surrendered to movement— as if this ritual, this wordless ceremony, was now the way to speak, to whisper private and sacred things, to be in touch with some otherness. Dancing as if the very heart of life and all its hopes might be found in those assuaging notes and those hushed rhythms and in those silent and hypnotic movements. Dancing as if language no longer existed because words were no longer necessary.

2. Claire in *A Delicate Balance,* by Edward Albee [25]

(*Claire is telling her brother-in-law, Tobias, what it is like when an alcoholic hits bottom.*)

CLAIRE: . . . Pretend you're very sick, Tobias, like you were with the stomach business, but pretend you feel your insides are all green, and stink, and mixed up, and your eyes hurt and you're half deaf and your brain keeps turning off, and you've got peripheral neuritis and you can hardly walk and you hate. You hate with the same green stinking sickness you feel your bowels have turned into . . . yourself, and *everybody.* Hate, and, oh, God!! you want love, l-o-v-e, so badly—comfort and snuggling is what you really mean, of course—but you hate, and you notice—with a sort of detachment that amuses you, you think—that you're more like an animal every day . . . you snarl, and *grab* for things, and hide things and forget where you hid them like not-very bright dogs, and you wash less, prefer to *be* washed, and once or twice you've actually soiled your bed and laid in it because you can't get up . . . pretend all that. No, you don't like that, Tobias?

3. Eddie in *Fool for Love,* by Sam Shepard [26]

(*After pushing his half-sister's boyfriend, Martin, against the wall and pulling him to the ground, Eddie tells the story of their father's mysterious walks and the beginning of his love affair with his half-sister.*)

EDDIE: But one night I asked him if I could go with him. And he took me. We walked straight out across the fields together. In the dark. And I remember it was just plowed and our feet sank down in the powder and the dirt came up over the tops of my shoes and weighed me down. I wanted to stop and empty my shoes out but he wouldn't stop. He kept walking straight ahead and I was afraid of losing him in the dark so I just kept up as best I could. And we were completely silent the whole time. Never said a word to each other. We could barely see a foot in front of us, it was so dark. And these white owls kept swooping down out of nowhere, hunting for jackrabbits. Diving right past our heads, then disappearing. And we just kept walking silent like that for miles until we got to town. I could see the drive-in movie way off in the distance. That was the first thing I saw. Just square patches of color shifting. Then vague faces began to appear. And, as we got closer, I could recognize one of the faces. It was Spencer Tracy. Spencer Tracy moving his mouth. Speaking without words. Speaking to a woman in a red dress. Then we stopped at a liquor store and he made me wait outside in the parking lot while he bought a bottle. And there were all these Mexican migrant workers standing around a pick-up truck with red mud all over the tires. They were drinking beer and laughing and I remember being jealous of them and I didn't know why. And I remember seeing the old man through the glass door of the liquor store as he paid for the bottle. And I remember feeling sorry for him and I didn't know why. Then he came outside with the bottle wrapped in a brown paper sack and as soon as he came out, all the Mexican men stopped laughing. They just stared at us as we walked away. And we walked right through town. Past the donut shop, past the miniature golf course, past the Chevron station. And he opened the bottle up and offered it to me. Before he even took a drink, he offered it to me first. And I took it and drank it and handed it back to him. And we just kept passing it back and forth like that as we walked until we drank the whole thing dry. And we never said a word the whole time.

4. Li'l Bit in *How I Learned to Drive,* by Paula Vogel[27]

(*Li'l Bit is describing a night she remembers from her childhood in the context of a driving lesson.*)

LI'L BIT: In a parking lot overlooking the Beltsville Agricultural Farms in suburban Maryland. Less than a mile away, the crumbling concrete of U.S. One wends its way past one-room revival churches, the porno drive-in, the boarded up motels with For Sale signs tumbling down. . . . it's a warm summer evening. Here on the land the Department of Agriculture owns, the smell of the leather dashboard. You can still imagine how Maryland used to be, before the malls took over. This countryside was once dotted with farmhouses—from their porches you could have witnessed the Civil War raging in the front fields. Oh yes. There's a moon over Maryland tonight, that spills into the car where I sit beside a man old enough to be—did I mention how still the night is? Damp soil and tranquil air. It's the kind of night that makes a middle-aged man with a mortgage feel like a country boy again.

5. Carol in *Red Cross,* by Sam Shepard[28]

(*She stands on the bed and acts out the speech as though she were skiing on a mountain slope.*)

CAROL: . . . I'll be at the top of this hill and everything will be all right. I'll be breathing deep. In and out. Big gusts of cold freezing air. My whole body will be warm and I won't even feel the cold at all. I'll be halfway down and then I'll put on some steam. A little steam at first and then all the way into the egg position. The Europeans use it for speed. I picked it up when I was ten. I'll start to accumulate more and more velocity. The snow will start to spray up around my ankles and across my face and hands. My fingers will get tighter around the grips and I'll start to feel a little pull in each of my calves. Right along the tendon and in front, too. Everything will be working at once. All my balance and strength and breath. The whole works in one bunch. There'll be pine trees going past me and other skiers going up the hill. They'll stop and watch me go past. I'll be going so fast everyone will stop and look. They'll wonder if I'll make it. I'll do some jumps and twist my body with the speed. They'll see my body twist, and my hair, and my eyes will water from the wind hitting them. My cheeks will start to sting and get all red. I'll get further and further into the egg position with my arms tucked up. I'll look down and see the valley and the cars and house and people walking up and down. I'll see all the cabins with smoke coming out the chimneys.

6. Premier in *WASP,* by Steve Martin[29]

(*Premier is a spaceman describing a vision to Son.*)

PREMIER: Her skin will be rose on white. She will come to you, her face close to yours, her breath on your mouth. She will speak words voicelessly, which you will understand because of the movement of her lips on yours. Her hand will be on the small of your back and her fingers will be blades. Your blood will pool around you. You will receive a transfusion of a clear liquid that has been exactly measured. That liquid will be sadness. And then, whatever her name may be—Carol, Susan, Virginia—then, she will die, and you will mourn her. Her death will be final in all respects but this: she will be alive and with someone else. But time and again, you will walk in, always at the same age you are now, with your arms open, your heart as big as the moon, not anticipating the total eclipse.

7. Juliet in *Romeo and Juliet,* by William Shakespeare[30]

(*To prevent her having to marry Paris, Friar Laurence has given Juliet a potion that will make her appear as dead. She will then remain in the family vault until Romeo comes from banishment to rescue her. She has said goodnight to her mother and her nurse and is now alone, realizing she must drink the potion.*)

JULIET: Farewell! God knows when we shall meet again.
 I have a faint cold fear thrills through my veins
 That almost freezes up the heat of life.
 I'll call them back again to comfort me.
 Nurse!—What should she do here?
 My dismal scene I needs must act alone.
 Come, vial.
 What if this mixture do not work at all?
 Shall I be marry'd then tomorrow morning?
 No, no! this shall forbid it, lie thou there.
       (*Laying down a dagger*)
 What if it be a poison which the Friar
 Subtly hath minister'd to have me dead,
 Lest in this marriage he should be dishonor'd
 Because he marry'd me before to Romeo?
 I fear it is, and yet methinks it should not,
 For he hath still been tried a holy man.
 How if, when I am laid into the tomb,
 I wake before the time that Romeo
 Come to redeem me? There's a fearful point!
 Shall I not then be stifled in the vault,
 To whose foul mouth no healthsome air breathes in,
 And there die strangled ere my Romeo comes?
 Or if I live, is it not very like
 The horrible conceit of death and night
 Together with the terror of the place—
 As in a vault, an ancient receptacle,
 Where for this many hundred years the bones
 Of all my buried ancestors are pack'd,
 Where bloody Tybalt yet but green in earth
 Lies fest'ring in his shroud, where as they say
 At some hours in the night spirits resort—
 Alack, alack! is it not like that I
 So early waking—what with loathsome smells
 And shrieks like mandrakes torn out of the earth,
 That living mortals hearing them run mad—
 O if I wake, shall I not be distraught,
 Environed with all these hideous fears,
 And madly play with my forefathers' joints
 And pluck the mangled Tybalt from his shroud
 And, in this rage with some great kinsman's bone
 As with a club dash out my desp'rate brains?

O look! methinks I see my cousin's ghost
Seeking out Romeo that did spit his body
Upon a rapier's point. Stay Tybalt, stay!
Romeo, Romeo, Romeo! Here's drink—I drink to thee.
                    (*Falls upon the bed*)

8. Romeo in *Romeo and Juliet*, by William Shakespeare[31]

(*Romeo, believing Juliet is dead, comes to the tomb to say farewell and to die at her side.*)

ROMEO: How oft when men are at the point of death
        Have they been merry—which their keepers call
        A lightning before death. O! how may I
        Call this a lightning? O my love, my wife!
        Death, that has suck'd the honey of thy breath
        Hath had no power yet upon thy beauty.
        Thou art not conquer'd—Beauty's ensign yet
        Is crimson in thy lips and in thy cheeks,
        And Death's pale flag is not advanced there.
        Tybalt, ly'st thou there in thy bloody sheet?
        O what more favor can I do to thee
        Than with that hand that cut thy youth in twain
        To sunder his that was thine enemy?
        Forgive me, cousin. Ah dear Juliet,
        Why art thou yet so fair? shall I believe
        That unsubstantial Death is amorous
        And that the lean abhorred monster keeps
        Thee here in dark to be his paramour?
        For fear of that I still will stay with thee
        And never from this pallet of dim Night
        Depart again, here, here will I remain
        With worms that are thy chambermaids, O here
        Will I set up my everlasting rest
        And shake the yoke of inauspicious stars
        From this world-weary'd flesh. Eyes look your last,
        Arms take your last embrace, and, lips (O you
        The doors of breath) seal with a righteous kiss
        A dateless bargain to engrossing Death!
        Come bitter conduct, come unsavory guide,
        Thou desp'rate pilot, now at once run on
        The dashing rocks thy seasick weary bark.
        Here's to my love! (*He drinks*) O true apothecary,
        Thy drugs are quick. Thus with a kiss I die. (*Falls*)

9. Find examples of imagery in the roles you are studying, and try to communicate as fully as possible the sensory experience the playwright intended to evoke.

Notes

1. Edward Bond, *Early Morning* (London: Calder and Boyars, 1968), pp. 21–22.

2. Jerzy Grotowski, *Towards a Poor Theatre* (New York: Simon & Schuster, 1968), p. 171.

3. George Bernard Shaw, *Complete Plays with Prefaces* (6 vols.; New York: Dodd, Mead, 1962), Vol. I, p. 347.

4. Arthur Kopit, *Indians* (New York: Hill and Wang, 1969), p. 9.

5. James Baldwin, *Blues for Mister Charlie* (New York: Dial Press, 1964), p. 63.

6. Christopher Fry, *The Lady's Not for Burning; A Phoenix Too Frequent; and an Essay "An Experience of Critics"* (New York: Oxford University Press, 1977), p. 54.

7. Sean O'Casey, *Three Plays* (New York: Macmillan, 1960), pp. 42–43.

8. Kopit, *Indians,* p. 47.

9. John Barton, *Playing Shakespeare* (London: Methuen, 1984), p. 55–56.

10. Ibid., p. 56.

11. Luigi Pirandello, *Right You Are If You Think You Are,* trans. Eric Bentley (New York: Columbia University Press, 1954), p. 19.

12. Friedrich Duerrenmatt, *Play Strindberg,* trans. James Kirkup (Chicago: The Dramatic Publishing Company, 1952), p. 57.

13. Duerrenmatt, *Play Strindberg,* p. 58.

14. William Shakespeare, *King Lear* (New Haven, CT: Yale University Press, 1947), p. 71.

15. William Shakespeare, *Measure for Measure* (New Haven, CT: Yale University Press, 1954), p. 46.

16. William Shakespeare, *The Merchant of Venice* (New Haven, CT: Yale University Press, 1923), p. 4.

17. Charles Gordone, *No Place to Be Somebody* (Indianapolis: Bobbs Merrill, 1969), p. 12.

18. Ossie Davis, *Purlie Victorious* (New York: Samuel French, 1961), p. 31.

19. Peter Brook, *The Empty Space* (New York: Atheneum, 1968), pp. 77–78.

20. Laurence Perrine, *Sound and Sense* (New York: Harcourt Brace Jovanovich, 1956), p. 40.

21. Sam Shepard, *Chicago and Other Plays* (New York: Urizen Books, 1981), p. 115.

22. O'Casey, *Three Plays,* p. 101.

23. Davis, *Purlie Victorious,* p. 31.

24. Brian Friel, *Dancing at Lughnasa* (New York: Dramatists Play Service, Inc., 1991), pp. 83–84.

25. Edward Albee, *A Delicate Balance* (New York: Atheneum, 1966), p. 23.

26. Sam Shepard, *Fool for Love* (San Francisco: City Lights Books, 1983), pp. 46–47.

27. Paula Vogel, *How I Learned to Drive* (New York: Dramatists Play Service Inc., 1997), p. 9.

28. Shepard, *Chicago and Other Plays,* pp. 101–102.

29. Steve Martin, *WASP and Other Plays* (New York: Samuel French, Inc., 1998), pp. 21–22.

30. William Shakespeare, *Romeo and Juliet* (New Haven, CT: Yale University Press, 1917), pp. 101–103.

31. Shakespeare, *Romeo and Juliet,* pp. 120–121.

PART THREE

The Actor and the Production

Richard Feldman

Will LeBow (foreground) as
Jean Paul Marat in the 2002 American
Repertory Theatre production of *Marat/Sade*.
Directed by János Szász.

CHAPTER 13

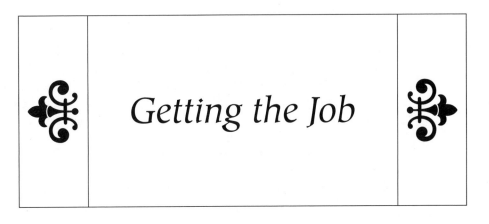

Getting the Job

. . . for every actor who gets hired for a part, fifty or a hundred or two hundred do not. An actor is forever trying to get a part; an actor is forever getting rejected, never knowing why, simply not wanted.[1]

Audition. The word itself sends a shock wave through every actor's body. The audition is entirely artificial; in many ways, it contradicts the technique training taught in legitimate acting classes. True, auditioning is a *form* of acting; however, it is not the same as performing in a play or film or on television, where you are engulfed into an imaginary world and "working off" your fellow actors. In the audition, there are no props, no set, no costumes. If you are lucky, the audition will take place in a theatre, but more times than not they will occur in an empty studio, hotel room, or conference hall. Indeed, auditioning is a necessary evil, and it will continue to plague actors until someone discovers a better way to cast a production.

No matter how great your talent, how extensive your training, how vast your experience — unless you are one of a few exceptions — you must audition to land a role. The actor's first encounter with the director is usually at this nerve-racking experience. Michael Shurtleff, whose book on auditioning has become the bible of the subject, warns, "In order to act, it is necessary to audition. . . . All the training in the world can go for naught if the actor in the reading situation can't convince the auditors he can perform the role." [2] Many good actors simply are not cast because they lack appropriate auditioning skills. It is naïve to think that directors and producers should simply have faith in your abilities and trust your résumé in lieu of auditioning. With hundreds of actors vying for the same role, it is a buyer's market. Directors will hire someone they *know* they can trust, and this trust will begin with the audition.

Your ability to audition with professional competence defines your life and career as an actor. It is your one opportunity to make a first impression. Directors will not hire someone who lacks self-confidence or is intimidated by the audition process. You must present yourself as a working professional. You must be tenacious, removing the concept of rejection from your vocabulary. You must believe in your own talent and experience, and you must seize the moment as it arises.

How do you set yourself apart from others who are equally talented and just as right for the role? How do you present yourself in a positive manner without sounding conceited? Obnoxious? Loud? You begin by knowing and liking yourself. You must know your strengths and weaknesses—both internal and external. You must be comfortable with your body. Whether you like it or not, you are "selling" your talent and body. And you must find creative ways to do so.

From the director's point of view, the audition is a simple, time-saving way to become familiar with numerous actors and to attempt to identify those who most closely resemble their concept of the characters in the play being cast. The director uses the audition to find an actor who has the talent and the technique to play a certain role, who is physically right for the part, and who will blend well with the other cast members. Of course, if the audition is for a repertory company or a stock company, the directors are also looking for versatility. They are not against you. In fact, they are on your side. They simply want to mount a successful production of the play, and to do so they need the right actors. They hope you will be "the one" for which they are searching; they are pulling for you.

In most auditions, whether for stage, television, or film, an actor presents a **cold reading** from the script. Often actors receive the scene when they arrive for the audition and have only a short time to look it over. At other times, they simply may be interviewed by the director or asked to do a prepared monologue or scene for the occasion.

It has become customary at many auditions attended by representatives from various companies that actors be allotted a total of three minutes, during which they present one dramatic and one comedic piece prepared before their arrival. At the Southeastern Theatre Conference Auditions, for example, the actor is allowed only ninety seconds to present a monologue and a song—and this includes the introduction, transition, and ending. After hearing the prepared auditions, companies conduct individual **callbacks** for further readings and interviews.

Usually, however, actors will audition for a particular production of a particular play. Most directors have their own system for holding auditions, and an actor should not be alarmed at one who uses unusual methods to determine a performer's suitability for a role. In *A Chorus Line,* a musical about dancers auditioning for a Broadway musical, the "director" asks the dancers to talk about themselves as well as to dance. Some of the dancers rise to the occasion; others do not.

Before launching directly into the preparation and presentation of the audition, let us take a moment to discuss the business.

Understanding the Business of Acting

Actors are artists. Many of them do not like to think of theatre as a business. The truth is, without business skills — particularly in the area of marketing — no one will ever see your talent. You may be an artist, but *you* are also a business. You are the CEO, the CFO, and the sole shareholder of "You, Inc." The studio system is dead. An agent or personal manager will only get you so far. You have only yourself to rely on. You must take charge of your own affairs. In doing so, you must have a plan — including both short-term and long-term goals. You must know where you hope to be in one year. Five years. Ten years. And you must have a well-formed strategy of how you intend to accomplish your goals. You do not have to live in New York, Chicago, or Los Angeles to begin working on your plan. Rather, you must make things happen for "You, Inc." one step at a time, beginning right now from wherever you are currently living.

As the CEO of your company, you must maintain your appearance. This does not mean that you have to present yourself as a right-winged, Rush Limbaugh conservative, but most working actors present themselves as working professionals. Think of top actors such as Denzel Washington, Tom Hanks, Julia Roberts, and Mel Gibson. They do not have conspicuous body piercing, tattoos, or alternative hairstyles. As beautiful as they are, they present themselves as someone with whom we can all relate. They are individuals, but each one of them could be our neighbor, our friend.

Top actors also maintain their physiques. You must get in shape and stay in shape. This is particularly true in television and film, where you are either physically fit and considered for **straight parts** or a **character actor,** who plays unusual or eccentric individuals. Our profession is not politically correct. Directors *are* looking at your body and how well you communicate with it. They *are* looking at your sexuality. They *are* judging your face, your hair, and your clothing. Therefore, if you wish to "make it" in this business, you must maintain your physical appearance.

As a working professional, you should also consider your office supplies and equipment. Agents and casting directors must have immediate access to you twenty-four hours a day, seven days a week. You must have:

✦ An answering service or machine with remote access.

✦ A pager or cell phone that you carry with you at all times.

✦ Access to a fax machine.

✦ Access to a computer and the Internet.

✦ An email address that you check several times each day.

✦ Paper and pens by all telephones.

✦ Maps of the city in which you are working and the ability to navigate from them.

✦ A record book and filing system for all items pertaining to your career. (Keep your receipts, for as a working actor, you are allowed tax breaks on your mileage, industry-related magazine and book purchases, research, educational expenses, etc.)

✦ A current subscription to various trade magazines and newsletters such as *Backstage, Black Talent News, Variety, Ross Reports, Latino Heat, Hollywood Reporter, Chicago Connection, American Theatre,* etc.

In other industries you have a business card, dossier, cover letter, letter of introduction and a résumé. As an actor you have your **headshot** and **résumé** to certify your professional background. They will not get you the job, but they might get you the audition. A good picture and résumé must create an interest in the eye and mind of the reviewer. The casting director must want to see the person behind the image in the photo and described on the résumé. If these marketing tools do not serve you well, you have done worse than waste your money; you have actually spent hard-earned cash to sabotage your own career. *Your headshot and résumé are your most important marketing tools.* Many times they are your *only* means by which to open the door to an audition that could lead to a job. If either one of these tools is not working for you, it is working against you. If your headshot fails to project your individuality, then you have paid someone a lot of money to obstruct your career. Remember, your picture and résumé are the only items you leave behind after the audition.

With regard to headshots, there are no "rules," but here are some general guidelines:

✦ Avoid the temptation to save money by using a friend who dabbles in photography. Hire a professional photographer with experience in shooting headshots. Look at his portfolios showing examples of his work. Ask for references. With headshots, as with so many things, "you get what you pay for."

+ The most basic or classic look is a **black and white** of the head and shoulders, with the focus on the face. Trends change, but this is always acceptable. In this market, actors do not use color pictures.

+ Your picture, whether smiling or serious, needs to have direct eye contact with the camera—and there needs to be something "going on" in your eyes. The phrase, "make love to the camera" may sound cliché, but that is exactly what you must do. A commercial look is usually a smiling or upbeat one, while a film look can be more serious. Many actors have two, even three different shots.

+ Have a natural look, and avoid using too much makeup. If you are uncomfortable doing your own, often the photographer can recommend a makeup artist.

+ Keep it simple. Avoid black and white clothing and busy patterns. Bring several tops with different collars and necklines to the photo shoot.

+ If shooting outside, rather than in a studio, avoid distracting backgrounds.

+ The classic size is **8"x10"**. These come with various border choices, so check with your agent or colleagues to verify the best choice for your market.

+ Have your name embossed on the front of all reproductions.

In short, a casting director wants to see a photograph that really looks like you, not someone on the cover of *Vogue* or *GQ*. Your individuality is what separates you from the crowd, and that individuality should be used and expressed in a professionally produced headshot showing you at your best.

Your résumé should contain the history of your theatrical life. At the most basic level, it should contain personal, descriptive information. It must tell the producer or director about your training and your experience and about the people with whom you've worked, the kinds of theatres and productions in your background, and your union affiliations (**SAG, AFTRA, Equity**), if any. The résumé serves as the chief source of information about you. It should be accurate and arranged in a manner that is easy to comprehend. Here are general guidelines with regard to résumés:

+ Put your résumé on your computer so that it can be updated regularly.

+ Keep it to a single page, and cut it to fit your 8"x10" headshot. Staple it to the backside of your photograph.

+ Specify your union affiliation (SAG, AFTRA, or AEA), if appropriate, directly under your name at the top of the page. If you are a member of the Equity Membership Candidacy (EMC) Program, you may list this.

+ Do not list your actual age or the age range you think you play. Why limit the director's vision or creativity?

Maia Rosenfeld

Figure 13.1 An actor's headshot, along with his or her résumé, is typically submitted when appling for an audition.

✦ Give the name, address, and telephone number of your agent and/or manager if you have one. You may wish to list your email address. *Do not list your actual home address or phone!* You do not know the people for whom you are auditioning, and you are putting yourself in danger by including this information. If you do not yet have an agent, use a Post Office Box and an answering service.

✦ List your most important credits, beginning with your strongest. Once you have gained experience, you will begin with your most recent credits.

✦ When starting out, do not be afraid to list small roles and **bit parts** (even background or "atmosphere" in film or TV, but be sure to specify it as **extra** work). You can list collegiate and other non-professional credits as long as you specify where the work was done.

✦ Credits should include the title of the piece, the role, and the director and/or producing organization.

✦ If you do not have any credits, list your classes and workshops. It shows you are committed to the business.

✦ Be honest. The theatre is a small, close-knit community in which everybody seems to know everyone else. Lying will only get you in trouble. Remember, everybody started once. There is no shame in being a beginner.

✦ List any special abilities you have: athletic skills, dancing, acrobatics, singing, dialects, bilingualism, musical instruments, magic, etc. Appraise yourself realistically and do not put down something you have only done once or twice. You may be expected to deliver on your special skills.

✦ Describe your professional training, educational background, etc. This is the best place to list your workshops, but keep it selective.

✦ List your height, weight, and hair and eye color.

Your résumé, like your picture, must give as truthful a view of you as possible. Padded lists of roles you have performed in acting class simply do not fool auditors. Do not be ashamed of who you are. Present yourself with pride.

The sample résumé on page 230 was prepared by a recent graduate to use in conjunction with auditions for summer jobs at professional or semiprofessional theatres. Although the needs of producing organizations vary, you should present your training and experience in the best possible light without overstating the case. Names and phone numbers of people who can vouch for your abilities are also useful.

Brooke Hildebrand

(573) 555-5555 (Service)

brookehildebrand@hotmail.com

Height: 5'6"   Hair: Brown
Weight: 135   Eyes: Brown

Regional

A CHRISTMAS CAROL	Mrs. Cratchit	Nebraska Theatre Caravan
STEEL MAGNOLIAS	Shelby	Country Theatre Workshop
BAREFOOT IN THE PARK	Corie	Country Theatre Workshop
HELLO, DOLLY!	Minnie Fay	Country Theatre Workshop
MUCH ADO ABOUT NOTHING	Hero	Players in the Park
ROMEO AND JULIET	Nurse	Players in the Park
MY FAIR LADY	Mrs. Higgins	Summer Music Theatre
THE SECRET GARDEN	Mrs. Medlock	Summer Music Theatre

Educational

THE MEMORANDUM	Jan Ballas*	WIU University Theatre
LOST IN YONKERS	Bella*	WIU University Theatre
THE SHADOW BOX	Maggie*	WIU University Theatre
THE MISER	Frosine	WIU University Theatre
COMPANY	Sarah	WIU University Theatre
THE COMEDY OF ERRORS	Amelia	WIU University Theatre
ARABIAN NIGHTS	Scheherazade	WIU Regional Touring Theatre
BEYOND THERAPY	Dr. Wallace	WIU Studio Theatre
INDEPENDENCE	Kess*	SE MO University Theatre
EVERYMAN	Everyman*	SE MO University Theatre
THE MUSIC MAN	Eulalie*	SE MO University Theatre
EMPEROR'S NEW CLOTHES	Ying*	SE MO University Theatre

*Kennedy Center / American College Theatre Festival Irene Ryan Nominations;
KC/ACTF Finalist 2000 & 2001; Alternate to Kennedy Center 2000

Training

MFA in Acting, Western Illinois University, 2001
BS in Education, Speech & Theatre, Southeast Missouri State University, 1998
Acting: Sonny Bell; Film: Gene Kozlowski; Movement: Ken Elston;
Voice: Matt Bean & Mim Canny

Special Skills

Dialects: Standard British, American Southern, Brooklynese; Improvisation;
Working with kids; Ten years of cello (I own my instrument)

Technical résumé and references available upon request.

If you are participating in a large audition site where many different casting directors will be present, do your "homework" before the audition. Secure the names and addresses of the theatres in which you have interest. Send ahead of time your résumé, headshot, and a simple cover letter explaining your background and interest in their company along with your audition number. The following represents a good example of a letter sent to the director before a production of Shakespeare in the Park's *The Tempest,* in Ft. Worth, Texas.

Dear Mr. Stilson,

    I am a second year MFA degree candidate at Columbia University. Training with Andrei Serban, Priscilla Smith, and Anne Bogart has given me the opportunity to study and perform Classic Greek, Spanish Golden Age, Chekhov, and Shakespearean plays. I have heard wonderful things about your company and understand you are producing Shakespeare's *The Tempest.* I would love the opportunity to be called back and meet with you in person at the Strawhat Auditions next week. I am #103. Enclosed, please find my headshot and résumé.

                                  Respectfully,
                                  Lauren Kerchoff

Similarly, you should always send a thank you note after the audition. You obviously cannot write to every company at a large audition site, but you should send a note to everyone who called you back—particularly if they *do not* cast you. Your note should be handwritten. Emails are not acceptable. The following are good examples of simple and yet effective thank you notes from that same production.

Dear Dr. Stilson,

    Thank you so very much for calling me back and interviewing me in Miami last weekend. Your comments proved invaluable, and your production of *The Tempest* sounds exciting. I truly hope to be a part of your company.

                                  Best regards,
                                  Emma Weller

> Dear Kenn,
>
>   Thank you for auditioning me at SETC. Although you have not cast me, I certainly hope you will keep me in mind for next year. I will be performing this summer at the Barn Theatre in Augusta, Michigan.
>
>   Sincerely,
>   Sarah Oathout

This is a professional business practice that will pay off.

Preparing for the Audition

Whether you are participating in one of the large **cattle-call** auditions or reading for a single role in a play, you will want to be ready to present one or more prepared monologues. Selecting this material is at the same time the most difficult and the most important task you will face. Guidelines and cheap advice about what works and what does not work are plentiful, but because directors vary so greatly in their taste and their needs, no definitive scheme exists. A few suggestions may help:

✦ Your material represents ninety percent of your time on stage; therefore, select something you like. You will be living with the piece for a considerable period of hard work. Do not add to the drudgery of it by starting with something you hate or with which you feel indifferent.

✦ Use material well within your grasp and understanding. Although "type casting" has developed a bad connotation, all actors should realize the range of roles for which they are best suited. Those roles constitute your "type." It is unwise to select an audition piece from material outside this range. The director may eventually cast you for a part that demands a considerable stretch in age and temperament, but you will show yourself best in roles that are close to what you believe to be your best aptitudes.

✦ Unless the director specifically requests them, avoid dialects, as they will needlessly complicate your presentation.

✦ Try to select material that will not be performed twenty times by other actors at the same audition. You cannot be clairvoyant, but new and alternative material will give you a distinct advantage. When several actors perform the same piece, the director not only tires of hearing it but also has an opportunity that would not otherwise be feasible to make a direct comparison between you and the other actors. Any selection taken directly from a monologue book is overused. Monologue books are good sources to find characters; however, we suggest you locate the full script and select another monologue by the same person.

✦ Sexually explicit or extremely offensive material can work against you, particularly if it is not based on humor. While eccentric selections may be attention-getters, remember that your material is a reflection of your taste. Auditors are not necessarily prudish, but in view of the brief time you have to present yourself, it is always best to leave a positive impression.

✦ Avoid climactic material that requires great depth or intensity of emotion. There simply is not enough time to achieve these emotional peaks effectively and honestly.

✦ Avoid dull and passive pieces that dwell on character or plot exposition. Sometimes referred to as "remember when" monologues, it is extremely difficult to engage your audience in such a short amount of time with these narrative pieces. Always look for speeches written in first person that deal with an immediate psychological or emotional problem rather than the telling of a story in past tense with no clearly defined objective.

✦ Your monologue should be from a well-written piece of literature and involve a character who is pursuing an immediate simple objective while working against an obstacle.

✦ Nearly anything you select as audition material will need to be "cut" to fit the playing time you are likely to be allotted at the audition. If you are given sixty seconds, your monologue should be no longer than forty-five seconds. If you are given two minutes, prepare ninety seconds. There is no such thing as a monologue that is too short. And actors who exceed an established time limit appear to be undisciplined and unlikely to follow direction.

✦ Edit for clarity. Selections should be self-explanatory with a distinct beginning, middle, and ending.

If you are choosing a song, all the above guidelines apply; however, you should also remember the following:

✦ Although good vocal quality is important, character always comes first. Character colors the voice and humanizes the song. Your song should "show off" your voice, but it also should reveal your acting skills.

✦ Choose a song that is stylistically similar to the show for which you are auditioning. Obviously, if you are auditioning for *Grease,* you will want to look at rock-and-roll songs, up-tempo songs, or ballads. If you are auditioning for *Big River,* perhaps a country-western or folk song would be more appropriate.

✦ Unless the director specifically requests it, do not audition with a song from the show being cast. However, you should *know* every song from that particular show for the callback.

✦ Avoid big production numbers and dance numbers. That is a separate audition.

✦ Avoid narration or story songs (i.e., Robert Preston songs). This will simply project your discomfort with singing.

✦ No signature songs! Some songs are simply off-limits because they have been eternally associated with the original performer. Therefore, unless you wish to be compared with Ethel Merman, do not audition with "There's No Business Like Show Business."

✦ Always be prepared to do more than one piece. Particularly in a callback situation, casting directors will inevitably ask to see additional pieces.

All actors should have an **audition portfolio** consisting of a variety of prepared monologues and songs. Your portfolio should consist of:

9 Monologues	*9 Songs*
1:30 contemporary comedic	16-bar up-tempo
1:30 Shakespeare comedic	16-bar ballad
1:30 contemporary dramatic	up-tempo standard
1:30 Shakespeare dramatic	ballad standard
:45 contemporary comedic	rock and roll
:45 Shakespeare comedic	50s (triplet feel)
:45 contemporary dramatic	patter song
:45 Shakespeare dramatic	classical aria
Shakespeare sonnet	country-western

Over half your Shakespeare should be in verse. You may choose other verse plays, but you should be careful to find good contemporary translations.

Even after you have a full complement of monologues and songs in your portfolio, early preparation is an absolute necessity for every audition. You should begin rehearsing your pieces weeks before the actual audition. Do not wait until the last minute! You should consider the following when rehearsing your prepared pieces:

✦ Study the entire script and analyze the actions and objectives of the character exactly as you would if you were preparing to perform the role in a production. Think of your audition as a "ninety-second, one-act play, starring you."

✦ For the most part, you should not expect to use furniture in your staging. Audition sites will sometimes allow you to use a straight-backed chair, but you should be careful not to use it as a "crutch" or as a device to hide behind during your presentation. It can weaken your audition. You should also know that casting directors sitting beyond the second or third row in a large conference hall would not be able to see you in a seated position.

◆ Your movement should clarify your simple objective, utilizing a minimum of space—preferably staying within a radius of five to ten feet.

◆ Focus your attention into the house, not in the wings.

◆ Avoid all gimmicks!

◆ No props should be used unless the item is something you might normally wear or carry (i.e., glasses, handkerchief, wristwatch, scarf, or jacket).

◆ Consider your audience. This is one of the most common responses given by adjudicators on critique sheets. Keep in mind that there are really very few actual monologues in modern drama, but rather they are duologues. There-fore, you must ask yourself, "To whom am 'I' speaking?" Are you speaking to the audience as a friend? Are you speaking to one person? A small group?

◆ Take dynamic risks. Human beings are big. They make big decisions. How many times have you heard someone say, "If you would put that on stage, nobody would believe it." This is nonsense. However, do not confuse risk taking with indicating—false, unmotivated speech and movement. Risk tak-ing is synonymous with decision making. Risk taking can be very subtle in-deed, just as it can be extremely overt. As long as you stay within the bounds of truth in imaginary circumstances, you *can* believe your actions.

◆ Explore the distinct tempo-rhythm of every character in your portfolio. In an audition situation, you are trying to show your range. The greatest actors are "chameleons." Each character they portray has a distinct tempo-rhythm that manifests itself through their speech, posture, walk, and gestures.

◆ Get a coach. Many audition sites such as SETC, CETA, NETC, UPTA, Strawhat, Midwest, and U/RTA feel so strongly about this issue that the name of the coach appears next to the actor's name on the audition form to ensure that the actor has had every benefit of proper preparation.

Auditioning

After agreeing to an audition, your presence is expected. If you are unable to at-tend, you must give them sufficient notice, and you must have a good reason for your absence. Your audition begins the moment you walk out your front door. There are many horror stories of actors who have had confrontations with people on their way to the audition, and that person turned out to be the casting direc-tor. Because you probably will not recognize the director, you must be nice to everyone (and we mean *everyone*). This is particularly true once you arrive at the audition check-in, where many times directors will wander through the lobby in-specting the talent. You must also arrive at least fifteen minutes early to fill out forms and adjust to your space. Nothing looks more unprofessional than tardi-ness. Once you have checked in with the stage manager and filled out appropriate paperwork, do not leave the audition site without permission. You must also be prepared to stay longer than expected. If you are scheduled to audition at three o'clock, do not schedule to be at work by four. If they request that you stay and you cannot, they will probably excuse you, but it will most likely cost you the job.

Remember, you are a professional in pursuit of a job, and your dress should reflect your professionalism. Consider the following with regard to dress:

◆ Your clothing should flatter your figure—whatever your body size and type—and expose your personality. Actresses may want to consider wearing a dress, being that most female characters will be in dresses in most plays written before the 1960s or set before that era.

◆ No jeans or sloppy clothing. Tyrone Guthrie was fond of saying that people who dress like slobs very nearly always turn out to be slobs.

◆ Some actors like to dress in a manner suggestive of the role for which they are auditioning. If you choose to do so, make your selection subtle so your "costume" will not overpower your performance.

◆ Avoid printed words and busy patterns on clothing, and avoid large, noisy jewelry. These can be major distractions, and they draw focus away from you.

◆ Wear appropriate footwear. Casting directors *do* look at your feet. No sneakers, flip-flops, sandals, or Birkenstocks. Fred Silver tells the story of a wealthy actor who "thought shoes were so important that he left his fortune to Actors' Equity Association, to set up a fund to provide shoes for actors so they could make rounds without ever having to look 'down at the heels.'" [3]

◆ If you wear a hat, they will assume you are bald. Hats will also create a shadow over the top portion of your face under lights.

◆ Be careful with glasses, as they sometimes cause a glare.

◆ If you are auditioning at a large cattle-call audition, always wear the same clothing that you wore at the initial audition to every callback.

Once you have signed in, use your techniques for relaxation to control your nervousness. Remember that relaxation involves both mind and body. You must be able to remove at will any condition that blocks your intellectual thought process or your ability to command your voice and body to perform at their full range of flexibility. Actors use a variety of methods to achieve total relaxation. For some, yoga or transcendental meditation provides the answer. Others prefer a vigorous routine of physical exercise. Find a method that works for you, and keep in mind that many audition sites provide a warm-up space with a piano.

If at all possible, you should preview the performance space before your audition. This will give you a decided advantage over those walking into the space for the first time. If you are allowed to watch the preceding auditions, you can learn from others' mistakes, and it will allow you to become more comfortable in the space.

Be careful not to fall into the trap of being "psyched-out" by the other actors. Actors talk while waiting to audition. They love to talk about themselves. Many young actors are intimidated by the "competition." They find it unbelievable that all these other actors—who are their own ages—have such composure and are thoroughly experienced professionals. People exaggerate to impress others. Do not accept everything you are told as the truth. Their credits are probably no more impressive than yours, and sometimes their credentials are simply fabricated. Trust yourself and your abilities. Do not denigrate your own past. You are not in competition with any one single person at the audition. The role is between you and the director. Remember this definition of success: "When Preparation Meets Opportunity." This is your opportunity; take advantage of it.

If you are singing, carefully and specifically go over your music with the accompanist as you wait in the wings or off to the side. Your music should be clearly marked, and it is your job to establish the tempo. You may tap it out for the pianist ahead of time. Also remember that the pianist will follow your lead during the audition, not the other way around. Your music must be in the correct key. You cannot expect an accompanist to transpose for you on sight. Finally, make sure to "back" or matt your music so it will stand by itself.

Upon entering the acting arena, smile and relax. Directors read a lot into the way an actor enters the stage. Try to control your nerves, and maintain a confident, pleasant, and positive persona. Before your introduction, make physical contact with the space. Place the chair in the appropriate place, even if this means moving it only a few inches. If you do not need the chair, move it out of your way. Find the light. Casting directors cannot understand actors who refuse to act in the light. Also, find your off-stage focal points to help you sustain belief in the fourth side. Remember, these focal points should be located in the auditorium (e.g., exit sign, column, door, or any clearly visible inanimate and stationary object).

As you begin to address the casting personnel, rid yourself of all pretenses. Be yourself. Do not apologize. This does not mean to literally say, "I'm sorry," but rather people apologize with their gait, their gestures, their eyes, and their vocal inflection. Relax. You are the reason they are there. One of the biggest fallacies is that actors feel that those watching are the competition and want them to fail. Everyone involved in the casting process wants you to succeed. In fact, they will "jump for joy" if they perceive you to be the next Gwyneth Paltrow or Al Pacino.

Stand during your introduction. Actors who walk into the space, sit down, and introduce themselves come across as being intimidated by the situation. If a stage manager announces your arrival and mispronounces your name, do not correct her or show irritation. Casting directors will not hire actors who seem to be "prima donnas" or "divas." Clearly and professionally state your name and number (if necessary). This is perhaps the most important part of your audition. Take a moment, and launch into your first monologue or song.

Your transition and exit are also extremely important parts of the audition process. Take your time between pieces. This is a common problem, usually caused by nerves or inadequate preparation, and it breaks the dramatic illusion. After you have completed your prepared material, you may wish to repeat your name (and number if you have one). This could be the last thing they hear you say as you exit the room. If time is called, do not keep going, even if it is the last sentence or last musical phrase. Simply say, "Thank you," and exit. Do not show frustration with the timekeeper (or the accompanist). You cannot blame him for your lack of preparation. Also, the auditors will sense your frustration, which may cost you a callback. Maintain your composure as you exit. Many casting directors look at the exit as the most important part of auditioning.

Cold readings require a different kind of effort. Most directors would certainly prefer that you not memorize the text, but you certainly may, and should, study the script if it is available before attending the auditions. The director will not expect a fully developed characterization in a cold reading. She will, however, expect you to make decisions about your character—even if they are wrong—and establish a relationship with your reading partner. She will also expect you to perform well under pressure and to show that you can quickly focus on an objective and perform it well enough to bring your words to life.

If you are allowed to hear others read, be wary of the tendency either to copy an effective decision or to try too hard to be different. Another warning: Do not attempt to guess what the director wants. Center your energies on understanding the script well enough to give an intelligent reading that shows you can make defensible choices. Believing is a part of auditioning, too. You must be able to believe in your abilities and in the words you are speaking.

Use your script in a cold reading, but do not be overly dependent on it. It is a map for your reading and interpretation. Hold it in one hand away from your body to free your ability to gesture. You should also make eye contact with your reading partner—*infect* him. Sometimes you will read with a casting assistant as you speak. Generally, they are not actors and will just "read." Do not fall into the trap of reading as they do. Trust your own instincts and deliver a full performance reading to the best of your ability.

Do not allow yourself to lose control of the reading. Listen to your monitor and react realistically to the situation. In other words, do not "ham it up." Less is usually better, depending on the material. Even in broad comedy, go only as far as the action and dialogue take you. Do not try to be funny. Simply play your objective, and rely on your technique.

Take your time. Never rush through your reading, unless the script states that the character is talking very fast. Take your moments. If you feel a rising nervous sensation, take a deep breath—never dropping character—and continue. Of course, you will make mistakes. All actors do throughout their careers. No matter what happens, stay focused. If you get a really bad start on a reading, it is perfectly permissible and entirely professional to say "I'd like to start over, please." Take a moment and begin again. You will be respected for this kind of command of your reading. After all, this is your time and maybe your only time for this person or production group. If you make multiple mistakes and cannot continue, simply say "Thank you. It was very nice meeting you." and leave. Never apologize! The casting director may not have even noticed your mistake. Often actors are cast in roles when they themselves felt they gave an awful reading.

Be proud of your work, and do not apologize for your presence!

EXERCISE

1. Using the above list, begin working on your portfolio. Find monologues and songs you believe would serve you well as audition pieces.

2. Prepare and perform in class a three-minute audition (non-singing) containing two pieces: one comic and one serious, and one from a classic and one from a modern play.

3. Prepare your résumé on your computer, and update it regularly as you achieve additional training and experience.

4. Research the professional photographers in your area who specialize in theatre, film, and television headshots. Peruse their portfolio and compare prices. As soon as you have the money, schedule an appointment.

5. Investigate your local audition scene. Find publications and hotlines that will inform you of upcoming events.

6. Research and make an appointment with a reputable agent for commercial work.

7. Investigate the combined audition sites listed in Appendix B. Plan to attend one or more of these auditions.

Notes

1. Michael Shurtleff, *Audition: Everything an Actor Needs to Know to Get the Part* (New York: Walker, 1978), p. 1.

2. Ibid.

3. Fred Silver, *Auditioning for the Musical Theatre* (New York: New Market Press, 1985), p. 138.

CHAPTER 14

Show Time!
Rehearsing and
Performing

You survived the audition. You landed the role. It is time to begin rehearsals; only now you have the advantage of working under the guidance of a director. A good director, who has thoroughly analyzed the script and who has fashioned a strong artistic vision, helps you shape your characterization so it will make the greatest possible contribution to the overall production. Directors will help you create characters that are true to the dramatist's intentions as they have interpreted them for that particular production.

The director's interpretation becomes the foundation for the master plan—a plan often intricately complicated in its detail—for coordinating all aspects of the production into an artistic whole. Your interpretation of your character is a vital part of that plan, and much rehearsal time is spent on its development and its relationship to the other characters in the play. To bring you to "performance level," the director will also devote rehearsal time to gaining clear speech, good projection, precise movement, rhythm, and energy.

The pre-rehearsal period—after you are cast and before rehearsals begin—is a time for you to learn about your role and the structure of the play as a whole. It is a time to read about the period of the play and, if appropriate, to study the art and general history of the period.

Ideally, you should study the play's structure before rehearsals. Discover how each character's action relates to the whole drama. Take a while to examine the play with fresh eyes—as if you had no role in it at all. *Being flexible toward* [*role early in rehearsals is as important as being solidly and comfortably prepared when rehearsals end.*

During the rehearsal period, you will join a team that consists of the director, the stage manager, the other actors, and, finally, the various production crews. All these people strive for a single goal: the creative and artistic expression of the play's super-objective. Although you are expected to analyze your role on your own, you must relate your performance to the director's concept. You must also learn how to use all the elements of modern theatre to reinforce your character, including lights, scenery, costumes, sound, and many more. You must learn to keep a cool head in a demanding and often pressure-packed group enterprise. Producing a play is a fine example of cooperative effort—a process described by Harold Clurman as "the relating of a number of talents to a single meaning."[1]

Although they often are not sharply defined and they may considerably overlap, five principal phases make up the rehearsal process:

1. Finding the meaning
2. Developing the characters
3. Creating and refining the form
4. Making technical adjustments
5. Polishing for performance

Finding the Meaning

If a production is to realize its possibilities, if it is to be the "relating of a number of talents to a single meaning," everyone working on the production must understand what that single meaning is. And everyone must understand how each particular part, small or large as it may be, contributes to the expression of it. Indeed, the final success or failure of the production will rest in all likelihood on that part of the rehearsal period devoted to finding the meaning of the play.

The director, the actors, and the designers come to an agreement about the meaning of the play. Their understanding may result from group discussions, in which everyone, having analyzed the play beforehand, stands ready to present his or her interpretation but willing to modify it if necessary. This, we warn you, is the least effective way to create a cohesive production. More often, production teams depend on directors to initially possess a more thorough knowledge of the play than anyone else and to share their vision with them at the first meeting. The various production personnel take the director's interpretation and superimpose their own ideas before taking them back to the director, who usually incorporates all or parts of each artist's contribution into the artistic whole. Usually, the schedule will call for a number of "reading rehearsals," in which actors sit in a circle reading aloud their individual parts and discussing the play with the director and with each other. Other members of the production team will often be invited to these sessions. Remember, however, you must always guard against sharing too much personal information about your character with the entire group. Again, recall our comments in Chapter 9 about mystery and secret.

The important thing is that everyone clearly understands what the play means. Until this common understanding has been reached, the group is likely to be working at cross purposes, and the rehearsals cannot proceed effectively.

Once the interpretation is set, the actors begin to search for their characters' motivating force and its relationship to the super-objective. Here again agreement between the actor and the director is necessary, and the reading rehearsals usually produce this understanding. At the same time, the actor begins to consider the problem of line interpretation—of relating the lines to the character's motivating force and to the meaning of the play as a whole.

There are two schools of thought with regard to the amount of table work. Some contemporary directors sit around a table with their cast and read and discuss the play for as much as a third of the entire rehearsal period, a practice Stanislavski used at the beginning of the twentieth century at the Moscow Art Theatre. He eventually realized—and most contemporary directors agree—that too much table work actually impedes the psychophysical process. Actors must learn "to act," not just discuss. Through actions, you are forced to consider the psychological motivation, thus finding a harmony between substance and shape. So, as we previously suggested, you must learn to analyze the script in juxtaposition with the physical exploration that occurs in rehearsals. The process of physical and psychological exploration is never finished, as new and deeper meanings are certain to reveal themselves during all kinds of rehearsals and, indeed, during performances.

Although the actor and director are teammates, sharing the goal of excellence, they have different responsibilities. The director is the team captain, who ultimately decides which particular actions move the play toward the desired effect. The director also interacts with other team members—set designer, lighting designer, costume designer, property master—and, most of all, with the playwright, either directly or through the play. A play is not just an imitation of an action but is also a work of art, requiring unity, structure, and focus that a director must create. The director guides actors in much the same way an acting teacher guides an acting class—supervising the production: inspiring an actor's own analysis, growth, and development, and serving as a formal friend.

College actors tend to expect directors to give them too much direction. Actors are creators. In addition to learning their role, showing up at rehearsals, and adapting to different directorial methods and to their fellow actors, they should be self-reliant. Self-observation is an important part of artistic growth. Actors who refuse to look objectively at their own work are destined to a life in community theatre. When asked to review their performance, they either say such things as "Fabulous," or "Great" or blame their lackluster work on the audience. Actors who cannot—or will not—articulate "what worked" and "what didn't work" will never grow. Actors who will not take responsibility for their own work will forever remain amateurs. As Uta Hagen said, "the actors will cease to improve in their parts unless they themselves have learned to recognize their flaws and how to correct them."[2] Truly professional actors understand that the director is there to guide them through the process, but they must have the ability to explore, make decisions, and evaluate their own work.

Developing the Character

With the meaning of the play in mind, the actor is ready to concentrate on characterization. At this time most actors find their greatest satisfaction as creative artists, and, as we have seen, the temptation is great to rush to this phase before the proper groundwork has been established. In this series of rehearsals, you explore you inner resources to discover how you can use your experiences to understand the problems of the character. You use your imagination to supply additional circumstances to round out the character's background and to aid yourself in believing the action. You observe people and objects to find helpful details. You continue to read, study paintings, and listen to music if you need to enlarge your experience to understand any aspect of the play.

By this time, you have completed the task of breaking your role down into units of action. You know the simple objective of each unit and can relate it to the character's motivating force. You devise a score of physical actions through which you can realize your objectives, and you explore various "tactics" working against obstacles in each unit, both at home by yourself and at rehearsals with the other actors.

At the same time, you are determining the motivation behind each line, discovering its subtext and verbal action, and relating it to the character's motivating force. If the character's speech differs from your own, you have the added task of learning to reproduce it believably by listening to speakers with a similar background or to recordings. Chances are that you will be called on during these rehearsals to have completed the memorization of your lines and cues.

As with the amount of table work, there are two schools of thought with regard to memorization of lines. Some directors warn against memorizing the lines before you know your subtext and have your inner monologues and inner images. They feel if you memorize the lines too early, your intonations may be entirely wrong. They believe that once you have done the necessary preparation, the lines will easily follow. Other directors, however, demand that you memorize the lines from the beginning. Stanislavski and Nemirovich-Danchenko debated this issue. Today, Russian directors agree with Nemirovich-Danchenko. "Before an actor can understand and make a dramatist's language, style and unique diction his own, the lines must first be memorized," wrote Sonia Moore. "Even if an actor understands a character's actions and motivations, without the text he will not be able to understand fully the subtext or its relationship to the text."[3] Both arguments are valid, and chances are you will develop a technique that falls somewhere in the middle. Regardless, you must take this responsibility seriously and complete it by the time you are asked to be "off book," a moment that varies from director to director.

Accurate memorization is your responsibility. You owe it to the dramatist, who is dependent on you for the truthful representation of the work, and you owe it to your fellow players, whose own lines must be motivated by what has gone before.

Creating and Refining the Form

"Art is search, not finished form," Yevgeny Vakhtangov was fond of saying. In the early stages of rehearsal, you are exploring the character, blocking the movement, inventing the business, creating the form. However, throughout the investigative process—a process that doesn't fully conclude until the lights fade on the final performance—you are refining the form. The period of first discovery is undoubtedly the most exciting part of the creative process, and at some point you will be asked to "freeze" your major movements. However, you must *never* allow your investigation of form to end. As long as you can improve, make new discoveries, enhance the second plan, and uncover better actions and tactics, the artistic development of your character will continue. You are not bound by your early discoveries. Theatrical form is never "set in stone." Through self-observation, you continue the *process of exploration,* for that is the entire purpose of rehearsals— no matter how close to opening night.

By using the technique discussed in this book, your work will never grow stale. However, once your verbal and physical actions become nothing more than mechanical repetition, your performance is dead. And it will grow worse with every subsequent presentation. The moment you stop "working," the truthfulness of your actions and subsequent emotions will become mere accidents. Art will only exist as long as there is exploration of outer form. Stanislavski referred to it as the state of "I am." He said, "Right here. Right now. Today." At every rehearsal, you must, as your character, relive the moments of action as if they were happening for the first time. You must continually ask yourself, "What would I do *if* I were this character in this circumstance?" What are "my" actions? What is "my" objective? What are "my" expectations? What am "I" willing to do to get what "I" want? What adaptations am "I" willing to explore?

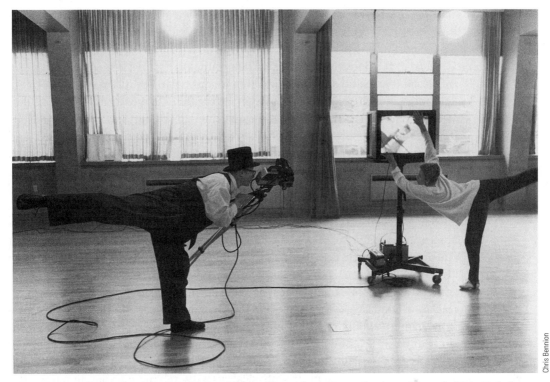

Figure 14.1 Bill Irwin in rehearsal of Seattle Repertory Theatre's production of *Largely/New York,* by Bill Irwin. Rehearsals are a time to experiment, to discover, to fail. The greatest creativity and artistic satisfaction come during working rehearsals.

You must play your objectives and work against your obstacles each time you put on your character's clothing. This is your path to uncovering the "mystery of inspiration." With the proper inner work at every rehearsal and performance, your work will remain fresh. Your character will continue to grow. Inspiration comes as a result of hard work! And repeated inspiration comes as a result of even harder work! That is the way it is—no matter how great your talent.

In the early rehearsals, the initial creation of form is a rewarding, and sometimes agonizing, process. It does not spring full-grown from the imaginations of either the actors or the director but grows slowly. It comes in bits and pieces and cannot be forced. Although parts of it may need to be "grafted on from the outside," as Stanislavski said in his supplement to *Creating a Role,* it cannot be wholly imposed in this fashion. It comes from the combined imaginations of the actors and the director, stimulated initially by the playwright and later by the responses of the actors to one another and to the products of other artists—props, settings, costumes, and lights, for example. It must develop organically as the character develops. Form grows out of character and character out of form, so, enigmatic as it sounds, what a character is determines what she does, and what she does determines what she is.

Most of the time, the ground plan determines the actor's large movements (entrances and exits, crosses from one area to another). The director and designers determine these before rehearsals begin, aware that the most important consideration in making the ground plan is the movement it will impose on the actors. The large movements become apparent as soon as the ground plan is explained, and the actors accept these new conditions and motivate them. In fact, the blocking, the ground plan, the director's concept, the scenic design, the costume design, the prop design, and the lighting design all join the playwright's words as part of the actor's given circumstances.

Some movements and other physical activities are inherent in the lines. Examples are crossing to answer the doorbell or telephone, serving tea, or less obvious indications such as Petruchio's threat to Katharina (*The Taming of the Shrew*): "I swear I'll cuff you, if you strike again" or Juliet's plea to Romeo: "Wilt thou be gone? It is not yet near day." Most acting editions of plays also describe physicalization in their stage directions, but the actor must examine this material carefully. In all likelihood it will relate to a ground plan and set of circumstances entirely different from those of the current production, and the director often may tell you to ignore it entirely. Even including all these sources, it is necessary to invent additional movement and physical activity, relying on your impulses. Remember that physical objectives help you believe in your character and express their desires in ways the audience can see and understand. During this part of the rehearsal period, often called *working rehearsals,* you and the director use your imaginations to devise movement and business that will give outer form to inner characterization.

You also use these rehearsals as a testing ground for what externals of manner, dress, action, and so forth you can use to reinforce the characterization. These externals are vital because, as we recall from earlier chapters, doing is believing. You are likely to believe the character to the extent you can translate the character's desires into action. Such small things as using a handkerchief, eating a sandwich, turning on a light, or writing down an address provide physical motivations on which you can concentrate your attention.

Determining the amount and nature of the physical activity is a matter to be settled between you and director. Good directors frequently make suggestions, but you have both the opportunity and the responsibility for originating small actions that will help create form. Nowhere is the quality of your imagination more evident than in this phase of your work. Of course, to claim the stage, all business must be justified in terms of the total meaning of the play and the production.

Costumes and properties are vastly important in creating the form of both the role and the production. If you establish a proper relationship to them, they become in themselves excellent "actors," and they are essential to the creation of physical image. Stanislavski wrote:

> A costume or an object appropriate to a stage figure ceases to be a simple material thing, it acquires a kind of sanctity for an actor. . . . You can tell a true artist by his attitudes towards his costume and properties.[4]

Making Technical Adjustments

Somewhere toward the end of the rehearsal period, you will begin to work in the setting, with the properties that will be used in performance, in costume, and under the lights. At this time, adjustments are always necessary. The furniture may take up more space than the small chairs and tables with which you have been working. Opening and closing actual doors may require more time than you have been allowing. The position of a piano may have to be changed to improve the sight lines for the audience. The manipulation of the clothing may require more care than anticipated. A climactic scene may have to be played farther downstage so that it may be lighted effectively. Such adjustments are an inevitable part of rehearsal. Experienced actors recognize the need for these changes and immediately find ways (sometimes by inventing additional "circumstances") to motivate them in terms of their characters' desires.

During "technical rehearsals" certain actions may have to be repeated over and over to allow the lighting and sound crews to coordinate their timing with that of the actors. You are responsible for handling these hardworking rehearsals calmly and pleasantly. Although it may seem that the development of the production has come to a standstill or actually regressed, you must remember that you have now had many weeks of rehearsals and that the technical production crews are attempting to catch up in one or two nights. You must recognize that the technical crew will catch up quickly. You must also know that only through these rehearsals can the entire company become the smooth-working team it will take to make the production a success.

Polishing the Performance

The final rehearsals, including the dress rehearsals, are devoted to polishing for performance. At this time, your blocking is set—although your "work" continues—and feelings of tentativeness must disappear. During the earlier rehearsals, you have made many discoveries. You have experimented with details of business, movement, and line reading. Throughout the entire period, you have explored details that will allow you to believe your character. These rehearsals are, in fact, a continual process of selection and rejection. By the time the play is ready for polishing, however, your major choices must be relatively firm. During the final rehearsals, you need to have confidence in your characterization and in the technical support for the production, as only then can you be comfortable and assured in your performance.

Much attention in the polishing rehearsals turns to *timing* and *projection,* although both will have been anticipated earlier.

Timing is a matter of pace and rhythm, pertaining to the tempo at which lines are spoken and business and movement are executed and to the rapidity at which cues are picked up. As long as you feel uncertain about the details of your performance, you cannot establish and maintain a tempo.

A sense of timing is one of the subtlest elements of stage technique. For its development, you must have experience before an audience. Too slow a tempo will not hold interest, but too fast a tempo will obscure the meaning. Too consistent a tempo will become monotonous; too varied a tempo will seem jerky and illogical. If you are slow to pick up cues, your rhythm will falter between speeches. If you are too fast in speaking your lines, their meaning will be blurred. To the expert ear, this blurring clearly indicates that you are not using your lines to accomplish a verbal action. Maintaining too constant a tempo indicates you are not hearing and feeling different tempo–rhythms for varying structural units.

An important consideration in timing is the use of *silences.* Many beginning actors tend to *pause*—an indication that "nothing" is happening—for their own convenience (because they are not breathing correctly, because they are not thinking fast enough, because they are not sure of what they are doing) without regard to dramatic effect. During silences, however, dramatic action is still being driven forward. Objectives are still being pursued. Nevertheless, silences should be used sparingly and *only when they are more effective than speech.*

Some playwrights are so conscious of the need to use silences effectively that they take great pains to indicate the proper place for them in their scripts. Actors performing in the plays of Harold Pinter, for example, will find silences to be as much a part of the dialogue as the words themselves.

Timing varies from play to play, from scene to scene, from character to character, and from audience to audience. Thought-provoking plays usually require a slower tempo than does farce, and expository scenes at the beginning almost always require a slower tempo than do climactic scenes at the end. One character moves and speaks more slowly than another, and one audience is quicker at grasping meanings than another. During the final rehearsals, the director will guide the cast in establishing effective tempos for the play, for different scenes, and for different characters. The actors alone have the responsibility to feel out the audience and make necessary adjustments from performance to performance.

Vocal projection is another variable element. A constant requirement of the theatre is that the audience hears and understands the lines. This requirement may be satisfied in a variety of voice levels, ranging from a shout to a whisper. Pro-

Figure 14.2 Avery Brooks as Oedipus in The Shakespeare Theatre's 2001 production of *The Oedipus Plays,* by Sophocles, a new translation by Nicholas Rudall. Directed by Michael Kahn. Whether a small, intimate scene or a large spectacle, the actors must project their individual characters into the audience.

jection does not mean talking loudly but describes the actor's effort to share every moment of the play with the audience. The play, the scene, the character, and the size and acoustical qualities of the auditorium will determine the degree of loudness that is most suitable. Again, variety is necessary. Nothing is more tiresome than listening over a period of time to an unvaried voice. Unmotivated, abrupt changes, on the other hand, are likely to startle the audience and attract undue attention.

Visual projection is equally important. The audience must see the action as clearly as they can hear the lines. Three requirements of movement, business, and gesture are:

1. They must be suitable to the character, the scene, the play, and the general style of the production.

2. They must be clearly seen.

3. Their significance to the total meaning must be readily comprehensible.

At final rehearsals, actors turn much of their attention to auditory and visual projection. The director carefully checks their effectiveness, but the final test can be made only by performing before an audience. To ensure that the cast will meet the test on opening night, producers and directors have preview performances or invite an audience to the final "run-throughs."

Working at Rehearsals

For a talented actor, well trained in techniques of their art, rehearsals are a happy time, though they are not always filled with fun. Preparing a play for production is at best hard work, often fraught with frustration. But during rehearsals you have the greatest opportunity for creative accomplishment. You should begin rehearsals resolved to use all your resources for the good of the production. What is best for the production should be the single criterion for choices, and nothing makes for a happier atmosphere than sharing this resolve with all members of the cast.

Rehearsals will proceed best if you establish a relationship with the director and with the other actors based on mutual respect. The director determines the working methods, the rehearsal schedule, and the distribution of rehearsal time among the different acts and scenes. You respect both the method and the schedule and cooperate with the director in their way of working. Needless to say, you attend rehearsals regularly and punctually. You are ready to work at the scheduled time, which means you arrive fifteen to thirty minutes early, warm up, and prepare for your first scene. You have an obligation to keep yourself healthy, rested, and in good spirits, so sickness, fatigue, or personal problems do not interfere. To the other actors, you are generous and demanding: insisting that they give their best, generous in giving your best to them.

At the first opportunity, you will also want to get to know the stage manager, to understand her importance to the production and to respect her authority. Although her specific duties vary from theatre to theatre and company to company, the stage manager is the person who, according to Lawrence Stern, "accepts responsibility that the rehearsals and performances run smoothly on stage and backstage."[5] Establishing the proper relationship with this individual is absolutely critical to a productive rehearsal and performance period.

Throughout each rehearsal, you are alert and committed to the work at hand. You give your entire attention to what is going on, both when you are in the scene and when you are waiting for an entrance. You mark directions in your script or in a notebook. Once blocking or business has been given by or worked out in conjunction with the director at rehearsal, you are responsible for retaining it. You bring a supply of pencils (with erasers) to rehearsal with you and record all movements in the margin of your script at the time you are blocked, using standard abbreviations. Drawing diagrams in the margin is a practical way of recording complicated blocking. You do more, though, than keep track of your blocking. You write down your units, objectives, subtext, comments, and interpretations until your copy of the script becomes a complete score for playing your role. That score becomes an invaluable source of reference during later rehearsals and performances. You take careful notes on your director's oral critiques and refer to them before the next time you rehearse the scene for which they were given. You study, absorb, experiment, probe, watch, listen, and create.

Rehearsals constitute a fluid process during which the production gradually emerges. For you, the actor, the process offers a chance to explore every facet of the character you are portraying. Layer by layer you develop the character and relate it to the performances of the rest of the company and the production as a whole. You recognize that early rehearsals must progress in bits and pieces; therefore, you are cautious of going too fast. Each moment of the play must be explored and the problems solved through trial and error. Early decisions can be only tentative; preliminary ideas about a character may actually be reversed as rehearsals progress. The production must develop organically. Without change at each rehearsal, satisfactory progress toward the final shape of the production bogs down.

Rehearsal expectations vary from company to company, but the work habits of all good actors reflect an attitude toward the theatre that is conducive to creativity and free from serious "acting traps" that shackle their efforts. What are these traps? Joseph Slowik has pinpointed four on which Grotowski regularly concentrated while Slowik was observing his company. They are *impatience, half-heartedness, poor work ethics,* and *substitution.*[6]

Impatience leads to a lack of technique, because it causes you to look for shortcuts that disrupt and emasculate your work. Stanislavski called this trap taking the "line of least resistance" in creating a character. The impatient actor relies on tricks, on work that has been successful in a previous characterization, or on actions that have been neither sufficiently grounded in the play's given circumstances nor properly articulated with the other performances.

Half-heartedness means giving less than maximum effort during rehearsals. Good actors simply do not work with anything less than their entire being. They know that truth and believability are difficult to achieve under any circumstances and that without maximum effort they simply will not appear.

Poor work ethics inevitably lead to a rehearsal atmosphere in which creativity cannot take place, in which actors will be afraid to take a chance. Sure signs of poor work ethics are resentment, back biting, buck passing, and unconstructive criticism, all mortal enemies of the trust necessary for success in the theatre.

Substitution is the most pervasive trap of all, but also the most difficult to define. Slowik said:

Anything less than [a] preciously recognizable human response is a substitute. It is something behind which the actor hides when he is empty.

When audiences seem to be satisfied with less than the "real thing" actors continue to hide behind substitution, building their careers on one of the most destructive enemies of creativity.[7]

Working at Home

You cannot accomplish all your work at rehearsals. Beginners too often neglect "homework." You must use rehearsals as an opportunity to test for the director and with the other actors what you have worked out by yourself. Dividing your role into units, discovering and stating the simple objectives, finding additional circumstances, setting the sensory tasks, and writing the subtext all are problems for you to discover, subject to the guidance of the director. You can also work by yourself on many of the specific problems that arise during rehearsal. Referring often to the notes you took at the oral critique, you work on the suggestions associated with your role and bring a fresh approach to the next rehearsal.

Playing the Part

We have seen that your first major concern during rehearsals is discovering the total meaning of the play by studying the script, examining other sources, and discussing the interpretation with the director and the other actors. In the kind of play that constitutes the great body of Western drama, both classic and contemporary—the kind of play in which the dramatist expresses his or her meaning by creating characters involved in some sort of conflict—you must next give immediate attention to understanding the character you are playing and to believing the character's speech and actions. In later rehearsals, you become increasingly concerned with projecting the character to the audience, and you continue to focus on these concerns during the entire run of the play. You must bring the character newly to life at every performance, confident that you are not only performing "natural" actions but also creating a theatrically effective form.

As the play is repeated in performance, the core—the super-objective, motivating forces, simple objectives, and overall physical form of the production—stays the same. Keeping it the same is one of your responsibilities. You are required to perform the play as rehearsed, and the Actors' Equity Association fines and ultimately suspends professionals who fail to respect their obligation. As we explained, however, this requirement does not mean that creativity (and exploration) ceases and that the robot-like actor repeats from memory what has been "set" in rehearsal. Rather, you commit yourself at each performance to accomplishing the character's objectives and to establishing relations with objects and other actors as if it were for the first time. Performance demands continual and

Linda Blase

Figure 14.3 A scene from the Dallas Theater Center's production of *The Front Page*. Note the joy with which these four actors perform their roles.

fresh adjustment to the stage life going on around you. To keep a performance the same, it must always be subtly different; mechanical repetition does not retain vitality.

Concentration is the keynote to success, but you must recall the earlier lesson in which we concluded that concentration must take place on two levels. Let us review this important, if sometimes confusing, duality.

On one level, you direct your attention to satisfying the desires of the character. You use your speech and actions to get what the character wants and attempts, to influence the behavior of the other characters as you try to satisfy your objective. By concentrating on this objective, you are able to believe your actions. They, in turn, produce feelings similar to the feelings the character would have if the situations were real. Your imagination also allows you to use the feelings that arise from your relationship to the other actors.

On another level, you concentrate on expressing the character in theatrical terms. The audience must hear the lines and see the actions. A tempo must be maintained that will be suitable to the play, stimulating to the audience, and dramatically effective. You do your part to create enough variety in the performance to ensure a continual renewal of the audience's interest. To maintain this level of concentration, you must develop what Lynn Fontanne called an "outside eye and ear" to guide you in playing your role. You have the dual function of being both character and interpreter.[8]

In some contemporary works, the creation of character in imaginary circumstances is a minimal part of your responsibility. You express your or the playwright's meaning to the audience in your own person. In these instances the audience becomes a part of the given circumstances of the play, and your task is to find every way possible to communicate with them directly, clearly, and forcefully.

You must serve your function with ease and authority. The audience experiences no pleasure watching a performer who is tense and strained and no comfort watching one who does not seem confident in her ability to perform with some degree of credit to herself. Concentration, again, is the keynote to relaxation. When you can turn your full attention to doing a job you know you are prepared to do, you forget your fears and your self-consciousness.

Although many of the suggestions we have made about performing a role are universal, conditions will certainly vary with the experience of the company, the sophistication of the audience, and whether the play is presented for a limited run, for a long run, or in repertory. These distinctions are too complex for inclusion in this text, but you should be prepared to seek advice from your instructor, your director, your stage manager, or a colleague who has experienced the particular conditions under which you will be performing. Keeping a role fresh during a long run is a particularly difficult problem and one that will tax your ability to generate anew exciting objectives and actions every time you step on stage. Naturally, each audience must believe you are performing the role for the first time and, for them, you are. Any reasonably accomplished actor can get excited about opening night; it is the fifth, or seventy-fifth, or three hundred seventy-fifth performance of the same role that taxes your technique.

One of the final tasks of the actor is to learn to handle criticism, both positive and negative. Although it would be foolish to say you should pay no attention to criticism from the press or your friends, it is important for you to establish the habit of acting for your fellow actors and your director rather than for the critics. Negative criticism is depressing and inevitably affects a show adversely. Praise or flattery usually adds fuel to the fires of self-esteem, a conflagration from which your enemies all too often emerge. Acting is a frightening art, the only one in which the moment of its final creation is also the moment of its acceptance or rejection by the public. Actors often suffer because the audience, on which they are dependent for their success, does not seem to view their art with the same respect it has for other artists. Uta Hagen explained the phenomenon this way:

> More than in the other performing arts the lack of respect for acting
> seems to spring from the fact that every layman considers himself a

valid critic. While no lay audience discusses the bowing arm or stroke of the violinist or the palette or brush technique of the painter, or the tension which may create a poor entre-chat, they will all be willing to give formulas to the actor. . . . And the actor listens to them, compounding the felonious notion that no craft or skill or art is needed in acting.[9]

This book has been dedicated to the purpose of helping you believe in your craft, your skill, and your art. *Believe* is the operative word, the linchpin, of its message. Without a believable foundation for character: believable actions; believable objectives; believable vocal, physical, and emotional technique; and above all, a belief in the script and one's fellow artists, you are doomed to failure. With them, you have a chance to create magic, to move an audience to a deeper understanding of the mystery and the majesty — as well as the failures and the foibles — of humankind.

Notes

1. Harold Clurman, *The Fervent Years* (New York: Knopf, 1945), p. 41.

2. Uta Hagen, *A Challenge for the Actor* (New York: Macmillan Publishing Company, 1991), pp. 292–293.

3. Sonia Moore, *Stanislavski Revealed* (New York City: Applause Theatre Books, 1991), p. 125.

4. Constantin Stanislavski, *An Actor's Handbook,* ed. Elizabeth Reynolds Hapgood (New York: Theatre Arts Books, 1963), p. 43.

5. Lawrence Stern, *Stage Management: A Guidebook of Practical Techniques,* 3rd ed. (Boston: Allyn and Bacon, Inc., 1987), p. 4.

6. Joseph Slowik, "An Actor's Enemies," paper delivered to the Mid-America Theatre Conference, Omaha, Nebraska, March 16, 1984.

7. Slowik, "An Actor's Enemies," p. 6.

8. Lewis Funke and John E. Booth, *Actors Talk About Acting: Fourteen Interviews with Stars of the Theatre* (New York: Random House, 1961), p. 67.

9. Uta Hagen with Haskel Frankel, *Respect for Acting* (New York: Macmillan, 1973), p. 3.

Suggested Plays for Undergraduate Scene Study

Three Women

Agnes of God, by John Pielmeier

And Miss Reardon Drinks a Little, by Paul Zindel

*Blue Blood, by Georgia Douglas Johnson

Candy and Shelley Go To The Desert, by Paula Cizmar

Catholic School Girls, by Casey Kurtti

Crimes of the Heart, by Beth Henley

Desdemona: A Play About a Handkerchief, by Paula Vogel

Eating Out, by Marcia Dixcy (Found in *25 Ten Minute Plays from Actor's Theatre of Louisville*)

Effect of Gamma Rays on Man-in-the-Moon Marigolds, The, by Paul Zindel

Eleemosynary, by Lee Blessing

Family Scenes, by Ivette M. Ramirez

Five Women Wearing the Same Dress, by Alan Ball

Independence, by Lee Blessing

Laundry and Bourbon, by James McLure

Maids, The, by Jean Genet

Miss Firecracker Contest, The, by Beth Henley

On the Verge, by Eric Overmyer

Shallow End, The, by Wendy MacLeod

Three Sisters, The, by Anton Chekhov

Uncommon Women and Others, by Wendy Wasserstien

Vanities, by Jack Heifner

Waiting for the Parade, by John Murrell

Women of Manhattan, by John Patrick Shanley

Three Men

Absurd Person Singular, by Alan Ayckbourn

American Buffalo, by David Mamet

Art, by Yasmina Reza

Biloxi Blues, by Neil Simon

Boy's Life, by Howard Korder

Compleat Works of Wllm Shkspr (abridged), The, by The Reduced Shakespeare Co.

Hurlyburly, by David Rabe

*Indian Wants the Bronx, The, by Israel Horovitz

Life in the Theatre, A, by David Mamet

Lone Star, by James McLure

Lost in Yonkers, by Neil Simon

*"Master Harold" . . . and the Boys, by Athol Fugard

Mister Roberts, by Thomas Heggen and Joshua Logan

Of Mice and Men, by John Steinbeck

Orphans, by Lyle Kessler

Pick Up Ax, by Anthony Clarvoe

Pvt. Wars, by James McLure

*T Bone N Weasel, by Jon Klein

True West, by Sam Shepard

Words, Words, Words, by David Ives (Found in *All in the Timing*)

Two Men / One Woman

*12-1-A, by Wakako Yamauchi

*And Palm-Wine Will Flow, by Bole Butake

Baltimore Waltz, The, by Paula Vogel

Beyond Therapy, by Christopher Durang

Boy's Life, by Howard Korder

Burn This, by Lanford Wilson

Chopin Playoffs, The, by Israel Horovitz

Copenhagen, by Michael Frayn

*Corner, The, by Ed Bullins (Found in *Black Drama Anthology*)

Cover, by Jeffrey Sweet (Found in *25 10 Minute Plays from Actors Theatre of Louisville*)

Cowboy Mouth, by Sam Shepard

*Fences, by August Wilson

*F.O.B., by David Henry Hwang

Fool for Love, by Sam Shepard

Hedda Gabler, by Henrik Ibsen

*House of Ramon Iglesia, The, by José Rivera

Hurlyburly, by David Rabe

Italian American Reconciliation, by John Patrick Shanley

Key Exchange, by Kevin Wade

Lost in Yonkers, by Neil Simon

LUV, by Murray Schisgal

Molly Sweeney, by Brian Friel

Murder at the Howard Johnson's, by Ron Clark and Sam Bobrick

Porno, by Mario Fratti

Prelude to a Kiss, by Craig Lucas

Proposal, The, by Anton Chekhov

Sight Unseen, by Donald Margulies

Six Degrees of Separation, by John Guare

*Slow Dance on the Killing Ground, by William Hanley

Speed-the-Plow, by David Mamet

Spoils of War, by Michael Weller

Strange Snow, by Steve Metcalfe

Words, Words, Words, by David Ives (Found in *All in the Timing*)

One Man / Two Women

*12-1-A, by Wakako Yamauchi

Abundance, by Beth Henley

Baby Dance, The, by Jane Anderson

Baby With The Bathwater, by Christopher Durang

Bosoms and Neglect, by John Guare

Candy & Shelley Go to the Desert, by Paula Cizmar

Coyote Ugly, by Lynn Siefert

Dinner With Friends, by Donald Margulies

Duck Pond, The, by Ara Watson (Found in *25*

10-Minute Plays from Actors Theatre of Louisville)

Extremities, by William Mastrosimone

Fox, The, by Allan Miller

*Home, by Samm-Art Williams

Lesson, The, by Eugène Ionesco

Lie of the Mind, A, by Sam Shepard

Odd Couple, The (Mail Version), by Neil Simon

*Our Lady of the Tortilla, by Luis Santeiro

Painting Churches, by Tina Howe

Pizza Man, by Darlene Craviotto

Rancho Hollywood, by Carlos Morton

Miss Firecracker Contest, The, by Beth Henley

Miss Lulu Bett, by Zona Gale

No Exit, by Jean-Paul Sartre

Proof, by David Auburn

*Raisin in the Sun, A, by Lorraine Hansberry

Redwood Curtain, by Lanford Wilson

Savage in Limbo, by John Patrick Shanley

*Shayna Maidel, A, by Barbara Lebow

Street Scene, by Elmer Rice

Vinegar Tom, by Caryl Churchill

Words, Words, Words, by David Ives (Found in *All in the Timing*)

Two Women

Bedtime, by Mary Gallagher (Found in *Plays for Actresses*)

*Blue-Eyed Black Boy, by Georgia Douglas Johnson

Brighton Beach Memoirs, by Neil Simon

Bright Room Called Day, A, by Tony Kushner

Candy and Shelley Go To The Desert, by Paula Cizmar

Catholic School Girls, by Casey Kurtti

Children's Hour, The, by Lillian Hellman

*Colored Girls Who Have Considered Suicide/When the Rainbow Was Enuf, For, by Ntozake Shange

*Colored Museum, The, by George Wolfe

Coupla White Chicks Sitting Around Talking, A, by John Ford Noonan

Crimes of the Heart, by Beth Henley

Early Girl, The, by Caroline Kava

Eleemosynary, by Lee Blessing

Family Scenes, by Ivette M. Ramirez

Flyin' West, by Pearl Cleage

Importance of Being Earnest, The, by Oscar Wilde

Last Night of Ballyhoo, The, by Alfred Uhry

Laundry and Bourbon, by James McLure

*Letters to a Student Revolutionary, by Elizabeth Wong

Lie of the Mind, A, by Sam Shepard

Low Level Panic, by Clare McIntyre

Mama Drama, by Leslie Ayvazian & Others

Miracle Worker, The, by William Gibson

Miss Firecracker Contest, The, by Beth Henley

Miss Lulu Bett, by Zona Gale

Mrs. Klein, by Nicholas Wright

My Sister in This House, by Wendy Kesselman

*Once Removed, by Eduardo Machado

Our Country's Good, by Timberlake Wertenbaker

Playing for Time, by Arthur Miller

Poof!, by Lyn Nottage (Found in *Plays for Actresses*)

Proof, by David Auburn

Sally and Marsha, by Sybille Pearson

Savage in Limbo, by John Patrick Shanley

*Shayna Maidel, A, by Barbara Lebow

Spike Heels, by Teresa Rebeck

Steel Magnolias, by Robert Harlin

Streetcar Named Desire, A, by Tennessee Williams

*Talented Tenth, The, by Richard Wesley

Top Girls, by Caryl Churchill

Watermelon Boats, by Wendy MacLaughlin (Found in *25 10 Minute Plays from Actors Theatre of Louisville*)

Weldon Rising, by Phyllis Nagy

What Mama Don't Know, by Jane Martin

Whose Life Is It Anyway, by Brian Clark (Female Version)

Wine in the Wilderness, by Alice Childress (Found in *Plays By & About Black Women*)

Women of Manhattan, by John Patrick Shanley

Two Men

Beggars in the House of Plenty, by John Patrick Shanley

Boy's Life, by Howard Korder

Chopin Playoffs, The, by Israel Horovitz

Day the Bronx Died, The, by Michael Henry Brown

Dance and the Railroad, The, by David Henry Hwang

Equus, by Peter Schaffer

Elephant Man, The, by Bernard Pomerance

Fences, by August Wilson

Grapes of Wrath, The, by John Steinbeck

Hidden In This Picture, by Aaron Sorkin (Found in

Best American Short Plays of the 1990s)

How I Got That Story, by Amlin Gray

Hughie, by Eugene O'Neill

Hurlyburly, by David Rabe

Joe Turner's Come and Gone, by August Wilson

K2, by Patrick Meyers

Living At Home, by Anthony Giardina

Lone Star, by James McLure

Man Enough, by Patty Gideon Sloan

Marriage, The, by Donald Greaves (Found in *Black Drama Anthology*)

Medal of Honor Rag, by Tom Cole

Of Mice & Men, by John Steinbeck

One Flew Over the Cuckoo's Nest, by Dale Wasserman

Orphans, by Lyle Kessler

Paul Robeson, by Phillip Hayes Dean

Pvt. Wars, by James McClure

Sizwe Banzi Is Dead, by Athol Fugard, John Kani, and Winston Ntshona

Soldier's Play, A, by Charles Fuller

Some Things You Need to Know Before the World Ends (A Final Evening With the Illuminati), by Levi Lee and Larry Larson

Suburbia, by Eric Bogosian

Tracers, by John DiFusco and others

True West, by Sam Shepard

Yankee Dawg You Die, by Philip Kan Gotanda

Zoo Story, by Edward Albee

One Man / One Woman

12-1-A, by Wakako Yamauchi

Angels in America: Millennium Approaches, by Tony Kushner

Before It Hits Home, by Cheryl West

Beyond Your Command, by Ralph Pape

Big Time, by Keith Reddin

Biloxi Blues, by Neil Simon

Boy's Life, by Howard Korder

Boys Next Door, The, by Tom Griffin

Blue Blood, by Georgia Douglas Johnson

Brilliant Traces, by Cindy Lou Johnson

Children of a Lesser God, by Mark Medoff

Chopin Playoffs, The, by Israel Horovitz

Closer, by Patrick Marber

Cowboy Mouth, by Sam Shepard

Coyote Ugly, by Lynn Siefert

Crucible, The, by Arthur Miller

*Death of the Last Black Man in the Whole Entire

World, The, by Suzan-Lori Parks

Desire Under the Elms, by Eugene O'Neill

Diary of Anne Frank, The, by Frances Goodrich and Albert Hackett

Dining Room, The, by A.R. Gurney

Dinner With Friends, by Margolis

Diviners, The, by Jim Leonard

Elephant Man, The, by Bernard Pomerance

Equus, by Peter Shaffer

Extremities, by William Mastrosimone

*Fences, by August Wilson

Fool for Love, by Sam Shepard

Frankie and Johnny in the Clair De Lune, by Terrence McNally

Glass Menagerie, The, by Tennessee Williams

Grapes of Wrath, The, by John Steinbeck

Heidi Chronicles, The, by Wendy Wasserstein

Henceforward, by Alan Ayckbourn

Hidden Parts, by Lynn Alvarez

How I Learned to Drive, by Paula Vogel

Hurlyburly, by David Rabe

Italian American Reconciliation, by John Patrick Shanley

Jack and Jill, by Jane Martin

Kentucky Cycle, The ("The Homecoming"), by Robert Schenkkan

Key Exchange, by Kevin Wade

Lady and the Clarinet, The, by Michael Cristofer

Last Night of Ballyhoo, The, by Alfred Uhry

Les Liaisons Dangereuses, by Christopher Hampton

Lie of the Mind, A, by Sam Shepard

*Marriage, The, by Donald Greaves (Found in *Black Drama Anthology*)

Miss Julie, by August Strindberg

Open Admissions, by Shirley Lauro (Found in *Off-Off-Broadway Play Festival, Volume 4*)

Owl and the Pussycat, The, by Bill Manhoff

Prelude to a Kiss, by Craig Lucas

Raised in Captivity, by Nicky Silver

*Rancho Hollywood, by Carlos Morton

Redwood Curtain, by Lanford Wilson

Royal Gambit, by Hermann Gressieker

Same Time, Next Year, by Bernard Slade

Sexual Perversity in Chicago, by David Mamet

Shadow Box, The, by Michael Cristofer

Shivaree, by William Mastrosimone

Shopping and F***ing, by Mark Ravenhill

Simpatico, by Sam Shepard

*Spanish Eyes, by Eduardo Ivan Lopez (Found in *Nuestro New York*)

Split Second, by Dennis McIntyre

Streetcar Named Desire, A, by Tennessee Williams

*Talented Tenth, The, by Richard Wesley

Three Sisters, The, by Anton Chekhov

27 Wagons Full of Cotton, by Tennessee Williams

Two-Character Play, The, by Tennessee Williams

Two for the Seesaw, by William Gibson

Waiting for Lefty, by Clifford Odets

*Wine in the Wilderness, by Alice Childress (Found in *Plays By & About Black Women*)

* *Denotes multicultural scripts*

Theatre Resources

Combined Audition Sites

California Educational
  Theatre Association
  (310) 372-0250 or
  (562) 692-0921, ext. 3451
  *http://www.cetaweb.org/
  aandi/*

East Central Theatre
  Conference
  (732) 381-2264
  *http://www.community.nj
  .com/cc/ectc*

Illinois Theatre Association
  (773) 929-7288, ext. 18
  & 19

Indiana Theatre Association
  (317) 940-6549
  *intheatre@netdirect.net
  http://www.intheatre.org/
  works.html*

League of Resident Theatres
  (LORT) Lottery
  Auditions
  Contact your nearest
  AEA.

Midwest Theatre Auditions
  (314) 968-6937
  *mwt@pop.webster.edu
  http://www.webster.edu
  .depts/finearts/theatre/
  mwta/content.html*

National Dinner Theatre
  Association
  (616) 781-7859

New England Theatre
  Conference
  (617) 424-9275
  *NETC@world.std.com
  http://www.netconline.org*

New Jersey Theatre Alliance
  (973) 593-0189
  *http://www.njtheatre
  alliance.org*

Northwest Drama
  Conference
  (208) 885-6197

Ohio Theatre Alliance
  (614) 228-1998
  *http://www.ohio
  theatrealliance.org*

National Outdoor Drama
  Auditions
  (919) 962-1328
  *http://www.unc.edu/depts/
  outdoor*

Rocky Mountain Theatre
  Association
  http://www.rmta.net

Southeastern Theatre
Conference
(336) 272-3645
http://www.setc.org

Southwest Theatre
Association
*http://www.southwest-
theater.com*

Strawhat Auditions
*http://www.strawhat-
auditions.com*

Theatre Alliance of Michigan
*http://www.theatre
allianceofmichigan.org*

Theatre Auditions in
Wisconsin
*http://www.dcs.wisc.edu/
lsa/theatre/auditions.htm*

Theatre Bay Area General
Auditions
(414) 957-1557
*http://www.theatrebayarea
.org*

Unified Professional Theatre
Auditions
(901) 725-0776
http://www.UPTA.org

University/Resident Theatre
Association (U/RTA)
National Unified
Auditions
(212) 221-1130
http://www.urta.com

Vermont Theatre Auditions
*http://www.newengland
wow.com/Auditions.htm*

News & Publications

Backstage & Backstage West
http://www.backstage.com

Broadway Play Publishing
*http://www.broadwayplay
publ.com/*

Chicago Tribune
*http://www.chicago.tribune
.com/*

Curtain Up
http://www.curtainup.com

Daily Variety
*http://www.magazania
.com/id/cji/group/2999*

Dramatic Publishing
*http://www.dramatic
publishing.com/*

Dramatists Play Service, Inc.
*http://www.dramatists
.com*

Los Angeles Times
http://www.latimes.com/

Music Theatre International
http://www.mtishows.com

New York Times
http://www.nytimes.com/

PerformInk
Chicago
*http://www.performink
.com/*

Playbill Online
http://playbill.com/

Rodgers & Hammerstein
Organization, The
*http://www.rnh.com/
index1.html*

Samuel French, Inc.
*http://www.samuelfrench
.com*

Theatre.com
http://vl-theatre.com/

*Theatre Communications
Group*
http://www.tcg.org

Theatre Design & Technical
Jobs Page, The
*http://home.earthlink.net/
~pshudson/jobs/jobs.htm*

Hollywood Reporter
*http://www.hollywood
reporter.com*

TheatreJobs.com
*http://www.theatrejobs
.com/*

Variety
http://www.variety.com

Village Voice
*http://www.villagevoice
.com/*

Washington Post
*http://www.washingtonpost
.com/*

Organizations & Conferences

AACT—American
Association of
Community Theatre
http://www.aact.org/

AEA—Actors' Equity
Association
*http://www.actorsequity
.org*
Western Region (Los
Angeles)
(213) 462-2334
Central Region (Chicago)
(312) 641-0393
Eastern Region (New
York)
(212) 869-8530

AFTRA—American Federation of Television and Radio Artists
http://www.aftra.org

AGMA—American Guild of Musical Artists
(212) 265-3687

AGVA—American Guild of Variety Artists
(212) 675-1003 or (818) 508-9984

ATHE—Association for Theatre in Higher Education
http://www.athe.org

British Equity
http://www.equity.org.uk/

CSA—The Costume Society of America
http://www.costumesociety america.com/

DGA—Directors Guild of America
http://www.dga.org

DGA—Dramatists Guild of America
http://www.dramaguild .com/

IATSE—International Alliance of Theatrical Stage Employees
http://www.iatse.lm.com/

KC/ACTF—Kennedy Center/American College Theatre Festival
http://www.kennedy-center .org/education/actf/

NEA—The National Endowment for the Arts
http://arts.endow.gov/

NTCP—Non-Traditional Casting Project
http://www.ntcp.org/index .html

SAFD—Society of American Fight Directors
http://www.safd.org

SAG—Screen Actors Guild
http://www.sag.org

SSDC—Society of Stage Directors and Choreographers
http://www.ssdc.org

USA—United Scenic Artists
http://www.usa829.org

USITT—United States Institute of Theatre Technology
http://www.ffa.ucalgary .ca/usitt/

WGA—Writers Guild of America
http://www.wga.org

Acting Links

Acting Depot
http://www.actingdepot .com/

Acting Links
http://acting.freeservers .com/Links.htm

ActorSource Homepage, The
http://www.actorsource .com/

Acting World
http://www.actingworld .com/links.htm

Actor Links
http://www.expage.com/ page/onthesetlinks

ActorPlace.com
http://www.actorplace.com

Actor Site, The
http://www.actorsite.com/

Actor's Guide to Los Angeles, The
http://www.geocities.com/ casunset1/actinla.html

Actors Northwest
http://www.actorsnw.com/

AWOL's Hundreds of Great Acting Links
http://www.redbirdstudio .com/AWOL/acting1.html

AWOL's Search Machine for Actors
http://www.redbirdstudio .com/AWOL/AWOL SearchForm.html

Business of Acting Links, The
http://www.castlelanevideo .com/BofA/links.html

Castnet.com
http://www.castnet.com/

The Improv Page
http://www.improvcomedy .org/

Page of Theatre Resources, A
http://www.english.upenn .edu/~schwebel/theater .html

Performing Arts Links
http://theatrelibrary.org/ links/index.html

Shakespeare's Monologues
http://www.shakespeare- monologues.org/

Showbizltd: The Official Database of the Entertainment Industry
http://www.showbizltd .com/

Starving Actors.com
  *http://www.starvingactors
  .com/*

Trained Actor, The
  http://trainedactor.com/

Victoria' Acting Links
  *http://www.geocities.com/
  patchessul/*

Theatre Groups & Organizations

Actors Theatre of Louisville
  Louisville, KY
  *http://www.actorstheatre
  .org/*

Alabama Shakespeare
  Festival
  Montgomery, AL
  *http://www.asf.net/ASF
  .html*

Alley Theatre, The
  Houston, TX
  *http://www.alleytheatre
  .org/*

Alliance Theatre Company
  Atlanta, GA
  *http://www.alliancetheatre
  .org/atc_main.asp*

American Conservatory
  Theater, The
  San Francisco, CA
  http://www.act-sfbay.org/

American Repertory Theatre
  Cambridge, MA
  http://www.amrep.org/

Arena Stage, The
  Washington, D.C.
  *http://www.arenastage
  .org/home1.shtml*

Arizona Theatre Company
  Tucson, AZ
  *http://www.aztheatreco
  .org/*

Arkansas Repertory Theatre,
  The
  Little Rock, AR
  http://www.therep.org/

Asolo Center for the
  Performing Arts
  Sarasota, FL
  http://www.asolo.org/

Barter Theatre
  Abingdon, VA
  *http://www.bartertheatre
  .com/*

Berkeley Repertory Theatre
  Berkeley, CA
  *http://www.berkeleyrep
  .org/*

Berkshire Theatre Festival
  Stockbridge, MA
  *http://www.berkshire
  theatre.org/*

Black Theatre Companies
  *http://www.bridgesweb
  .com/blackcomp.html*

California Theatre Center
  Sunnyvale, CA
  http://www.ctcinc.org/

Casa Mañana Theatre
  Ft. Worth, TX
  *http://www.casamanana
  .org/*

Center Stage
  Baltimore, MD
  *http://users.erols.com/
  cntrstage/index.html*

Contemporary Theatre, A
  Seattle, WA
  http://www.acttheatre.org/

Cincinnati Playhouse
  Cincinnati, OH
  http://www.cincyplay.com/

Cleveland Playhouse, The
  Cleveland, OH
  *http://www.cleveland
  playhouse.com/*

Coconut Grove Playhouse
  Coconut Grove, FL
  *http://www.cgplayhouse
  .com/*

Dallas Theater Center
  Dallas, TX
  *http://www.dallastheater
  center.org/index2.html*

Denver Center Theatre
  Company
  Denver, CO
  *http://www.denvercenter
  .org/*

Florida Stage
  Manalapan, FL
  *http://www.floridastage
  .org/*

George Street Playhouse
  New Brunswick, NJ
  *http://www.georgest
  playhouse.org/*

Goodman Theatre
  Chicago, IL
  *http://www.goodman-
  theatre.org/*

Goodspeed Opera House
  East Haddam, CT
  http://www.goodspeed.org/

Great Lakes Theater Festival
  Cleveland, OH
  *http://www.greatlakes
  theater.org/*

Guthrie Theater, The
  Minneapolis, MN
  *http://www.guthrietheater
  .org/*

Hartford Stage Company
Hartford, CT
http://www.hartfordstage
.org/

Huntington Theatre
Company
Boston, MA
http://www.bu.edu/
huntington/

Indiana Repertory Theatre
Indianapolis, IN
http://www.indianarep
.com/

La Jolla Playhouse
La Jolla, CA
http://www.lajolla
playhouse.com/

La MaMa e.t.c.
New York City, NY
http://www.lamama.org/
set.htm

Long Wharf Theatre
New Haven, CT
http://www.longwharf.org/

Lorraine Hansberry Theatre
San Francisco, CA
http://www.lorraine
hansberrytheatre.com/

McCarter Theatre
Princeton, NJ
http://www.mccarter.org/
welcome.cfm

Manhattan Theatre Club
New York City, NY
http://www.manhattan
theatreclub.com/

Mark Taper Forum
Los Angeles, CA
http://www.taperahmanson
.com/

Milwaukee Repertory
Theatre
Milwaukee, WI
http://www.milwaukeerep
.com/

Missouri Repertory Theatre
Kansas City, MO
http://www.missouri
reptheatre.org

New Dramatists
New York City, NY
http://newdramatists
.org/ndintro.html

New Harmony Theatre, The
Evansville, IN
http://www.usi.edu/nht/
index.asp

Old Globe Theatre
San Diego, CA
http://www.oldglobe.org/

Oregon Shakespeare Festival
Ashland, OR
http://www.osfashland.org/

Orlando-UCF Shakespeare
Festival
Orlando, FL
http://www.shakespearefest
.org/

PCPA Theaterfest
Santa Maria, CA
http://www.pcpa.org/

Philadelphia Theatre
Company
Philadelphia, PA
http://www.phillytheatreco
.com/

Pioneer Theatre Company
Salt Lake City, UT
http://www.ptc.utah.edu/

Pittsburgh Public Theater
Pittsburgh, PA
http://www.ppt.org/

Playwrights Horizons
New York City, NY
http://www.playwrights
horizons.org/

Portland Center Stage
Portland, OR
http://www.pcs.org/main
.shtml

Public Theater/New York
Shakespeare Festival
New York City, NY
http://www.publictheater
.org/

Repertory Theatre of St.
Louis, The
St. Louis, MO
http://www.repstl.org

Roundabout Theatre
Company
New York City, NY
http://www.roundabout
theatre.org/

St. Louis Black Repertory
Company
St. Louis, MO
http://www.stlouisblackrep
.com

San Jose Repertory
San Jose, CA
http://www.sjrep.com/

Seattle Repertory Theatre,
The
Seattle, WA
http://www.seattlerep.org/

Shakespeare Theatre, The
Washington, D.C.
http://www.shakespeare
theatre.org/

South Coast Repertory
Costa Mesa, CA
http://www.scr.org/

Southern Repertory Theatre
New Orleans, LA
http://southernrep.com/

Stage West/Ft. Worth
Shakespeare Festival
Ft. Worth, TX
http://www.stagewest.org/

Steppenwolf Theatre
Company
Chicago, IL
*http://www.steppenwolf
.org/*

Syracuse Stage
Syracuse, NY
*http://www.syracusestage
.org/*

Tennessee Repertory
Theatre
Nashville, TN
http://www.tnrep.org/

Theatre Three
Dallas, TX
*http://www.theatre3dallas
.com/*

Trinity Repertory Company
Providence, RI
*http://www.trinityrep
.com/*

Utah Shakespearean Festival
Cedar City, UT
http://www.bard.org/

Walnut Street Theatre
Philadelphia, PA
*http://www.wstonline.org/
index.shtml*

Williamstown Theatre
Festival
Williamstown, MA
*http://www.wtfestival.org/
home.html*

Yale Repertory Theatre
New Haven, CT
http://www.yalerep.org/

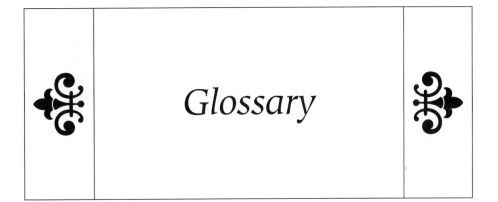

Glossary

abstraction A commonly misunderstood principle in which the actor observes an object for the purpose of taking away from it ("seizing and noting") qualities that will be useful in developing a character.

action Either physical or verbal, action happens in and is dictated by circumstances. Not to be confused with *physical movement* (a mechanical act), action has purpose and is motivated by the character's *simple objective*.

action verb Verb that motivates a sequence of smaller actions. "To provoke," "to seduce," "to belittle," "to protect" are examples of action verbs that stir the actor's imagination and germinate subsequent actions. (See *objective, simple* and *static verb*.)

adaptation The ability to adjust and sometimes abandon the present plan of actions when confronted with the unexpected. Sometimes referred to as *tactics* and "How?" (See *transacting* and *expectation*.)

ad lib Coming from the Latin ad libitum ("at pleasure"), the term applies to lines supplied by the actor wherever they may be required, as in crowd scenes or to fill in where there would otherwise be an undesirable pause.

adjustment The technique that allows actors to hold fast to the reality of their roles while altering *objectives* or *actions* to fit the changing circumstances of the scene. (See *adaptation*.) It also refers to an actor's physical alteration to accommodate a new position by a fellow actor to be in a position beneficial for the audience's viewing.

Adler, Stella One of the great American acting teachers of the twentieth century. Founding member of the influential Group Theatre in the 1930s along with Harold Clurman, *Lee Strasberg,* Cheryl Crawford, Luther Adler, Robert Lewis, *Sanford Meisner,* and later Elia Kazan.

affective memory *Stanislavski* term used to indicate both *sense memory* and *emotional memory.*

analogous emotion (See *emotional memory.*)

animated listening Hagen term that demands the interpretation of what is being said to us as it interacts with our own battery of psychological and mental actions.

animated talking The need to talk as instigated by our wishes and substantiated by the actions and experiences we are having in the present or by a reminder of a past experiences. (See *communion.*)

antithesis Setting one word or phrase against another word or phrase. Shakespeare's line, "Suit the action to the word, the word to the action," is an example of an antithetical phrase.

aside An onstage line shared with the audience but supposedly unheard by the other actors on stage. Although a regular convention in plays of the seventeenth, eighteenth, and nineteenth centuries, modern dramatists rarely use asides.

audition A tryout for a film, TV, or stage role. Usually auditions involve a presentation of prepared material and reading from a script, but they can also require *improvisation.*

audition portfolio Prepared audition material, consisting of a variety of monologues and songs, that can be used at any given tryout.

beat A short silence in the dialogue (e.g., "hold the moment a beat before continuing); also the smallest whole unit of a play. (See *unit of action.*)

bio Short for actor biography. A *résumé* in narrative form, usually for a printed program or press release.

bit part A small role with few lines.

blocking The director's arrangement of the actors' movements on stage with respect to one another and the stage space.

Blocking helps tell the story, develop characterization, set mood and atmosphere, and create suspense. The term *blocking* is also often used in two additional ways: as a synonym for *covering* and as a term for situations in which actors find it psychologically difficult or even impossible to remember a line or perform a required action.

build To increase the intensity of a line or physical action to reach a climax.

business, stage Small actions, such as smoking, eating, slapping, falling, crying, using a fan, and tying a necktie are known on the stage as business.

callback Any follow-up interview or *audition.*

casting director The person responsible for choosing the initial performers for later consideration by the producer or director.

catharsis Aristotelian term referring to a cleansing or purging of emotions.

cattle call An open *audition* where anyone can attend.

centering A term synonymous with proper alignment and good posture. Rather than posture that is stiff or artificially frozen, centering involves the correct alignment of our vertebrae that is our body's natural position.

character autobiography A method by which actors explore their characters' *second plan* and world of the play by asking questions such as "Who am I?" "What are my circumstances?" "What are my relationships?" and "What do I want?" The autobiography should be written in first person from the character's point of view.

character breakdown The description of a character for casting purposes.

character part Contrasted to *straight part,* a role usually depicting an elderly, unusual, or eccentric individual.

cheating A term used without any derogatory meaning when an actor plays in a more *open* position, or performs an action more openly, than complete realism would permit. Although a common staging technique, it may seriously hinder the *communion* between actors.

circles of attention The range of concentration on stage of an action, person, object, or event. *Stanis-lavski* described three circles of attention: small, medium, and large. (See *concentration.*)

clear stage A direction to leave the stage, given by the stage manager for everyone not immediately involved in the action.

closed A position in which the actor is turned away from the audience.

cold reading Unrehearsed reading of a scene, usually at an *audition.*

cold submission Sending an unsolicited *headshot* and *résumé* to an industry professional.

commenting A technique by which actors "distance" themselves from their roles, continually pointing out the significance of each action in relation to the total meaning of what the characters are doing and saying.

communion To give to or to receive from a person, object, or image something, even briefly, constituting a moment of spiritual intercourse. A state of absolute connection with self, the other actors, and the audience. (See *animated listening* and *animated talking.*)

company A group of actors who perform together either in an individual play or for a season. Sometimes called a troupe.

composition The physical arrangement of set, *props,* and actors.

concentration Giving complete attention to something. The ability to concentrate is a key part of effective acting. Also referred to as focus or directing attention. (See *circles of attention.*)

conflict Two opposing forces in comedy or drama.

contact sheet Numerous small images of potential *headshots* printed on 8"x10" paper. They usually require the use of a magnifying glass to evaluate them. Also known as proofs.

counter A movement in the opposite direction in *adjustment* to the *cross* of another actor. The instruction usually given is counter left or counter right. If only a small adjustment is necessary, the actor should make it without being told and is referred to as *dressing the stage.*

cover The movement of another actor into a position between you and the audience, thus obstructing you from view; also a term used to define the speech or action invented by an actor to keep the audience from detecting a mistake.

creative state A concentrated state of relaxation in which actors can attain their utmost capacity for accomplishing any activity—the kind of relaxation in which actors are most ready to react, like a cat in front of a mouse hole.

cross Movement from one area to another. When noting a cross in your script, the standard abbreviation is X.

cue An impulse derived from another person's actions on stage that motivates a verbal or physical response. A cue may come at the end of another person's speech or action, but many times this impulse occurs before the other actor has completed her speech or action. Thus, the words and actions may be overlapped. (See *telescoping.*)

cue-to-cue A rehearsal where actors are asked to play only the moment leading up to and during a section of the play where technical elements

are incorporated into the production.

curtain call The appearance of actors on stage after the performance to acknowledge the applause of the audience. Actors are required to remain in costume and makeup and to take the calls as rehearsed without variation. The term applies whether or not a curtain has been used.

dialogue The characters' lines spoken by actors in a play.

discovery Any new information an actor learns about the character in the rehearsal or performance process or the character learns about himself, others, or events during the course of the play.

double To play more than one role in a single play.

dress stage A direction requesting the actors to adjust their positions to improve the *composition* of the stage picture. If only a small *adjustment* is necessary, the actor should make it without being told.

elements of drama As defined in Aristotle's *Poetics,* the elements of drama in order of importance include: plot, character,

thought, diction, music, and spectacle.

emotional memory A personal emotion, also referred to as an *analogous emotion,* that helps an actor find a similar stage emotion. The situation does not have to be the same, but a comparable emotion is important. It is also imperative to note that time is an excellent artistic filter for emotional memories, and an actor must have come to closure with the particular event (e.g., the death of a parent) before using it on stage.

ensemble The actors' internal and external reactions to one another in a mutual endeavor to project the super-objective of a play. (See *transacting* and *communion.*) Also a theatrical presentation in which the stress is on the performance of the group rather than the individual.

Equity Actors' Equity Association (AEA). The union representing stage actors.

Equity waiver In 99-seat (or less) theatres that were otherwise professional, over which Equity waives contract provisions under certain circumstances.

Now officially called "Showcase Code," the term "Equity waiver" is still used informally.

exit To leave the stage; also an opening in the setting through which actors may exit.

expectation While remaining in *Stanislavski's* present state of "I am," the character's continuous state of anticipation of what will happen next. (See *transacting* and *adaptation*.)

external technique The development of the body and voice as responsive and expressive instruments; vocal dexterity, speech, movement, and gestures are the actor's principal means of external expression.

extra A small non-speaking part (e.g., soldiers, townspeople, ladies-in-waiting, etc.). (See *bit part*.)

fourth side In both interior and exterior settings, the imaginary side(s) of the room or environment that is undefined and left to the imagination of the actor. The actor, however, must make the fourth side specific by use of focal points.

give, take When two actors are not equally *open*, the one who receives a greater emphasis is said to *take* the scene. The other is said to *give* the scene.

given circumstance Any unchangeable fact that affects the playing of the scene; the who, what, when, and where of a scene.

ground plan The arrangement of doors, windows, steps, levels, furniture, and so forth for a stage setting; also a diagram showing the arrangement of these elements.

Hagen, Uta Preeminent German-born actress known for her portrayals of Blanche Du Bois in *A Streetcar Named Desire*, Martha in *Who's Afraid of Virginia Woolf?*, and more recently Mrs. Klein in *Mrs. Klein*, Hagen is perhaps known best as a great teacher of acting at her second husband's HB Studio and through her two books, *A Challenge for the Actor* and *Respect for Acting*.

headshot A general term for an actor's picture used for *auditioning* and marketing purposes. These black and white photos are also referred to as 8x10s—the picture's dimensions—and glossies. Other actor pictures include three-quarter shots that show more of the body, and composite shots, which are a series of photos on one sheet representing an actor's different looks.

historical imagination Hagen term. Unlike the scholar's approach to history, with its literal-minded and plodding accuracy, historical imagination is a totally subjective approach to convince yourself that "you" exist in the world of the play. Historical facts are not the issue but rather the external behavior of a unique individual in a particular social order with its own culture, values, fashion, and mores. (See *style*.)

improvisation Spontaneous invention of lines and business without a fixed text.

inciting incident The precise event that serves as the catalyst for the *action* of the play.

indicating A derogatory term in psychologically motivated acting in which actions are presented without *objectives*. Actors who are indicating are "showing" the audience what their character is supposed to be feeling rather than playing the logical *score* of actions.

inner monologues The unspoken flashes of thoughts and images that underscore the character's every action, inner monologues occur while speaking, listening, and experiencing any action. It is important to note, however, that thinking moves with the speed of light and is not based on verbally organized ideas.

inner objects *Hagen* term that refers to envisioning and forming a specific mental picture for an exact purpose that helps an actor to trigger actively traveling thoughts.

inspiration The goal of *Stanislavski's System.* When actors find a consistent and repeatable conscious means to subconscious creativity, they are said to be inspired.

internal technique An actor's keen understanding of human psychology, *historical imagination,* and learning how to control and to make effective use on stage of *affective memory.*

journey The changes a character makes while pursuing the *throughline of action.*

justification A validation of and strong belief in every action that an actor makes for the character in pursuit of each *simple objective.*

magic if Stanislavski term used to describe the process by which actors place themselves in the given circumstances of the scene. The actor asks, "What would I do *if* I were this character in this circumstance?" The *magic if* is the key to unlocking the actor's imagination.

Meisner, Sanford One of America's great acting teachers who sprang from the Group Theatre of the 1930s. His focus on "the reality of doing" spawned many acting exercises widely used in current teaching.

Method Acting Developed by *Lee Strasberg* and based on early teachings of *Stanislavski,* it is an internal approach to acting that—although very similar to *System Acting*—gives primary focus to *affective memory.*

Method of Physical Actions The heart of the *Stanislavski System,* it is the actor's logical sequence of actions that leads to the stirring of emotions, thoughts, imagination—all the psychic forces. (See *psychophysical union.*)

monologue A character's continuous dialogue without interruption of another character; also a speech delivered while alone on stage.

Moore, Sonia The most critically acclaimed American teacher of the *Stanislavski System.* Other than *Stanislavski's* own published works, the most widely read interpretation of his techniques remains Sonia Moore's pioneering studies, *The Stanislavski System* and *Stanislavski Revealed.*

motivating force What your character wants overall. It is sometimes referred to as the character's *super-objective* and is expressed in much the same way as the *simple objective.* (See *super-objective, spine, throughline of action,* and *simple objective.*)

mugging A derogatory term for exaggerated facial expressions.

Nemirovich-Danchenko, Vladimir Russian cofounder—with *Constan-*

tin *Stanislavski*—and literary manager of the Moscow Art Theatre from 1898 until his death in 1943.

noun name A single word that characterizes a *unit of action* (e.g., "Confession," "Celebration," "War").

objective, simple A character's quest at any given moment expressed and pursued by use of an *action verb* that motivates a sequence of simple actions (e.g., to provoke, to belittle, to seduce). A simple objective is the best-known translation of *Stanislavski's* term *zadacha* (problem). Also referred to as goal, motivation, desire, impulse, intention, intended victory, and according to Robert Lewis, spinach. (See *action verb* and *static verb*.)

observation "Seizing and noting" the outer world to use for later reference on stage. *Stanislavski* referred to this as storing.

obstacle A physical or psychological obstruction that hinders the character from completing an *action*. Obstacles provide conflict and heighten the dramatic effect; the greater the conflict, the more interesting the scene.

open An on-stage position in which the actor is facing toward the audience, or nearly so. To open is to turn toward the audience.

operative word A key word or logical accent within the structure of each phrase of dialogue.

opposite A contradiction between the text and the *subtext* which makes the word or action unexpected, vivid, and significant.

pacing The rate of speed at which the actors speak their lines, pick up their cues, act upon their impulses, telescope the dialogue, and hold the moments of silence. Frequently heard directions are "Pick up the pace" or "The pace is too slow (or too fast)." (See *tempo-rhythm*.)

parent union An actor's first union that may provide eligibility into other acting unions.

particularization *Hagen* term referring to the making of each event, each person, and each place down to the smallest physical object as specific as possible. Nothing should be left general

or taken for granted—even in early rehearsals.

pension and health payment An additional amount of money paid by the employer to cover employee benefits under union contract.

physical movement A physical *action* stripped of any context or meaning. (See *action*.)

"pick up cues" A direction for the actor to begin a counteraction immediately on the impulse to do so—whether it be internally within another person's verbal or physical action (see *telescoping*) or at the end of a fellow actor's *action*. Beginning actors tend to be slow in picking up cues, with the result that they often fail to maintain a tempo fast enough to hold the interest of the audience.

places A direction given by the stage manager for everyone to be in the proper position for the beginning of an act.

pointing Giving special emphasis to a word, phrase, or *action*.

postcard A 4"x6" picture of an actor with name and other information, intended to remind industry professionals of an actor's recent credits and other news (e.g., a stage production in which the actor is performing).

projection Using external technique to propel thoughts and ideas to the audience. Projection deals with dimension, energy, and clarity that can communicate the meaning to an audience of a certain size occupying a certain space.

properties Tangible on-stage objects, properties or "props" are divided into several categories: hand, personal, costume, and stage.

psychological action A character's inner thoughts that manifest themselves through physical *actions*. (See *psychophysical union.*)

psychophysical union *Stanislavski* term that refers to the inseparable connection between internal experience and its external expression. Through the *Method of Physical Actions* an actor has a conscious means to the subconscious. Every mental process, every feeling and thought, decision and evaluation, is immediately transmitted through the body in visual

expression. (See *Method of Physical Actions.*)

public solitude Achieved when actors are fully focused on their immediate action without any attempt to amuse the audience. When actors are in the state of public solitude they commune with their partner(s), themselves, and the audience — the very place where many people believe "theatre" happens. (See *communion.*)

reincarnation *Stanislavski* term that translates as actors' means of changing their own distinctive qualities into those of the character. Reincarnation occurs when the actors have the ability to think, feel, and behave as their characters.

resonance An opening of the oral cavities amplifying the vocal sound and giving it strength, tone, timbre, and personal quality.

résumé List of credits, training, and special skills usually attached to an 8"x10" *headshot*. Résumés are also cut to 8"x10". (See *headshot* and *bio.*)

risk taking A term synonymous with definitive decision making. Risk taking

may be very subtle indeed; however, decisions may be as infinitely large as human beings. As long as risks are truthful, *actions* will not be *indicated*. Risk taking is not to be confused with overused risqué choices. (See *indicating.*)

run-through An uninterrupted rehearsal of a scene, an act, or the entire play. In contrast is the "working" rehearsal, in which either the director or the actors may stop to work on details.

scale Minimum payment for services under union contracts.

score of physical actions A list of the character's psychological and physical *actions* forming a sequence that is logical and appropriate for the situation and are capable of being carried out. (See *Method of Physical Actions* and *psychophysical union.*)

second plan *Nemirovich-Danchenko's* term used to help explain inner images and *inner monologues*. The existence of characters on stage is only a small part of their whole life; the second plan includes their life before the play and after it. It also incorporates the events that occur off stage during the course of the selected life. Like *Stanislavski*, Nemirovich-Danchenko believed the audience must be made aware of the whole inner life of the characters, their entire destiny, while they are on stage.

sense memory The use of past sensations—taste, touch, sound, smell, and sight—as a means to *substitute* the qualities of one thing for another (e.g., drinking water as if vodka or burning your finger on a stove that is not actually lit). (See *substitution*.)

share When two actors are both open to the same degree, allowing the audience to see them equally well.

showcase A stage show designed to promote actors by allowing them to perform in short venues with industry attendance.

spine A term used by Harold Clurman, one of the founders of the Group Theatre, that refers to the play's central idea; it is like a spine in the human body that holds the other parts together. (See *superobjective*.)

stage directions *Stage right* refers to the actor's right as he stands on stage facing the audience. *Stage left* is the actor's left. *Downstage* is toward the audience, and *upstage* is away from the audience. *Below* means the same as "downstage of," and *above* is the same as "upstage of." *In* refers to toward the center of the stage, whereas *out* means away from center.

standard union contract The standard format/contract approved by the unions and offered to most union performers before the job.

Stanislavski, Constantin Russian cofounder—with *Vladimir Nemirovich-Danchenko*—and director of the Moscow Art Theatre from 1897 until his death in 1938. The creator of the world's first and best known systematized study of the acting art. Most of today's acting technique training is a derivative of Stanislavski's System.

static verb Verbs that do not motivate immediate and simple actions. Take, for example, the word "power." To say "I wish power" is too general. If you phrase it as a question, "What must I do to obtain power?" it will move you more toward purposeful activity; however, the word "power" remains too large and relatively static. Other examples of static verbs include: run, sit, jump, hit, and read. (See *action verb* and *objective, simple*.)

stealing An unobtrusive adjustment that will not receive the audience's attention; or to take the audience's attention when it should be elsewhere.

straight part A role without marked eccentricities, normally a young man or young woman. (See *character part*.)

Strasberg, Lee One of the founders of the Group Theatre and later the Actors Studio and developer of what came to be known as *Method Acting*, an internal approach based on the early teaching of *Stanislavski* emphasizing *affective memory*.

strategy The overall plan of attack to overcome the forces working against them. (See *adaptation*.)

style A term referring to individuality and distinctive manner of expression. Style cannot be predetermined and, according to *Uta Hagen,* is a label given to a finished work by critics, scholars, and viewers. "It does not belong in the vocabulary of a creator." Considering style at any point in the creative process will result in stereotypes and predetermined actions and gestures. Style should also not be confused with genre (e.g., realism, absurdism, epic, Shakespearean, etc.). (See *historical imagination.*)

substitution Using experiences different from the *given circumstances* to help find true emotion in a scene.

subtext The actor's continuous flashes of thoughts that gives meaning to the *dialogue* and the *stage directions.* Referred to by *Stanislavski* as "illustrated subtext," an actor must have specific images for everyone and everything that is spoken, heard, or experienced on stage. (See *inner monologues.*) Subtext also refers to behavior.

super-objective *Stanislavski* term (*sverkhzadacha* or "super-problem") for the play's central theme or intent that runs throughout the plot; what the author wanted to say. Also referred to as a character's long-range goal. (See *motivating force, throughline of action,* and *spine.*)

suspension of disbelief The term that refers to the audience's willingness to temporarily accept the actions on stage as truth, although they never completely forget they are watching fiction.

System Acting *Stanislavski's* technique training that permits the actor to create a character, to reveal the life of a human spirit based on laws of the organic nature of the actor and that gives primary focus to the play's *given circumstances,* the *Method of Physical Actions,* and *psychophysical union.*

tactics (See *adaptation* and *strategy.*)

tag line The last line of a scene or an act. It usually needs to be *pointed.*

"take five" The announcement of periodic five-minute breaks.

talent agent The liaison between the actor and casting director. Union-affiliated talent agents can only accept 10% commission from their clients.

talent manager Another form of representation for the actor, managers do not have a set commission base nor do they have any union affiliations, but they usually work more closely with individual actors.

telescoping Overlapping speeches so one actor speaks before another has finished. It is a realistic technique for providing the illusion of accelerated *pace* and building a climax.

tempo-rhythm *Stanislavski's* term for the combined rhythmic flow and the speed of execution of the physical action (including speech) in a given scene. In life any little change of circumstance stirs a different tempo-rhythm. Rhythm expresses inner experience, and control over it is one of the conditions for mastering the *inner technique.* Overcoming *obstacles* by use of *tactics* should be of tremendous help in changing the tempo-rhythm.

through-line of action The chain of logical, purposeful, consecutive *simple objectives* that gradually disclose the *super-objective.*

The movement of the inner life of your character, and through this the play is understood by the spectator.

top To "build" or intensify a line or physical action higher than the one that preceded it.

trades Short for "trade papers." The newspapers and periodicals such as the *Hollywood Reporter* and *Variety* that specifically feature information on the entertainment industry.

transacting Purposeful action with *expectations* followed by *adaptation* or counteraction as a result of another actor's unexpected *actions*. Actors must have the ability to adjust their actions to the needs of the moment; therefore, adapting to other characters turns *ac-*

tions into transactions. (See *adaptation* and *expectation.*)

transference *Hagen* term to convey from one person, place, or situation to another. Transfer from your own life to the very origins of your character, to ensure faith in the reality of your new existence. Similar to *emotional memory* but more inclusive.

transition A stasis, a momentary vacuum, that comes from a strong impulse for new action.

tryouts See *audition.*

understudy A performer hired to do a role if the lead player is unable to perform.

unit of action The smallest whole division of a play—one in which there is a distinct beginning, middle, and end. The

principal character in each unit—sometimes referred to as the driving force—pursues a *simple objective* while working against an obstacle. Also referred to as a *beat.*

upstaging When one actor takes a position that forces the second actor to face upstage or away from the audience. Because the downstage actor is put at a disadvantage, upstaging has an unpleasant connotation and is generally to be avoided.

waiver Union-approved permission for deviation from the terms of a standard contract.

walk-on (See *extra* or *bit part.*)

workshop A class where actors can learn from industry professionals, often for a limited number of sessions.

Bibliography

These books and articles, representing much of the modern theory of acting, should provide informative and interesting reading. (*Note:* Various transliterations of Constantin Stanislavski's name can prove confusing. In the body of the text, we opt for the spelling used in the preceding sentence. In the Bibliography, we use the spelling selected by the author we are citing.)

Boal, Augusto. *Games for Actors and Non-Actors.* Translated by Adrian Jackson. London and New York: Routledge, 1992.
Described as a "book for all those who are interested as a force for change," this collection of exercises and improvisations is extremely useful as a supplement to the exercises in *Acting Is Believing.*

Brook, Peter. *The Empty Space.* New York: Atheneum, 1968.
An influential director and experimentalist discusses what makes theatre vital and what makes it deadly. Throughout are many penetrating comments about the art and craft of acting.

Brown, Richard P. (ed.). *Actor Training.* Vols. 1–3. New York: Drama Book Specialists, 1968–1976.

This series deals with approaches to acting through group improvisation, through emphasis on performer rather than on character, and through attempts to objectify subjective experience.

Chaikin, Joseph. *The Presence of the Actor.* New York: Atheneum, 1972.
A valuable aid to the understanding of self-exploration as a means

of breaking away from convention and cliché.

Chekhov, Michael. *To the Actor.* New York: Harper & Row, 1953.
A creative approach by a student of Stanislavski and a one-time member of the Moscow Art Theatre. The concepts, especially the "psychological gesture," are imaginative. The exercises are stimulating, providing excellent problems in improvisation.

Cole, Toby (ed.). *Acting: A Handbook of the Stanislavski Method.* New York: Lear Publishers, 1947.
A group of articles describing principles and practices derived from Stanislavski. I. Rapoport, "The Work of the Actor," is particularly useful.

——— and Helen Krich Chinoy, (eds.). *Actors on Acting.* New York: Crown Publishers, 1949.
The long subtitle is significant: *The Theories, Techniques, and Practices of the Great Actors of All Times As Told in Their Own Words.* A selection of material by and about actors from Plato to José Ferrer.

Duerr, Edwin. *The Length and Depth of Acting.* New York: Holt, Rinehart and Winston, 1962.
An account of acting and actors from the Greeks to the present. Of value both as history and as analysis of the actor's problems and objectives, but Duerr's apparent anti-Stanislavski bias damages the book's usefulness.

Funke, Lewis, and John E. Booth. *Actors Talk About Acting.* New York: Random House, 1961.
Taped interviews with fourteen "stars of the theatre": Anne Bancroft, Morris Carnovsky, Katharine Cornell, José Ferrer, Lynn Fontanne and Alfred Lunt, John Gielgud, Helen Hayes, Bert Lahr, Vivien Leigh, Paul Muni, Sidney Poitier, Maureen Stapleton, and Shelley Winters. The interviews provide some understanding of these actors' creative processes.

Gordon, Mel. *The Stanislavsky Technique: Russia; A Workbook for Actors.* New York: Applause Theatre Book Publishers, 1987.
A compendium of the actor-training systems of Stanislavski, Vakhtangov, and Michael Chekhov. Gordon arranges the material both chronologically and topically, so the reader can see how the techniques the United States imported from Russia evolved and compare the subtle differences in approach of the three most famous theorists.

Grotowski, Jerzy. *Towards a Poor Theatre.* New York: Simon & Schuster, 1968.
Articles by and about the famous Polish innovator. They describe a theatre devoid of commercialism, demanding the ultimate in personal dedication and rigorous physical and vocal training.

Hagen, Uta. *A Challenge for the Actor.* New York: Macmillan, 1991.
Distinguished both as actress and teacher, Hagen talks about acting in both conceptual and practical terms. A stimulating and rewarding book for the serious student.

Hethmon, Robert H. (ed.). *Strasberg at the Actors Studio.* New York: Viking, 1965.
Tape-recorded sessions at the Actors Studio, giving Lee Strasberg's comments and criticisms of scenes and exercises presented by studio members. The comments reveal remarkable understanding of the actor's problems and offer much practical help, especially in inducing relaxation and freeing the imagination.

Lewis, Robert. *Method—— Or Madness?* New York: Samuel French, 1958.
Eight witty and illuminating lectures explaining Stanislavski's principles and describing their use

and misuse by American actors.

Magarshack, David. *Stanislavsky on the Art of the Stage.* New York: Hill and Wang, 1961. Includes a posthumous collection of Stanislavski's lectures under the title "The System and Method of Creative Art." The introduction is a clear summary of the so-called Stanislavski system.

Marowitz, Charles. *The Act of Being.* New York: Taplinger Publishing, 1978. This lively book takes a historical look at acting from Stanislavski to Grotowski, in search of a workable acting theory for the present-day actor. It is especially useful for its explorations of the changing actor/director/playwright/audience relationships.

———. *Stanislavsky and the Method.* New York: Citadel Press, 1964. Helpful application of Stanislavski's principles to various acting problems, including the playing of Brecht and Shakespeare.

Moore, Sonia. *Stanislavski Revealed.* New York: Applause, 1991. A breakthrough study revealing the subtle tissue of ideas behind what Stanislavski regarded as his "major breakthrough," the Method of Physical Actions. Sonia Moore devoted a decade of work in her world-famous studio to an investigation of Stanislavski's final technique. The result is the first detailed discussion of Moore's own theory of psychophysical unity.

———. *The Stanislavski System.* New York: Penguin, 1984. Other than Stanislavski's own published work, this is the most widely read interpretation of his techniques.

Parke, Lawrence. *Since Stanislavski and Vakhtangov; the Method as a System for Today's Actor.* Hollywood, CA: Acting World Books, 1985. Although Parke's approach is more esoteric than most, his step-by-step method of preparing the actor for performing a role is solidly based on Stanislavski's tradition. His concept of *obstacles* is a particularly useful addition to the methodology favored by this text.

Samuels, Steven (Ed.). *Theatre Profiles 10: The Illustrated Reference Guide to America's Nonprofit Professional Theatre.* New York: Theatre Communications Group, 1992. This semiannual publication attempts to document the world of the nonprofit professional theatre. This edition features listings for 229 theatres across America and includes important names of people to contact for information about employment and other operational aspects. *Theatre Profiles 11* should be available by the time this edition of *Acting Is Believing* goes to press.

Shurtleff, Michael. *Audition: Everything an Actor Needs to Know to Get the Part.* New York: Walker, 1978. In our discussion about auditioning, we referred to this book as the bible of all books on the subject. In his chatty, informative style, Shurtleff takes the actor through the entire process of auditioning, defines the kinds of auditions the actor is likely to encounter, and gives tips about how the actor can give himself the best chance to be successful.

Stanislavski, Constantin. *An Actor's Handbook.* Edited and translated by Elizabeth Reynolds Hapgood. New York: Theatre Arts Books, 1963. Described accurately on the title page as "an alphabetical arrangement of concise statements on aspects of acting." The statements have been selected from the whole body of Stanislavski's writings.

———. *An Actor Prepares.* Translated by Elizabeth Reynolds Hapgood. New York: Theatre Arts Books, 1936.
The most widely known in England and America of Stanislavski's works. It sets forth the principles of the "inner technique" and describes the concepts of sensory recall, emotion memory, relaxation, concentration, units and objectives, super-objectives, communion, adaptation, and through-line of action.

———. *Building a Character.* Translated by Elizabeth Reynolds Hapgood. New York: Theatre Arts Books, 1949.
Less well known than *An Actor Prepares* but vital to an understanding of Stanislavski's principles. It is concerned with developing an "outer technique" and is a necessary supplement to the earlier work.

———. *Creating a Role.* Translated by Elizabeth Reynolds Hapgood. New York: Theatre Arts Books, 1961.
How to work on a role from a first reading through various necessary stages of development.

Tulane Drama Review 9: 1 and 2 (Fall and Winter 1964).
These issues, entitled "Stanislavski and America," marked the one hundredth anniversary of Stanislavski's birth. They contain articles and interviews about Stanislavski's principles and their uses by prominent actors, directors, and teachers.

Additional Sources

Aaron, Stephen. *Stage Fright: Its Role in Acting.* Chicago: University of Chicago Press, 1986.

Adler, Stella. *The Technique of Acting.* New York: Bantam Books, 1978.

Alterman, Glenn. *The Job Book I, The Job Book II.* Lyme, NH: Smith and Kraus, 1995.

Artaud, Antonin. *The Theater and Its Double.* Translated by Mary Caroline Richards. New York: Grove Press, 1961.

Babson, Thomas. *The Actor's Choice: The Transition from Stage to Screen.* Portsmouth, NH: Heinemann, 1996.

Balk, H. Wesley. *The Complete Singer-Actor: Training for Music Theater.* Minneapolis: University of Minnesota Press, 1985.

Ball, David. *Backwards & Forwards: A Technical Manual for Reading Plays.* Carbondale: Southern Illinois University Press, 1983.

Barton, John. *Playing Shakespeare.* London and New York: Methuen, 1984.

Barton, Robert. *Acting: Onstage and Off.* Second Edition. Fort Worth: Harcourt Brace Jovanovich, 1993.

Benedetti, Robert L. *The Actor at Work.* Eighth Edition. Boston: Allyn and Bacon, 2001.

Blum, Richard A. *American Film Acting: The Stanislavski Heritage* (Studies in Cinema no. 28). Ann Arbor, MI: UMI Research Press, 1984.

Blunt, Jerry. *Stage Dialects.* San Francisco: Chandler Publishing, 1967.

Brestoff, Richard. *The Great Acting Teachers and Their Methods.* Lyme, NH: Smith and Kraus, 1995.

Boleslavsky, Richard. *Acting: The First Six Lessons.* New York: Theatre Arts Books, 1933.

Bruder, Melissa, et al. *A Practical Handbook for the Actor.* New York: Vintage Press, 1986.

Charles, Jill. *Directory of Theatre Training Programs.* Eighth Edition. Dorset, VT: Theatre Directories,

American Theatre Works, Inc., 2002.

Charles, Jill, & Tom Bloom. *The Actor's Picture/Résumé Book.* Dorset, VT: Theatre Directories, American Theatre Works, Inc., 1991.

Cohen, Robert. *Acting One.* Palo Alto, CA: Mayfield Publishing, 1984.

———. *Acting Professionally: Raw Facts About Careers in Acting.* Second Edition. Palo Alto, CA: Mayfield Publishing, 1990.

Cole, David. *Acting as Reading: The Place of the Reading Process in the Actor's Work.* Ann Arbor: University of Michigan Press, 1992.

Corrigan, Mary (ed.). "Casting: A Survey of Directors' Viewpoints." *Theatre News,* January-February 1983, pp. 6–7.

Corson, Richard. *Stage Makeup.* Sixth Edition. Englewood Cliffs, NJ: Prentice-Hall, 1981.

Donohue, Jim. "Learning Lines with Meaning: A Method for Memorizing." *Dramatics,* January 1988, pp. 28–36.

Ellis, Roger. *An Audition Handbook for Student Actors.* Chicago: Nelson-Hall Publishers, 1986.

Finchley, Joan. *Audition!* Englewood Cliffs, NJ: Prentice-Hall, 1984.

Friedman, Ginger Howard. *The Perfect Monologue.* New York: Limelight Edition, 2000.

Goldman, Michael. *The Actor's Freedom.* New York: Viking, 1975.

Grote, David. *Script Analysis: Reading and Understanding the Playscript for Production.* Belmont, CA: Wadsworth, 1985.

Hagen, Uta, with Haskel Frankel. *Respect for Acting.* New York: Macmillan, 1973.

Harrop, John, & Sabin R. Epstein. *Acting with Style.* Second Edition. Englewood Cliffs, NJ: Prentice-Hall, 1990.

Henry, Mari Lyn, & Lynne Rogers. *How to Be a Working Actor.* Third Edition. New York: M. Evans and Company, 1994.

Hobbs, Robert L. *Teach Yourself Transatlantic: Theatre Speech for Actors.* Palo Alto, CA: Mayfield Publishing Company, 1986.

Hooks, Ed. *The Audition Book.* New York: Back Stage Books, 1996.

Hull, S. Loraine. *Strasberg's Method As Taught by Lorrie Hull: A Practical Guide for Actors, Teachers and Directors.* Woodbridge, CT: Ox Bow Publishing, Inc., 1985.

Hunt, Gordon. *How to Audition.* New York: Harper & Row, 1977.

Johnstone, Keith. *Impro: Improvisation and the Theatre.* London: Faber and Faber, 1979.

Kahan, Stanley. *Introduction to Acting.* Third Edition. Boston: Allyn & Bacon, 1991.

King, Nancy. *A Movement Approach to Acting.* Englewood Cliffs, NJ: Prentice-Hall, 1981.

Lessac, Arthur. *Body Wisdom: The Use and Training of the Human Body.* New York: Drama Book Specialists, 1981.

———. *The Use and Training of the Human Voice.* New York: Drama Book Specialists, 1967.

Levin, Irina and Igor. *Working on the Play and the Role: The Stanislavsky Method for Analyzing the Characters in a Drama.* Chicago: Ivan R. Dee, 1992.

Lewis, Robert. *Advice to the Players.* New York: Harper & Row, 1980.

Linklater, Kristin. *Freeing the Natural Voice.* New York: Drama Book Specialists, 1976.

Lounsbury, Warren C. *Theatre Backstage from A to Z.* Seattle: University of Washington Press, 1967.

Machlin, Evangeline. *Dialects for the Stage.* New York: Theatre Arts Books, 1975.

McTigue, Mary. *Acting Like a Pro: Who's Who, What's What, and the Way Things Really Work in the Theatre.* White Hall, VA: Betterway Publications, 1992.

Manderino, Ned. *The Transpersonal Actor.* Los Angeles, CA: Manderino Books, 1985.

Markus, Thomas. *The Professional Actor from Audition to Performance.* New York: Drama Book Specialists, 1978.

Martinez, J. D. *Combat Mime: A Non-Violent Approach to Stage Violence.* Chicago: Nelson-Hall, 1982.

Matson, Katinka. *The Working Actor: A Guide to the Profession.* New York: Viking, 1976.

Meisner, Sanford, and Dennis Longwell. *Sanford Meisner on Acting.* New York: Vintage Books, 1987.

Miles-Brown, John. *Acting: A Drama Studio Source Book.* London: P. Owen, 1985.

Moore, Sonia. *Training an Actor.* New York: Penguin, 1979.

Morris, Eric. *Being and Doing: A Workbook for Actors.*
Los Angeles: Spelling Publications, 1981.

Moston, Doug. *Coming to Terms With Acting: An Instructive Glossary: What You Need to Know to Understand It, Discuss It, Deal With It and Do It.* New York: Drama Book Publishers, 1993.

Novak, Elaine Adams. *Performing in Musicals.* New York: Schirmer Books, 1988.

Olivier, Laurence. *On Acting.* New York: Simon and Schuster, 1986.

Pisk, Litz. *The Actor and His Body.* New York: Theatre Arts Books, 1975.

Poggi, Jack. *The Monologue Workshop.* New York: Applause, 1990.

Rendle, Adrian. *So You Want to Be an Actor?* London: A. C. Black, 1986.

Richardson, Don. *Acting Without Agony: An Alternative to the Method.* Boston: Allyn and Bacon, 1988.

Rizzo, Raymond. *The Total Actor.* Indianapolis: The Odyssey Press, 1975.

Rolfe, Bari. *Movement for Period Plays.* Oakland, CA: Personabooks, 1985.

Russell, Douglas. *Period Style for the Theatre.* Boston: Allyn & Bacon, 1980.

Schechner, Richard. *Environmental Theatre.* New
York: Hawthorn Books, 1973.

Silverberg, Larry. *The Sanford Meisner Approach, An Actor's Workbook.* Lyme, NH: Smith and Kraus, 1994.

———. The Sanford Meisner Approach, Workbook Two: Emotional Freedom. Lyme, NH: Smith and Kraus, 1997.

Silver, Fred. *Auditioning for the Musical Theatre.* New York: Newmarket Press, 1985.

Sonenberg, Janet. *The Actor Speaks.* New York: Crown, 1996.

Spolin, Viola. *Improvisation for the Theatre.* Evanston, IL: Northwestern University Press, 1963.

Stern, Lawrence. *Stage Management: A Guidebook of Practical Techniques.* Third Edition. Boston: Allyn and Bacon, Inc., 1987.

Strasberg, Lee. *A Dream of Passion: The Development of the Method.* Edited by Evangeline Morphos. Boston: Little, Brown, 1987.

Swift, Clive. *The Job of Acting: A Guide to Working in Theatre.* London: Harrap, 1976.

Taylor, John Russell. *The Penguin Dictionary of the Theatre.* Baltimore: Penguin, 1966.

Thomas, James. *Script Analysis for Actors, Directors and Designers.* Boston: Focal Press, 1992.

Woods, Leigh. *On Playing Shakespeare: Advice and Commentary from Actors and Actresses of the Past.* New York: Greenwood Press, 1991.

Yakim, Moni. *Creating a Character: A Physical Approach to Acting.* New York: Back Stage Books, 1990.

Index

Page numbers in italics refer to photographs.